Why We Love
Disney

This book is part of the Peter Lang Media and Communication list.
Every volume is peer reviewed and meets
the highest quality standards for content and production.

PETER LANG
New York • Washington, D.C./Baltimore • Bern
Frankfurt • Berlin • Brussels • Vienna • Oxford

ANDI STEIN

Why We Love Disney

The Power of the Disney Brand

PETER LANG
New York • Washington, D.C./Baltimore • Bern
Frankfurt • Berlin • Brussels • Vienna • Oxford

Library of Congress Cataloging-in-Publication Data

Stein, Andi.
Why we love Disney: the power of the Disney brand / Andi Stein.
p. cm.
Includes bibliographical references and index.
1. Walt Disney Company. 2. Walt Disney Company—History.
3. Amusements—United States—History. I. Title.
PN1999.W27S72   384'.80979494—dc22   2010046194
ISBN 978-1-4331-0898-3 (hardcover)
ISBN 978-1-4331-0897-6 (paperback)

Bibliographic information published by **Die Deutsche Nationalbibliothek**.
Die Deutsche Nationalbibliothek lists this publication in the "Deutsche
Nationalbibliografie"; detailed bibliographic data is available
on the Internet at http://dnb.d-nb.de/.

Cover photo by Cesar Rubio, courtesy the Walt Disney Family Museum

© 2011 Andi Stein
Peter Lang Publishing, Inc., New York
29 Broadway, 18th floor, New York, NY 10006
www.peterlang.com

Printed in the United States of America

Table of Contents

Figures

Acknowledgments

Many thanks go to all those interviewed for this book who generously shared their Disney impressions and experiences.

Thanks to Andi Wang and The Walt Disney Family Museum for permission to use photographs from the museum's collection.

Much appreciation goes to Janet Wasko at the University of Oregon and Coral Ohl at California State University, Fullerton, for their reviews of the book proposal and finished manuscript.

Thanks to Sophie Appel, Peter Lang Publishing design and production supervisor, for guidance with the book's production.

Finally, I am extremely grateful to editor Mary Savigar at Peter Lang Publishing for offering me the opportunity to write this book. It has been a great experience, and I truly appreciate the encouragement and support.

Why We Love Disney: An Introduction

The line began to form by 8:00 a.m., more than two hours before the scheduled opening of the auditorium doors. It made its way along the wall, then spilled into the lobby of the Anaheim Convention Center. Eventually, people began talking to each other—introducing themselves, chatting about their shared interests, and comparing notes on their reasons for coming.

As it drew closer to the appointed start time of the event, anticipation began to build. The chatter and buzz grew louder. When the doors to the auditorium finally opened, the level of excitement in the building was almost palpable.

Surprisingly, the guest of honor the crowds were waiting for wasn't a rock star or a famous dignitary. He was Bob Iger, CEO of The Walt Disney Company. Iger had come to kick off the D23 Expo, the Disney Company's first convention for members of its new D23 Fan Club. Disney fans from all over the country had come to hear what Iger had to say about the company's plans for the future.

Iger's talk was to be only the beginning of a four-day extravaganza that would include insights into Disney's history as well as a glimpse at what was to come pertaining to the company's films, TV shows, consumer products, and theme parks. It would showcase the many different aspects of Disney for its loyal followers and give those who were less familiar with the company an overview of the multiple facets of the Disney enterprise.

A few of the fans who showed up that day at the D23 Expo might have been labeled by some as Disney "fanatics." But, many were simply moms and dads with children in tow, or individuals whose interests in Disney hearkened back to their own childhoods. What joined them together was their love for a company that, over the last 85+ years, has managed to capture the hearts of young and old alike with its vast array of family entertainment-related products and services.

Disney Company Background

Since the creation of Mickey Mouse in the late 1920s, the world has been captivated by the creations that began with the imagination of a man named Walter Elias Disney. Today, the image of Mickey Mouse is recognized worldwide as the symbol of a company equated with wholesome family entertainment.

The Disney Company's beginnings date back to 1923, when Walt Disney and his brother Roy began producing short cartoons in their Uncle Robert's garage in Los Angeles. After the debut of Mickey Mouse in *Steamboat Willie* in 1928, Walt Disney and his associates formed the Walt Disney Studio and began creating what was ultimately to become a legacy of animated characters featured in engaging, heartwarming, stories.

When Disney debuted *Snow White and the Seven Dwarfs* in 1937, it was the first time the world had seen a full-length animated feature film. The movie set a standard for the industry that was to influence the future of animated films, both for the Disney Studio as well as for its competitors.

Film and Television

For many years, animated films were at the heart of the Disney Studio's operations. The company became known for films that featured colorful characters, excellent storytelling, and the inevitable happy ending.

"You go to a Disney movie to feel good," said Joe Alfuso, a Los Angeles-based composer. "There's always a feeling that's great—love, compassion, hope, belief in the future. The whole idea of falling in love...ultimately, it's what we all want, it's what we're all looking for—a life full of love and fun and excitement and hope."[1]

By the 1950s, the company had branched out to live action films and into the "new" medium of television. For many growing up in the 1950s and 1960s, their memories of Disney are tied to *The Mickey Mouse Club* or the weekly *Disneyland* anthology television program.

Don Bitz remembers watching the *Disneyland* programs as a youngster. "Those influenced my character and my interests and my appreciation for nature and animals and history. It all really came out of those TV shows," he said.[2]

Theme Parks

For some, the *Disneyland* program introduced them to what was to be perhaps the most lasting of Walt Disney's contribution to the entertainment industry—a theme park called Disneyland. When Disneyland opened in Anaheim, Calif., in 1955, it was unlike any amusement park the world had ever seen.

Like the Disney Company's films and television programs, the park was geared toward families, especially those looking for a leisurely way to spend their time in a wholesome, family-friendly environment. People immediately took to a shine to Disneyland because it provided an escape from reality into a realm of fantasy, a chance to relax and revel in the stories associated with their childhood memories.

"It's a nice, safe place to be," explained Disneyland patron Milt Thurman. "It's not today, it's not tomorrow, it's forever. It's just a great place," he said.[3]

Disneyland was only the beginning of what has since become a network of 11 Disney theme parks, including international parks in Tokyo, Paris, and Hong Kong. Eight of the 11 parks rank among the top 10 most attended theme parks in the world.[4]

Corporate Growth

After the death of Walt Disney in 1966, the Disney Company continued to grow and change with the times. New leadership brought new ideas. Since then, the company has stretched itself far beyond the parameters of films, television programs, and theme parks into arenas such as travel, sports, radio, and online media. At the same time, the foundation of its business—the art of family-friendly storytelling—remains at its core.

The Disney Company is involved in so many different areas of the entertainment industry that it manages to offer something for practically everyone, even those who may not consider themselves Disney fans. For example, Disney merchandise such as clothing, toys, stationery, jewelry, and even food products is consumed by people of all ages.

The company owns its own cable channel, the Disney Channel, which shows a series of TV sitcoms and made-for-TV movies that appeal to teens and "tweens." At the same time, Disney also owns ESPN, considered a leader in sports television programming and popular with all sorts of individuals who may never have set foot in a Disney theme park. With all its diverse assets, in 2010, the Walt Disney Company ranked as the number one entertainment corporation in the world.[5]

Disney Fans

One factor that sets Disney apart from other large, global corporations is the multifaceted nature of its consumers. For instance, there are those who are keenly interested in anything and everything put forth by the Disney Company simply because it *is* Disney.

The D23 Fan Club was launched by the Disney Company in 2009 in response to the interests of these many fans and followers. (The "D" stands for Disney; "23" represents 1923, the year Walt Disney moved to California and started his West Coast studio.) In fact, D23 is just one of many Disney fan clubs that exist all over the world.

The Disneyana Fan Club—formerly the National Fantasy Fan Club (NFFC)—is another group populated by lovers of Disney products. The club was started by a handful of friends and Disney fans in the mid 1980s and has grown to include thousands of members who belong to chapters throughout the United States, Canada, Australia, and Japan. The group holds its own convention every summer in Anaheim, Calif.

Don Bitz is the membership coordinator of the Los Angeles chapter of the Disneyana Fan Club. "It's really diverse, a lot of people with different interests," he said. "Some people are collectors, some are interested in visiting the parks, and for some it's more of a social thing.

"The Disney fan kingdom has grown to an amazing level," he added. In addition to the clubs, he said, there are a lot of different fan websites such as LaughingPlace.com, MousePlanet.com, and MiceAge.com.[6]

The Disneyana Fan Club has chapters around the world and sponsors a variety of activities and special events for members.

Some fans go to great lengths to express their love of Disney. Roe Weatherspoon of Fullerton, Calif., won a "Best in Show" award at the 2010 Orange County Fair for a map of Disneyland she constructed of mosaic tiles and Disney pins. According to the *Orange County Register*, she spent nearly $3,000 and 1,200 hours putting the project together.[7]

George Reiger could be considered the ultimate Disney fan. According to an article in the Allentown *Morning Call*, the Pennsylvania resident makes regular pilgrimages to Disney's Florida parks and has decorated his home with Disney collectibles and memorabilia. What identifies him instantly to others as a Disney fan, however, are the many Disney tattoos he has all over his body—more than 2,400.[8]

While Weatherspoon, Reiger, and others like them may be quite exuberant in expressing their devotion to the Disney Company, most typical Disney fans are merely consumers of the organization's many different forms of media and entertainment. Their reasons for partaking of Disney products spring from their own personal interest in the "warm and fuzzy" nature of these products, or, in some cases, from their desire to provide their families with a source of good, clean, family entertainment. It is these individuals whom the company caters to by continuing to develop new wares to keep people coming back for more.

Did You Know?

When D23 was launched in 2009, it became the Disney Company's first official company-wide fan club.

Why Do We Love Disney?

While there is no doubt that the Disney Company has left an indelible mark on the field of entertainment and on those who consume it, the bigger questions are, why and how? Why do so many people love Disney? How has the Disney Company managed to transform itself into the entertainment powerhouse the world knows today and garner such a loyal following?

Much of the early credit for the company's success stems from the creative ideas put forth and carried out by Walt Disney and his associates. It can also be attributed to the management and marketing strategies used by both Walt and Roy Disney to grow the company.

These strategies were honed by Michael Eisner, who became Disney CEO in 1984. Eisner and his management team led the expansion of the Disney Company far beyond the scope of its early beginnings. Eisner's 20 year reign as Disney CEO helped make the Disney Company a household brand. Today, his successor, Bob Iger, continues the company's growth as he leads it into the future.

In building its brand, the Disney Company has perfected the art of synergy, the integration of individual parts to form something greater than the whole. This has been a key element of the organization's success in building global awareness of and appreciation for Disney products. This type of corporate synergy is something that has set the Disney Company apart from the pack in many respects and has been emulated but never equaled by other corporations.

Focus of the Book

The purpose of this book is to delve into the many different aspects of the Disney Company and to show how the organization's innovative management and marketing practices have helped make Disney the powerful brand it is today. The book will start at the beginning with the early days of Walt Disney, show the evolution of the company, and discuss the products and services Disney has created and marketed over the years to build its brand. It will also show the impact these products and services have had on Disney consumers. Following is a description of the topics that will be addressed in each chapter.

Disney History: The Walt Disney Years

The Disney Company began with the creative ideas of a man named Walt Disney. Chapter 2 provides background information on the early years of the Disney Company and the efforts Walt and his brother Roy put into transforming these ideas into a full-fledged business. The chapter will describe the growth and development of the organization under the direction of Walt Disney until his death in 1966.

Disney History: The Post-Walt Years

After Walt Disney died, the Disney Company experienced a period of uncertainty that lasted for nearly two decades. In the mid-1980s, the hiring of Michael Eisner as Disney CEO marked a new beginning for the organization, one that included tremendous growth and expansion. Chapter 3 will address the changes the company went through under the leadership of Michael Eisner and will discuss the outlook for the company's future under current CEO Bob Iger.

Disney Characters

Colorful characters have been one of the main reasons people have loved Disney since the company's beginnings. Chapter 4 will examine the creation of some of Disney's most popular characters, including Mickey Mouse, Donald Duck, and Winnie the Pooh. It will explain how and why these characters have come to mean so much to so many people. Information will be included about the company's character franchises like the Disney Princesses and Disney Fairies. The chapter will also discuss the franchise potential of its recently acquired characters from Marvel Entertainment.

Disney Films

The Disney Company was an early pioneer in the creation of animated films, beginning with Mickey Mouse cartoons, Silly Symphony cartoon shorts, and the release of the first feature-length animated film, *Snow White and the Seven Dwarfs*. The company also ventured into the live action "family fare" film market in the 1960s. It later added several more sophisticated film companies to its repertoire with the addition of Touchstone Pictures and Miramax. Chapter 5 will examine the role films have played in the growth of the Disney Company and the impact the company has had on the film industry.

Disney Television

As with films, television has been significant in generating the public's interest in Disney. Chapter 6 will look at how Walt Disney was able to harness the power of television in the 1950s to promote his Disneyland theme park, capture the attention of a generation with *The Mickey Mouse Club*, and regularly attract weekly audiences to his *Disneyland* television program. It will also look at the company's creation of the Disney Channel in 1983, and the acquisition of Capital Cities/ABC in the late 1990s.

Disney Theme Parks

Theme parks are the backbone of the Disney Company. Chapter 7 will discuss the beginnings of Disneyland in Anaheim, Calif., and will explain how this park led to the birth of the modern-day theme park. An overview of the company's parks in Florida, Japan, France, and Hong Kong will be provided, along with information about some of the challenges that have resulted from the expansion of the Disney theme park concept into international arenas.

Disney Music

Music has played an important role in many different aspects of the Disney Company. Disney's focus on music has included the creation of Academy Award–winning songs, the development of Walt Disney Records, the launching of Radio Disney, and the promotion of performers such as Hannah Montana and the Jonas Brothers. Chapter 8 will look at how music figures into Disney's operations and will discuss how the company has leveraged its music products to reach audiences throughout the world.

Disney Theater and Live Entertainment

The Disney Company's entree into theater and live entertainment in the 1990s offered audiences a new way to experience its well-known stories and characters. In addition, Disney's restoration of Broadway's New Amsterdam Theatre in the mid-1990s for the launch of its own productions helped pave the way for a new generation of Broadway shows. Chapter 9 will examine the influence Disney has had on Broadway theater productions with the launching of shows such as *Beauty and the Beast, The Lion King,* and *Mary Poppins.*

Disney Travel and Tourism

Disney's ventures into the travel and tourism market include the establishment of Disney Cruise Line as well as Adventures by Disney escorted tour packages. The company also does a brisk business through its Disney Vacation Club program. Chapter 10 will offer an overview of Disney's presence in the travel and tourism industry.

Disney Sports

Over the years, Disney has made several attempts to penetrate the sports market with a variety of sports-related ventures. Chapter 11 will provide a look at some of these, including the Disney Company's brief ownership of two sports teams, the Mighty Ducks and the Anaheim Angels. The chapter will also look at the company's influence on sports television programming through its ownership of ESPN, and its participation in the youth sports market with its Florida-based ESPN Wide World of Sports complex.

Disney Home Entertainment and Interactive Media

Disney has developed its home entertainment and interactive media business into one of the company's fastest-growing segments. The variety of home entertainment products offered by Disney ranges from high-tech diversions such as DVDs, video games, and social networking websites to more traditional forms of media like books and magazines. Chapter 12 will look at the company's approach to home entertainment media to show what has made this sector of the company so successful.

Disney Marketing and Promotion

Much of Disney's success can be attributed to innovative marketing and promotional practices. The Disney Company is a master at synergizing the components of its business to create overlaps that appear seamless from one product to the next. Chapter 13 will provide an overview of the famous Disney synergy and will offer examples of how the company has successfully engaged audiences through advertising, marketing, and promotion.

Disney Merchandising

Since the early days of the company, Disney has long specialized in product merchandising, beginning with the sales of Mickey Mouse tablets and watches in the 1930s. Chapter 14 will examine the various ways Disney has sold its merchandise to the public. The chapter will include information about Disney's targeted merchandising as well as the company's Disney Stores.

Disney and the Global Marketplace

Disney characters, films, and merchandise are known to audiences all over the globe. The company has put a great deal of effort into establishing a foothold in many different countries in order to make itself into a globally recognized brand. Chapter 15 will discuss the popularity of the Disney brand around the world and will analyze what the company has done to make its products so appealing to international audiences.

Did You Know?
The *Orange County Register* runs a newspaper column and online blog called "Around Disney."

Alternative Perspectives

Although this book is called *Why We Love Disney*, it must be acknowledged that not everyone *does* love Disney. Some, in fact, are quite critical of the company.

A wide range of books, websites, and magazine and newspaper articles written over the years have expressed the point of view that Disney is not the wholesome provider of family entertainment it claims to be. Some see the company as a big, bad corporation that manipulates children and their parents, getting them to consume products that communicate harmful messages to young minds.

What makes the Disney Company so interesting to study is that it does provoke such lively debate. This book itself is only the latest in a long line of publications, documentaries, and even college courses that focus on the influence of the organization. While it espouses a certain point of view, there are many other books worth reading that offer a myriad of perspectives on Disney. For this reason, a list of suggested readings about Disney is provided at the end of this book.

Conclusion

In the end, the fans who stood in line to see Bob Iger on the first day of the D23 Expo were not disappointed. Iger talked about some of the plans that lay ahead for Disney, including the development of the company's latest addition to its entertainment repertoire—Marvel Entertainment. Disney's purchase of Marvel had been announced just a few weeks before the Expo.

Iger also showed the audience a preview of the company's forthcoming animated feature, *The Princess and the Frog*, a film that was to signify Disney's return to its roots in hand-drawn animation after several years of sole reliance on computer technology for its animated films.

Iger stressed to the audience the core philosophy underlying Disney's multidimensional magic kingdom. "We all work toward one goal—bringing together artistry and technology and innovation to tell a great story," he said. This stems from an "unprecedented desire to create and imagine coming from every corner of the Disney Company."[9]

This book will provide a glimpse into the corners of the company by telling Disney's own story and discussing the influence the Disney Company has had on the business of entertainment. ♦

Figure 1: Disney Fan Clubs and Websites

Disney Fan Clubs

D23–The Official Disney Fan Club–http://d23.disney.go.com
Disneyana Fan Club–www.disneyanafanclub.org
Disney Fan Club (social networking)–www.disneyfanclub.org

Disney-Related Websites

AllEars.Net–www.allears.net
DIS–www.wdwinfo.com
Hidden Mickeys Guide–www.hiddenmickeysguide.com
LaughingPlace–www.laughingplace.com
MiceAge/MiceChat–www.miceage.com
MousePlanet–www.mouseplanet.com
MouseSavers–www.mousesavers.com
Passporter–www.passporter.com
WDWMagic–www.wdwmagic.com
Yesterland–www.yesterland.com

Notes

1.   Joe Alfuso, telephone interview, June 21, 2010.
2.   Don Bitz, in-person interview, July 18, 2010.
3.   Milt Thurman, telephone interview, August 2, 2010.
4.   See Themed Entertainment Association/AECOM, 2009 *Themed Index: The Global Attractions Attendance Report*, 2009, 11-12.
5.   "Fortune 500 Ranked Within Industries," *Fortune*, May 3, 2010, F-35.
6.   Don Bitz, in-person interview, July 18, 2010.
7.   See Deepa Bharath, "Creative Women Emerge Winners at the Fair," *Orange County Register*, 6 August 2010.
8.   See Tim Blangger, "All Disney, All the Time," *The Morning Call*, 15 July 2006, D3; See also Mike Schneider, "Disney Retains its Magical Pull," *Houston Chronicle*, 8 May 2005, 18.
9.   Bob Iger, public presentation at D23 Expo, Anaheim, Calif., September 10, 2010.

2

Disney History: The Walt Disney Years

Many authors, biographers, and historians have attempted to chronicle the story of Walt Disney and the company he founded. What makes the story so complex is that it is actually two stories: the tale of Walt Disney's personal influence on the business he created, and the discussion of what has happened to this company since his death in 1966.

Although Disney certainly did not build his empire alone, there is no doubt that much of what is known of the company today began with his ideas, creativity, and genius. Therefore, in order to understand the innerworkings of the existing Disney Company, it is necessary to start at the beginning.

The genesis of the Disney Company began with one person's imagination and determination and his ability to follow his dreams and make many of them come true. This effort was backed by a supporting cast of thousands—animators, engineers, songwriters, executives, merchandisers, family members, and the like—who were able to help him accomplish much of what he set out to do in his lifetime and even beyond.

As a result, Walt Disney was able to break new ground in many different areas of the entertainment industry, sometimes in bold and innovative ways. His early efforts provided the foundation for the multimedia enterprise that exists today.

This chapter will provide background on the life of Walt Disney and his role in the founding and growth of The Walt Disney Studios, which is known worldwide as The Walt Disney Company. It will examine the evolution of the organization under the watchful eye of its founder and chronicle the many achievements that helped Disney make his mark on the world of entertainment. The following chapter will focus on the post-Disney years and will look at what the company has become today.

The Early Years

Walter Elias Disney was born in Chicago on December 5, 1901. He spent part of his formative years growing up on a farm in a small town called Marceline, Mo. Although this was only a brief period of his youth, it helped shape some of the ideas and values that later influenced his work and attitudes about what he considered the ideal American way of life.

Disney was the fourth of five children. His mother Flora was German-American, and his father Elias was Irish-Canadian. Disney had three older brothers—Herbert, Raymond, and Roy—and a younger sister, Ruth. Roy was among his biggest supporters and was later to become his lifelong business partner.[1]

During his youth, Disney's father moved the family several times back and forth between Kansas City, Mo., and Chicago. Drawing, sketching, and photography were always keen interests of Disney's. While attending high school in Chicago, he drew cartoons for the school paper and also took art classes at night at the Chicago Institute of Art.

During World War I, Disney tried to enlist in the armed services but was turned away because he was only 16. Instead, he volunteered for the Red Cross and went to France as an ambulance driver from 1918-1919. After the war ended, he moved to Kansas City to look for work.

Disney was hired to create advertisements for the Pesmen-Rubin Commercial Art Studio and later by the Kansas City Film Ad Company, where he learned how to animate cartoons. It was during this time that he met fellow artist Ubbe Iwwerks (who later shortened his name to Ub Iwerks), who was to be instrumental to his future career.

The pair formed a company called Laugh-O-Gram films and began creating cartoon shorts. Although the business was eventually forced to close because of financial problems, the experience led to Disney's decision to take the next step and head west to Hollywood to try and make it in the film industry.

Getting Started in Hollywood

In 1923, Walt Disney boarded a train bound for Los Angeles with some samples of his work and $40 to his name. Disney's brother Roy had already relocated to southern California and had encouraged Walt to join him there. Disney moved in temporarily with his Uncle Robert and rented space in his uncle's garage, where he and Roy built their first primitive animation studio.[2]

Walt Disney's first studio in his Uncle Robert's garage has been preserved and is now part of the Stanley Ranch Museum in Garden Grove, Calif.

The Alice Comedies

Prior to dissolving Laugh-O-Grams, Disney and Iwerks had put together a short film called *Alice's Wonderland*. The film combined live action and animation and featured a four-year-old girl named Virginia Davis as "Alice." Disney first filmed Davis against a white backdrop and then added animated background scenes and characters.

After relocating to Hollywood and unable to find the kind of studio work he desired, Disney ultimately sent the Alice film he and Iwerks had created to Margaret Winkler, a New York film distributor. She liked the film and agreed to hire Disney on a contract basis to produce an additional 12 Alice comedies at $1,500 apiece.

Roy Disney agreed to become his brother's business manager, and the two moved into a new building and officially declared themselves open for business on October 16, 1923. This is credited as the founding date of the Disney Company. Although originally called the Disney Brothers Cartoon Studio, the brothers eventually changed the company's name to The Walt Disney Studios.[3]

Walt and Roy began hiring employees to work on the project, including several "ink and paint girls." One of these was Lillian Bounds, whom Walt Disney later married in 1925. Eventually, he also convinced his former partner, Ub Iwerks, to relocate to Los Angeles and join the business. In 1926, the brothers moved the company to a new studio on Hyperion Avenue in Los Angeles.

Between 1923-1927, the studio produced 56 Alice comedies. Although the films were not great moneymakers, they justified themselves in other ways, explained historians Russell Merritt and J.B. Kaufman.

> All in all, Disney could well afford to be proud of the Alice films. During the course of their production he had proven himself as a producer, and had built up an animation studio that was the equal of any in the business.[4]

Oswald the Rabbit

Soon after the Alice series ended, Disney and company began work on a new character, Oswald the Lucky Rabbit, a roly-poly rabbit with long black ears and lots of energy. Margaret Winkler and her new husband, Charles Mintz, offered Disney a one-year contract to produce 27 Oswald cartoons, which they then distributed to Universal Pictures. Oswald was well received by the public right from the start.

Oswald was also Disney's first creation to be featured on merchandise, according to biographer Bob Thomas. "Oswald first appeared on a chocolate-coated marshmallow candy bar made by the Vogan Candy Corporation of Portland, Oregon, the wrapper bearing the message: 'Watch for OSWALD in Universal Pictures.' The Philadelphia Badge Company also issued a button with Oswald's likeness, and the Universal Tag and Novelty Company offered an Oswald Stencil Set."[5]

When it came time to renew the contract for the Oswald cartoons in 1928, however, Disney was in for a nasty surprise. Mintz met with Disney in New York and informed him that he wanted Disney to come to work directly for him and his wife. He told the young entrepreneur he had already hired away most of Disney's studio animators who had agreed to make the move.

When Disney refused, Mintz dealt him a final blow. He informed him that he could no longer produce the Oswald cartoons on his own, as he did not own the rights to the Oswald character—they belonged to Universal. He suggested to Disney that if he turned down this offer, his career in animation was likely finished.

After trying to negotiate with Mintz to no avail, Disney called his brother Roy in California. Roy confirmed that most of their animators, with the exception of Ub Iwerks, had deserted them to go and work for Mintz. Disney then boarded a train for Los Angeles, disappointed and resigned to the fact that he now needed a new idea to keep his business going.

The Birth of Mickey Mouse

Over the years, the story of Walt Disney's solution to his Oswald dilemma is one that has become enshrouded in a combination of fact and myth. Even the company's official biography of Disney is a bit vague about the details. Here is one version that has been recounted in a number of books written about the man.

After his final meeting with Charles Mintz in New York, a dejected Walt Disney and his wife Lillian got on a train and headed west. During the train ride, Disney began doodling to try and come up with a new cartoon character. The result was a drawing of a little mouse. When Disney suggested he be called "Mortimer," his wife thought "Mickey" would be a more suitable name.

Other versions of the story suggest that while Disney may have come up with the idea for a cartoon mouse, it was actually Ub Iwerks who designed the character once Disney returned to Hollywood and told him about it. Regardless of the real story, one fact was clear—Walt Disney was determined not to be sidelined by his loss of Oswald. He was ready to get back on the horse and try again.

If anything, this experience taught Disney a valuable lesson that was to guide the philosophy of the company forever: Never give up control. This philosophy underlies many of the company's activities, particularly when it comes to copyright and trademark-related issues.

Upon Disney's return to Hollywood, he and Iwerks began working on their new creation. They developed two cartoons based on Mickey Mouse—*Plane Crazy* and *Gallopin' Gauchos*. While the films received a positive response from those who viewed them, the studio was unable to find a distributor willing to invest in them.

Around the same time Disney was working on Mickey Mouse, the first movie with sound—*The Jazz Singer*—had been released and was rumored to have the potential to revolutionize the film industry. Disney and Iwerks were in the midst of working on a third Mickey Mouse cartoon when they decided to rework it to include synchronized sound.

The result proved to be worth the extra effort. *Steamboat Willie*, starring Mickey Mouse, debuted at the Colony Theater in New York City on November 18, 1928. The *New York Times* called it "an ingenious piece of work with a good deal of fun."[6] A new star was born, and Walt Disney was about to enter the next phase of his career.

Silly Symphonies

Mickey Mouse firmly established the Disney Studios as a leader in the development of animation. He also provided a secondary source of income for the studio through the sale of Mickey Mouse-related merchandise. This will be discussed further in Chapter 14.

Building on the success of the cartoon mouse, Disney, Iwerks, and studio animators began producing short cartoons called Silly Symphonies. These films "experimented with sound, music, and images to create moods and emotions, rather than humor as in other Disney productions," according to author Janet Wasko.[7]

Disney and his animators used these films to test out animation techniques they were able to incorporate later into feature-length films. Disney won his first Academy Award for Best Cartoon in 1932 for the Silly Symphony *Flowers and Trees*. More information about the Silly Symphonies will be provided in Chapter 5.

Snow White and the Seven Dwarfs

By this time, Disney's professional and personal lives were beginning to solidify. His studio had grown in size from 6 to 187 employees in less than a decade, according to biographer Bob Thomas.[8] He and his wife Lillian had a daughter, Diane, in 1933, and adopted a second daughter, Sharon, in 1936. Now he was ready for a new challenge—the production of his first full-length, animated feature.

One evening in 1934, Disney called his animators into his office and began to act out the story of *Snow White and the Seven Dwarfs*. He described the plot and characters and explained how the story might be transformed into an animated film. His audience was sold on the concept and began work on the film within the year.

Snow White and the Seven Dwarfs was Disney's biggest undertaking to date as well as his costliest. Many were skeptical about the film's potential to make money, including his brother Roy, who managed the business side of the studio. Roy sought out funds from the Bank of America and other sources to finance the film. Profits from sales of Mickey Mouse merchandise also helped fund the venture.

The production was such a risky undertaking that it was dubbed "Disney's Folly" by many in the business, who were dubious and yet curious to see if Disney could pull it off. Their curiosity was soon fulfilled.

Snow White and the Seven Dwarfs opened at the Carthay Circle Theater in Los Angeles on December 2, 1937, and was hailed as a masterpiece by critics. As one writer noted, "The studio would continue to turn out shorts for many years to come, but from that time on, the name 'Disney' meant feature-length, animated films."[9]

The film earned the studio $8 million within six months of its release. It won a special Academy Award the following spring, which was presented to Walt Disney by actress Shirley Temple and consisted of an Oscar accompanied by seven "junior" Oscars. This award is now on display at the Walt Disney Family Museum in San Francisco. More information about *Snow White and the Seven Dwarfs* will be discussed in Chapter 5.

With the profits from the film, the Disney brothers were able to move into a larger studio on Buena Vista Street in Burbank, where the company headquarters remains today. The success of *Snow White* led to work on the production of two additional full-length features released in 1940, *Pinocchio* and *Fantasia*. But, outside circumstances began to affect the atmosphere within the studio, which led to more difficult times ahead.

Studio Strike

At the end of the 1930s, the Second World War in Europe was having an impact on the distribution of Disney films to the European market, which was virtually closed for business. As European sales had made up approximately 45% of the Disney Studio's revenues for *Snow White*, this threatened to have severe consequences for the company's finances and led to some belt-tightening within the organization.[10]

At the same time, growing discontent with salaries at the company led to an attempt to unionize Disney employees in the spring of 1941. This resulted in a bitter strike that lasted nearly four months and had a long-lasting impact on the company. About one-third of Disney's employees walked out, including some of his key animators. This disrupted the studio's work on its latest film, *Bambi*, which was not released until the summer of 1942.

Though the strike was eventually settled, it came at a high cost, according to Bob Thomas.

> The 1941 strike had a profound effect on Walt, shaping his attitude toward politics and his relations with his employees. He was pushed further toward conservatism and anti-communism. And he suffered disillusion in his plans to make the Disney studio a worker's paradise.... Never again would the studio's creative people know the same free, intimate relationship with Walt that had existed in the studio during its formative years.[11]

Disney was absolutely convinced the strike was a communist-led effort, something he vehemently opposed. Many years later in 1947, he willingly testified before the House Un-American Activities Committee and reiterated his belief that communism had been the force behind the strike.[12]

South American Goodwill Tour

One of the factors that helped in the settlement of the strike was the removal of Walt Disney from the scene. In August of 1941, Disney was encouraged by the U.S. State Department to take a group of animators on a goodwill tour to South America. The stated purpose was to build a relationship with his South

American audience and possibly shoot some footage that could be used in future films. In reality, explained biographer Tom Tumbusch, "The Department was worried about Nazi sympathizers in South America and felt a visit from Walt Disney would help."[13]

At first, Disney resisted the idea, but with the encouragement of his brother Roy, he agreed to the trip. The tour served a dual purpose, as it also got Disney out of the way so that Roy could work toward a resolution of the studio strike.

While on tour, Disney was able to gather live action footage that was later integrated into two feature films, *Saludos Amigos* (1943) and *The Three Caballeros* (1945). The films proved popular in both South and North America when they were released to the public.

Impact of World War II on the Studio

After Disney's return from his South American tour, the studio released *Dumbo* in October 1941, which was the first film in several years to make a profit for the company. Two months later, on December 7, 1941, the Japanese invaded Pearl Harbor, and the United States officially became part of World War II the following day.

Immediately after the U.S. declaration of war against Japan, the military moved into the Disney Studios and transformed it into what biographer Steven Watts called a "wartime industrial plant."[14] Disney shifted the studio's production efforts from developing animated feature films to creating a series of training and educational short films for the U.S. government and American public.

Some of these were intended to promote patriotism and encourage the public to join in the fight against the war effort by engaging in activities such as conserving resources and paying income taxes. A number of them featured Donald Duck, one of Disney's most popular characters at the time. The most well known of these was *Der Fuehrer's Face*, which inspired an accompanying theme song by Spike Jones and won an Academy Award in 1943.

The Post-War Years

Disney's contribution to the war effort was impressive and resulted in more than a multitude of films. However, the war brought the studio's production of animated features to a virtual standstill and left the company with financial woes that plagued the organization for many years after the war. It was not until the early 1950s that the company was able to fully resume its release of feature-length animated films and begin to regain its financial footing.

Return to Animated Features

Disney reestablished itself as a leader in animation with the company's release of *Cinderella* in 1950. The film introduced Disney's second princess and contained many of the same story elements that had made *Snow White and the Seven Dwarfs* such a success.

Cinderella did well at the box office, which helped the organization in several ways, noted Tom Tumbusch. "Cinderella regained the public's confidence in Disney family entertainment and the profits were used to reduce the company's debt...."[15]

More animated films soon followed—*Alice in Wonderland* (1951), *Peter Pan* (1953), *Lady and the Tramp* (1955), and *Sleeping Beauty* (1959). Although none performed as well as *Cinderella*, the films kept the Disney name prominent and helped the company regain its position in the industry.

Live Action Films

It was during this same period that the studio began producing live action films for the first time in the company's history. Several live action/animation combinations such as *Song of the South* (1946) and *So Dear to My Heart* (1948) had been released in the past, but the studio had never attempted a straight live action feature. Although Walt Disney was not a big fan of live action, he realized that these films were much less expensive to produce and had the potential to make money that could be used to finance the animated features he preferred.

True-Life Adventures

In addition to full-length live action features, in the late 1940s, Disney began producing a series of nature featurettes after returning from a trip to Alaska. In the late 1940s, he hired Alfred and Elma Milotte to go to Alaska and film different aspects of Alaskan wildlife, especially seals. The footage was edited, and a story line was then added.

The result was *Seal Island* (1948), the first of a nature series called True-Life Adventures. The film won an Academy Award in 1949 and was just the beginning of Disney's venture into a succession of 13 short and full-length nature films. More information about the True-Life Adventures will be discussed in Chapter 5.

The Creation of Disneyland

Although the company was starting to turn a profit again by the early 1950s, Walt Disney's heart was not completely into what was going on at the studio. Instead, he had begun to contemplate expanding his business beyond the production of films and venturing into a much broader entertainment arena.

A New Kind of Family Entertainment

As mentioned earlier, Disney had two daughters, Diane and Sharon. As a father typical of his times, he frequently spent Sunday afternoon with them, sometimes accompanying them to local amusement parks. As his children played on the rides, Disney would sit on a bench, bored, wishing these parks offered some form of entertainment for adults as well as children.

As a result of these outings, Disney began formulating the ideas for what was to become his biggest project to date—the creation of a family-oriented amusement park that would embody all the Disney Studio had come to represent: fun, entertainment, and the promotion of family values. It would be a park with a theme, based on the films and characters that had put the Disney Company on the map. He planned to call the park "Disneyland."

When he pitched his idea to his brother Roy and others in the company, he was met with a great deal of negativity. The idea of a theme park was so far removed from the kind of business the company operated, and the potential costs of building such an enterprise seemed staggering.

Not to be deterred, Disney formed a second company, WED Enterprises (for Walter Elias Disney) and used it as a basis of operations for financing and developing his theme park project. He sold his vacation home in Palm Springs, Calif., and borrowed money against his life insurance policy to raise money for the venture. Then he found a site in Anaheim, Calif., a 160-acre orange grove, where he planned to build the park.

Television and Disney Magic

One factor that helped pave the way for the construction of Disneyland was the introduction of television. By the early 1950s, television was proving to be a popular medium with the public, and many film studio executives were cautiously waiting to see how much this newfangled contraption would impact their businesses.

Disney had already made his first foray into television in 1950 when he produced a one-hour television special for NBC called *One Hour in Wonderland*. The show was essentially a promotional piece for his forthcoming film, *Alice in Wonderland*. But, it allowed him to test the new medium to see how far-reaching an impact it might have on the American public.

As he began developing the ideas for his Disneyland theme park, Disney realized that television could be the ace in the hole he needed to finance the project. With Roy Disney as the chief negotiator, the studio struck a deal with television network ABC, which would bring in revenue for the building of the park while at the same time introduce the Disney company to a new audience through the small screen.

In exchange for ABC's $500,000 investment in the Disneyland park, Disney agreed to produce a weekly television show called *Disneyland*. The program provided an anthology show series for ABC, but it also allowed Disney to promote the construction of his park to a national audience via the show.

Disney also agreed to produce a second television show, a children's program called *The Mickey Mouse Club*. This proved instrumental in building a bigger fan base for and greater awareness of the company. Additional information about Disney's early involvement with television will be provided in Chapter 6.

The Opening of Disneyland

Once the financing was secured, work on Disneyland progressed. The park cost $17 million to build and was completed within a year. Disneyland officially opened for business on July 17, 1955. On the first day alone, 28,000 people passed through its gates, and thousands more watched the opening on television. Within six months, a million people had visited the park.[16] More detailed information about Disneyland will be provided in Chapter 7.

What made the park special was that it was a three-dimensional depiction of many of the stories and characters the public already knew about and loved through Disney's films. This helped generate interest and build momentum with the public. As a result, millions of people have continued to flow into the park in the more than 50 years that have passed since its opening day.

Disneyland did more than just allow Walt Disney to see his fantasy theme park project brought to life. It moved the company in a whole new direction and was just the beginning of what was to be an ongoing expansion of the company's entertainment undertakings for many years to come.

Did You Know?
Roy Disney purchased the first admission ticket to Disneyland in 1955, #000001. He paid $1.00 for it.

1964 World's Fair

With the formation of WED, Disney was able to hire technical and creative personnel to develop the exhibits for the Disneyland park. These individuals became known as Disney "Imagineers," a term that is still used by the company today.

Audio-Animatronics

One of the projects spearheaded by these Imagineers was the development of a new type of animation technology called "audio-animatronics." The process used robotic technology to make inanimate objects appear lifelike, giving them the ability to move and speak as though they were alive.

The first audio-animatronics figures appeared at the Disneyland park in the Enchanted Tiki Room, an attraction featuring moving, talking, and singing birds and flowers. The Tiki Room figures charmed the public, and Walt Disney hoped to keep developing the technology to give it more exposure.

A Worldwide Stage

The 1964 New York World's Fair gave Disney the platform he needed to broaden his audience and test out his new creations. When the fair was in its planning stages, Roy and Walt negotiated with several organizations to develop exhibits for them that would be seen by thousands of fair attendees.

One of these was an exhibit sponsored by the State of Illinois called, "Great Moments with Mr. Lincoln." Using the audio-animatronics technology, the attraction featured a life-sized replica of President Abraham Lincoln as its centerpiece.

A second exhibit designed for General Electric was called the "Carousel of Progress." It presented a look at how electricity had changed the world over time and included scenes featuring audio-animatronics families representing different time periods.

For the Ford Motor Company, Disney contributed an exhibit called the "Magic Skyway," a journey through time where fair-goers began by encountering life-like prehistoric creatures and ended their ride in a futuristic city.

The fourth exhibit to use the audio-animatronics technology was a boat ride sponsored by Pepsi-Cola in conjunction with UNICEF. Called "It's a Small World," it showcased audio-animatronics replicas of children from all over the world wearing native dress and singing a song by the same name written by Richard M. and Robert B. Sherman. The ride and the song have since become forever associated with Disney.

After the World's Fair ended, two of the exhibits, "Great Moments with Mr. Lincoln," and "It's a Small World," were relocated to Disneyland, as were the prehistoric figures from the Magic Skyway ride. The Carousel of Progress was later recreated at both Disneyland and Walt Disney World with General Electric as a sponsor.

The World's Fair offered great exposure for the Disney Company, as it illustrated the potential of the audio-animatronics technology to worldwide audiences. The fair also underscored the importance of Disney's involvement in building corporate partnerships, which was to play a key role in the development of future Disney theme parks. More about this will be discussed in Chapter 13.

Mary Poppins

As public interest in animated films began to decline in the 1960s, the Disney Studio started making more and more live action films to remain financially solvent. Although Walt Disney was now less involved in the film part of the business than he had been in the company's earlier years, one of his last films was, in fact, a movie that is often hailed as the best of his career—*Mary Poppins*.

Mary Poppins returned the studio to its live action/animation roots, which dated back to the early days of *Alice's Wonderland*. Based on the P.L. Travers books about a magical English nanny, the film was in many ways a personal coup for Disney, as it had taken him nearly 20 years to secure the rights from Travers to produce the film.

Actor Dick Van Dyke was chosen to portray Bert the chimney sweep, and English actress Julie Andrews, a newcomer to the silver screen who had made a name for herself on Broadway in *Camelot* and *My Fair Lady*, became Mary Poppins.

When it opened at Grauman's Chinese Theater in Los Angeles on August 27, 1964, *Mary Poppins* was hailed by critics. It was nominated for 13 Academy Awards and won five, including Best Actress for Julie Andrews.

Plans for the Theme Park of the Future

By the early 1960s, Disneyland was running smoothly, and Walt Disney was ready to move on to the next phase of his theme park plans. His goal was to build another park on the East Coast for those who were unable to experience what he had created in California.

Disney was unhappy with what he called the "Las Vegas honky tonk" that had been built up on the land surrounding Disneyland since 1955—motels, souvenir shops, and cheap eateries.[17] He wanted his new park to have plenty of space for development, so that it would truly feel like a "magic kingdom."

He began purchasing parcels of land in central Florida, using a variety of assumed names to avoid arousing suspicion of those in the area. By the time he was finished, the company owned 43.5 square miles of land near Orlando, Fla. According to author Janet Wasko, he purchased the land "at around $200 per acre—a price that would have been considerably higher had Disney involvement been known."[18]

Disney had a vision for his new venture that would combine a second Disneyland theme park with what he called the "Experimental Prototype Community of Tomorrow" (Epcot). This was to be an actual city where people could live, work, and build a sense of community. It was to include internationally themed plazas containing shops and restaurants reminiscent of faraway places such as Great Britain and Scandinavia.

Although Disney was not able to realize this dream in his lifetime, parts of his vision were later incorporated into the World Showcase section of the Epcot theme park and Celebration housing community, both of which will be discussed in Chapter 7.

The End of an Era

Disney was unable to see his dream of an experimental community fulfilled because of his unexpected death in December 1966. A longtime smoker, Disney was diagnosed with lung cancer in early November 1966. Surgery to remove one of his lungs revealed the severity of his illness, and his doctors estimated he had between six months to two years left to live.

Although he was able to return to work for a brief stint several weeks after surgery, he returned to the hospital shortly afterward and died on December 15, 1966, of acute circulatory collapse.[19]

The response to Disney's death was a mixture of shock, sadness, and disbelief. Because his illness had been so brief, many people, including his family members and employees, were unprepared for the end.

The Walt Disney Family Museum in San Francisco includes a gallery that focuses on Disney's death. It is filled with memorabilia from all over the world in the way of personal letters and telegrams, newspaper articles, and even editorial cartoons reacting to his death. All of it shows just how far-reaching Disney's influence was.

In the years following Walt Disney's death, his brother Roy went ahead with plans to build a second theme park in Florida. It opened on October 1, 1971, and was named Walt Disney World as a tribute to the man who had conceived it. Roy Disney died two months later on December 20, 1971.

Conclusion

As noted at the beginning of this chapter, many have written in depth about the life of Walt Disney and the impact he had on the formation of what is today The Walt Disney Company, one of the most influential entertainment companies on the planet. Steve Segal, animator and animation instructor at the Academy of Art University and the California College of the Arts, called Disney's influence "immeasurable." He said, "Most everybody has been to some degree influenced by the work of Walt Disney."[20]

Disney was a complex figure, and many have tried to analyze and explain him based on what is known of both his professional and personal lives. Although this chapter by no means does justice to the life of Walt Disney, it provides an overview of the man and the long-lasting legacy he created.

For many years after his death, when tough decisions needed to be made at the company, the question was often posed—"What would Walt do?" The next chapter will examine how the Disney Company continued without Walt and how this question influenced many of the activities that took place within the organization after his death. ♦

Figure 2: Timeline—The Walt Disney Years

- 1901   Walter Elias Disney born December 5
- 1918   Joins World War I Red Cross Ambulance Corps
- 1919   Forms Laugh-O-Gram Films with Ub Iwerks
- 1923   Moves to Hollywood and starts business with brother Roy; signs contract to produce Alice Comedies
- 1925   Marries Lillian Bounds
- 1927   Creates Oswald the Lucky Rabbit
- 1928   Mickey Mouse debuts in *Steamboat Willie*
- 1932   *Flowers and Trees* released, wins Academy Award
- 1937   *Snow White and the Seven Dwarfs* released, wins Academy Award
- 1941   Studio strike; Disney goes on South American Goodwill Tour; U.S. Army takes over studio during WW II
- 1948   First True-Life Adventure, *Seal Island*, released, wins Academy Award
- 1950   First live action film, *Treasure Island*, released
- 1954   Premiere of *Disneyland* weekly television series
- 1955   Disneyland opens; premiere of *The Mickey Mouse Club*
- 1963   First use of audio-animatronics at Disneyland
- 1964   Disney exhibits debut at New York World's Fair; *Mary Poppins* released, wins 5 Academy Awards
- 1965   Disney buys land in Orlando, Fla., for construction of Experimental Prototype Community of Tomorrow
- 1966   Walt Disney dies December 15

Notes

1. Much of the biographical information about Walt Disney is drawn from the following sources: Bob Thomas, *Walt Disney: An American Original* (New York: Disney Editions, 1994); Tom Tumbusch, *Walt Disney The American Dreamer* (Dayton, OH: Tomart Publications, 2008); Steven Watts, *The Magic Kingdom: Walt Disney and the American Way of Life* (Columbia, MO: University of Missouri Press, 1997); Michael Barrier, *The Animated Man: A Life of Walt Disney* (Berkeley, CA: University of California Press, 2007); and Neil Gabler, *Walt Disney: The Triumph of the American Imagination* (New York: Vintage Books, 2006). Information also was drawn from sources on the company's website: The Walt Disney Company, "Company History," http://corporate.disney.go.com/corporate/complete_history_1.html; "Walt Disney: A Biography," http://disney.go.com/vault/read/walt/index.html.

2. See Wade Sampson, "The Little Disney Garage Nobody Wanted," *MousePlanet*, http://www.mouseplanet.com/8366/The_Little_Disney_Garage_Nobody_Wanted; and http://www.ci.garden-grove.ca.us/?q=/HistoricalSociety/disney.

3. The Walt Disney Company, "Company History," http://corporate.disney.go.com/corporate/complete_history_1.html.

4. Russell Merritt and J.B. Kaufman, *Walt in Wonderland: The Silent Films of Walt Disney* (Baltimore, MD: Johns Hopkins University Press, 1993): 82.

5. Bob Thomas, *Walt Disney: An American Original* (New York: Disney Editions, 1994): 85.

6. Mordaunt Hall, "The Screen," *The New York Times*, 19 November 1918, 16.

7. Janet Wasko, *Understanding Disney* (Cambridge, England: Polity Press, 2001): 11.

8. See Thomas, *Walt Disney: An American Original*, 123.

9. Jean-Pierre Isbouts, *Discovering Walt: The Magical Life of Walt Disney* (New York: Disney Editions, 2001): 34.

10. See Thomas, *Walt Disney: An American Original*, 161.

11. Ibid., 171.

12. See Steven Watts, *The Magic Kingdom: Walt Disney and the American Way of Life* (Columbia, MO: University of Missouri Press, 1997): 284.

13. Tom Tumbusch, *Walt Disney the American Dreamer* (Dayton, OH: Tomart Publications, 2008): 60.

14. Watts, *The Magic Kingdom: Walt Disney and the American Way of Life*, 229.

15. Tumbusch, *Walt Disney the American Dreamer*, 64.

16. Ibid, 387.

17. See Tumbusch, *Walt Disney the American Dreamer*, 119.

18. Wasko, *Understanding Disney*, 23.

19. See Thomas, *Walt Disney: An American Original*, 354.

20. Steve Segal, telephone interview, October 7, 2009.

3

Disney History: The Post-Walt Years

In the years following the death of Walt Disney, the Disney Company struggled to find its way without its founder. In the immediate years after Walt's death, Roy Disney attempted to finish some of the projects started by his brother, including the opening of a new theme park in Florida.

After Roy's death in 1971, a management team composed of executives who had worked under the two brothers tried to move the company forward with much difficulty. Tensions within the organization led to conflict and turmoil. Leadership changed hands several times between 1971 and 1984, resulting in inconsistencies in the decision-making process. Threats of corporate takeover also colored the climate within the organization.

It was not until 1984 that a new leader entered the picture, one who would shape the Disney corporate landscape for the next two decades. The hiring of Michael Eisner as Disney CEO led to a resurgence in the company's profits and heralded a vast corporate expansion that included Disney's film, theme park, and television divisions. Eisner's team also brought new ideas and new properties into the fold, including ventures in theater, travel, and sports.

Eventually, however, Eisner fell out of favor with Disney's board of directors, and by the mid-2000s, it was time for yet another change. Bob Iger became Disney CEO in 2005, and in the last few years, he has begun to develop new projects and initiatives that will help pioneer the company through the 21st century.

This chapter will continue the discussion of the history of the Disney Company, focusing on the years since Walt Disney's death in 1966. It will address the various individuals who have left their imprint on the company and explore how their actions have transformed the organization into the corporate giant it has become today.

Life After Walt

The suddenness of Walt Disney's death left many in the company at a loss. Because Disney had not fully revealed the severity of his illness, there had been no discussion of corporate succession planning prior to his demise. Even after being released from the hospital in the weeks before he died, Disney had shown up at the office, eager to continue working on his plans for his Florida theme park.

Roy Disney in Charge

After his brother died, Roy Disney tried to pick up where Walt had left off. Roy was 73 years old and had been hoping to retire, but he agreed to continue at the company to try and make his brother's dream come true.

Roy and Walt had not always agreed on the running of their business and had some bitter clashes over the years, particularly in light of issues related to the Disneyland park. But, Roy felt an obligation to his brother to try and see his vision through to completion.

Rather than run the entire company operation by himself, Roy Disney put together a committee of people who had worked closely with Walt. These included Walt's son-in-law Ron Miller, Card Walker, Donn Tatum, and Roy's own son, Roy E. Disney Jr.

Over the next five years, he devoted himself to the construction of the theme park component of the Florida enterprise. Given the complexity and costs of the rest of the vision, Epcot, Walt's experimental community, would have to come later.

Walt Disney World opened on October 1, 1971. Just two months after the park's debut, Roy Disney was dead, leaving the future of the Disney Company in question.

Struggling to Regroup

One of the political ramifications of the conflicts between the two brothers over the years, according to author Jon Lewis, was that the company had become polarized into what he called "Walt men" and "Roy men."[1] This was to affect the leadership of the company after Roy Disney's death.

Donn Tatum assumed the role of CEO, and Card Walker took charge of the studio in 1972. The two, along with Ron Miller, fell into the "Walt men" category. They were countered by a group led by Roy Disney's son, Roy Jr., who was a company vice president and who had a seat on the board—a spot secured for him by his father in 1967.[2]

Conflict between Miller and Roy Disney Jr. ultimately led to the latter's resignation from the studio in 1977. As Lewis explained:

> Despite their considerable personal differences, Miller and Roy Jr. had much the same vision for the company, but both at the time, and for different reasons, found themselves hamstrung by the late Walt Disney, who still guided the faltering company's every move.[3]

Roy Disney Jr. subsequently went into the investment business, launching Shamrock Holdings with entertainment lawyer Stanley Gold. Their business partnership was to have an impact on the company several years later.

Resistance to Change

The Disney Company struggled throughout the 1970s, particularly within the film division. At the insistence of Card Walker, who took over from Tatum as CEO in 1976, the company continued to produce G-rated family-friendly films even though the times and tastes of audiences demanded more sophisticated movies. As a result, most of the films produced during this period had lackluster box office performance.

While other film studios were turning out such blockbuster hits as *Star Wars* and *Jaws*, Disney had little to offer in the way of competition.[4] Disney's answer to *Star Wars* was *The Black Hole*, a science-fiction thriller, which promptly died at the box office when it was released in 1979. Even the release of *Tron*—a film filled with innovative, computer-generated special effects that debuted in 1982—had little impact on the movie-going public.

In the meantime, the opening of Epcot in Orlando, Fla., on October 1, 1982, added a third theme park to the company's holdings. This was followed by the launch of Tokyo Disneyland in 1983, which was to be run by the Oriental Land Co. as part of a licensing agreement with the Disney Company. The new parks brought in additional revenue for Disney, but it wasn't enough to restore the organization to its prior secure financial footing.

A Last Resort

Ron Miller became company CEO in 1983, and tried to set things right but with little success. Much of the corporate decision-making continued to be based on the approach of "What would Walt do?" This hampered the organization's ability to keep up with the times.

To his credit, Miller was able to accomplish several achievements during his brief tenure as CEO—the creation of the Disney Channel in 1983, and the launching of Touchstone Pictures in 1984. He also got the company into the home video market, which ultimately became an extremely lucrative arm of the business.

Touchstone Pictures was Disney's answer to the changing film market. It allowed the organization to begin issuing more adult-oriented films that could carry PG-13 and R ratings, making them more appealing to teenagers and adults. Touchstone's first release, *Splash,* in 1984 starred Tom Hanks and Darryl Hannah. It was the first solid hit the company had released in years.

Ironically, on the same day *Splash* was released, Roy Disney Jr. resigned from the Disney board of directors, setting the stage for a major corporate shift that would have a long-term effect on the company's leadership.

Changes in Leadership

Over the years, Roy Disney Jr. had become increasingly dissatisfied with the management of his family's business. In 1984, he set in motion a chain of events that would ultimately restructure the organization.

Working with business partner Stanley Gold, through a series of stock purchases and negotiations, Disney aligned himself with three of the company's major stockholders to threaten a corporate takeover. One of these investors was Bass Brothers Enterprises of Fort Worth, Tex. As a result of a series of carefully calculated stock transactions, noted author Janet Wasko,

"Bass Brothers Enterprises ended up with around 25 percent of the Disney stock, enough to control the company and to appoint their own managers."[5]

When the dust settled, Ron Miller was out as CEO. In his place, the Disney board of directors selected two Hollywood veterans, Michael Eisner, formerly of Paramount Pictures, and Frank Wells, formerly of Warner Bros. Eisner was named Disney CEO, and Wells became president. The move satisfied Roy Disney Jr., who eventually regained his seat on the board of directors, along with his colleague Stanley Gold.

A New Era: The Eisner Years

Eisner and Wells both had impressive track records prior to arriving at Disney. Eisner had worked in programming at ABC alongside executive Barry Diller. After Diller moved to Paramount Pictures in 1974, Eisner followed him two years later and became company president. Wells started out as an entertainment lawyer and eventually moved to Warner Bros., where he worked as a studio vice president. He became president in 1973.[6]

Though the pair did not know each other well before arriving at Disney, they quickly became an efficient team and set about trying to make changes for the better within the organization. To accomplish this, they brought over a number of executives from Paramount, including Jeffrey Katzenberg, who was hired to oversee the studio's film and television divisions. Roy Disney Jr. was also brought back into the fold to run the company's animation division.[7]

Reviving the Film Division

Eisner, Wells, and Katzenberg began by focusing on building up the company's fledgling Touchstone Pictures label. Katzenberg had a reputation for being a driven and tough taskmaster, and he immediately went to work applying these skills to Disney.[8]

Part of his strategy was to hire talent who were not blockbuster marquee stars. Instead, he focused on individuals whose careers were struggling, such as Bette Midler and Richard Dreyfuss, whom he hired for *Down and Out in Beverly Hills*, released in 1986. This approach enabled the studio to pay less for actors and earned the new regime a reputation of being notoriously tightfisted when it came to hiring.

These early efforts paid off in box office returns, however. In addition to *Down and Out in Beverly Hills*, some of Touchstone's early hits were *Ruthless People* (1986), *Three Men and a Baby* (1987), *Outrageous Fortune* (1987), and *Tin Men* (1987). *Ruthless People* was the highest grossing film in the first three years of Katzenberg's tenure at the studio.[9]

On the animation front, Roy Disney Jr. focused his energies on developing a new direction for animated films, one that was more in keeping up with the times. According to the *Los Angeles Times:*

> Disney persuaded the new regime to invest about $10 million in a digital ink and paint system developed by Pixar, a seemingly minor decision that proved to be a turning point in the company's fortunes. It would lay the foundation of Disney's relationship with the firm that pioneered computer-generated animation.[10]

The system was called the Computer Animated Production System (CAPS).

The first blockbuster animated film to result from Roy Disney Jr.'s efforts was *The Little Mermaid* (1989), based on a classic fairytale by Hans Christian Andersen. The film was the first animated hit the company had seen in many years. It paved the way for others that followed such as *Beauty and the Beast* (1991), *Aladdin* (1992), and *The Lion King* (1994).

Did You Know?

Former Disney CEO Michael Eisner worked at all three television networks—NBC, CBS, and ABC—before joining the Disney Company in 1984.

New Directions in Television

As noted in Chapter 2, Walt Disney had led the company into the world of television back in the mid-1950s with the creation of his weekly anthology series, *Disneyland*. The program had aired steadily on all three of the major networks since its inception but was discontinued in 1983, when Ron Miller launched the cable television Disney Channel, leaving the company without a network presence.

Eisner and Wells felt a return to network television would be in the company's best interests. They formed a television production unit called Touchstone Television, which began producing shows such as *The Golden Girls* and *Empty Nest*. They also brought back a new version of the weekly Disney television program with Michael Eisner serving as host just as Walt Disney once had done.

Theme Park Expansion

Theme park expansion was another part of the efforts to revive the company's sagging bottom line. The new leadership began adding attractions to both the Disneyland and Walt Disney World parks. A new Florida park, Disney-MGM Studios, was opened in 1989. In addition, the company opened its second international theme park—Euro Disney—outside Paris in 1992, as a means of giving the company a larger global presence.

Disney Theatrical Productions

Following the success of the animated film *Beauty and the Beast* in 1991, the company launched a Broadway production based on the movie in 1994. This was the beginning of a new corporate division called Disney Theatrical Productions. The division was responsible for the development and production of a variety of Broadway musicals based on some of Disney's well-known animated films, including *The Lion King*.

Developing Corporate Synergy

It was during the late 1980s and early 1990s that the term "corporate synergy" began to creep into the vocabulary of those writing about the Disney organization. Part of this was the approach taken by Eisner and his associates of integrating all aspects of the business for cross-promotional and ultimately moneymaking purposes.

As one writer observed, "Eisner and his team of executives created the concept of entertainment merchandising, spinning off books, toys, theme-park attractions and Broadway shows based on Disney movies."[11] Synergy became an enduring watchword at the Disney Company, one that is today an integral part of company operations. It will be discussed further in Chapter 13.

As a result of all these efforts, in the first 10 years of what became known as "Team Disney," under the leadership of Michael Eisner, the Disney Company's revenues went from $1.7 billion to $25.3 billion.[12] After years of setbacks, it appeared as though the company was well on its way to becoming a major player in the entertainment industry.

Reversal of Fortune

By the early 1990s, however, the golden glow was beginning to wear off Disney's dynamic duo. Profits began to dip as a result of an economic recession that affected consumer spending. Several of the large-scale films produced by the company during this time, such as *Dick Tracy* (1990) and *The Rocketeer* (1991), had disappointing box office returns. Euro Disney got off to a disastrous start and needed a financial bailout a few years later.

A proposed deal to acquire the Muppets from The Jim Henson Company fell through when Henson suddenly died in 1990, and Eisner and Henson's heirs were unable to agree on the terms of the sale. It would take another 14 years before the Disney Company was eventually able to acquire the Muppets in 2004.

Then in 1994, tragedy struck when Frank Wells was killed in a helicopter accident, leaving the company without a second-in-command. Jeffrey Katzenberg was keenly interested in the position, but Eisner rejected his bid for the job. As a result, Katzenberg left the company to form DreamWorks, which was to provide major competition to Disney on the animated film front in later years. Katzenberg also filed a lawsuit against Disney, which was eventually settled for approximately $250 million.[13]

Eisner ultimately hired his longtime friend Michael Ovitz for the president's job. Ovitz was a former talent agent who came from the Creative Artists Agency and did not fit well into the Disney regime right from the start. Within 15 months he was gone, exiting the company with a $140 million severance package, which sparked a shareholder lawsuit that was not resolved until 2005.[14]

Major Acquisition

In the midst of all the turmoil, Eisner was able to engineer what some believe to be his greatest achievement—the $19 billion acquisition of Capital Cities/ABC in 1995. Eisner had long been interested in expanding Disney's television division and had previously attempted to buy NBC from General Electric without success.

"The move greatly enhanced the company's position in television, sports programming, and international marketing, as well as adding publishing and multimedia to its operations," explained Janet Wasko.[15]

The acquisition included not only the entire array of ABC's holdings but the cable channels Lifetime, Arts and Entertainment, and ESPN. Disney's acquisition of Capital Cities/ABC made the company, for a brief period, the largest entertainment company in the world.[16]

New Corporate Ventures

As the 1990s progressed, Eisner began to expand the company's holdings even further. In 1998, the Disney Company moved into the travel business with the establishment of the Disney Cruise Line and began offering vacation packages to the Caribbean. The cruise line has since grown to include four passenger ships and itineraries in Mexico, Alaska, and the Mediterranean.

A second component of the travel business, an escorted tour company called Adventures by Disney, was added in 2005. More information about Disney's travel activities will be provided in Chapter 10.

Disney also made inroads into the world of professional sports in 1993, when Eisner negotiated the purchase of a National Hockey League expansion team, which he named The Mighty Ducks after a Disney film of the same name. This was followed a few years later by the purchase of an interest in the Anaheim Angels in 1995. Though both of these enterprises had strong starts, they ultimately became money-losing rather than money-making ventures. By 2005, both teams had been sold.

Relationship with Pixar Animation

As mentioned earlier, Roy Disney Jr. persuaded Eisner to have the company invest in a computer graphics animation system, which had been developed by Pixar Animation Studios, a relatively new company owned by Steve Jobs, co-founder and CEO of Apple Computer. Disney signed a contract with Pixar for the development of a new process called the Computer Animated Production System (CAPS). This system could be used to replace the traditional hand-drawn animation coloring process and proved to be a major innovation in the field of animation.

One of Pixar's employees was John Lasseter, a former Disney staff member who developed Pixar's first full-length animated feature film, *Toy Story*. As part of an agreement with Disney, when *Toy Story* was completed in 1995, Disney distributed the film.

Did You Know?

John Lasseter first worked for Disney as a Disneyland Jungle Cruise boat operator and Walt Disney Studios junior animator before moving on to Pixar in 1984.

With the success of *Toy Story*, Pixar and Disney then signed a long-term agreement that would cover Pixar's next five films. "The two companies split costs and profits 50-50, including merchandise.... Pixar produced the films while Disney handled all marketing and distribution duties," according to Hoovers.[17]

Pixar became an animation powerhouse, turning out one blockbuster hit after another and often surpassing Disney's own animated films in box office returns. As the time drew closer to the end of the agreement between the two companies, Steve Jobs wanted to negotiate a new deal, one that would give Pixar 100% of the profits and pay Disney a distribution fee. Eisner wouldn't hear of it, and in 2005, Jobs threatened to take his business elsewhere after the last film of the agreement, *Cars*, was released the following year.

Conflict and Change

As Michael Eisner continued to expand Disney's holdings, the relationship between him and Roy Disney Jr. began to deteriorate. Disney felt Eisner's focus had become more about acquiring other businesses rather than maintaining the quality of the company's core entertainment properties. He was quoted as calling Eisner "rapacious, soul-less and always looking for the 'quick buck' rather than long-term value."[18]

With his business partner and fellow board member Stanley Gold, Disney launched a campaign to replace Eisner as Disney CEO and unseat him as Chairman of the Board, thereby attempting to oust the man he had helped bring into the company 20 years earlier. After a period of intensive lobbying, Disney once again was successful in shaking things up at the company, just as he had done in 1984.

At a shareholder's meeting in Philadelphia in 2004, the Disney board of directors announced that it had issued a 45% vote of no-confidence against Michael Eisner. The board also announced its plans to separate the CEO position from that of Chairman of the Board, stripping Eisner of his role as Chairman and replacing him with long-time board member and former U.S. Senator George Mitchell.[19]

This was a tremendous blow to Eisner and a signal that his days at the Disney Company were numbered. Eisner's term as CEO was slated to end in 2006. On September 9, 2004, he announced his plans to retire when his contract expired. In the end, he left the company a year early on September 30, 2005. He was replaced by Disney president Bob Iger, who assumed the role of CEO the following day.

The Eisner era had come to an end. Once again, it was time for new leadership and a possible new direction for the Disney Company.

New Beginnings: The Iger Years

Disney's new CEO, Bob Iger, wasted no time in rolling up his sleeves and getting to work. Iger had come into the Disney fold through ABC, where he worked in news, sports, and entertainment programming. He eventually became ABC's president and chief operating officer in 1994. Then in 2000, he was named president and chief operating officer of the Disney Company.[20]

Move into New Media

Iger was known for his keen interest in technology, and he made that a priority as he began mapping out the future of the Disney Company. Shortly after becoming CEO, he agreed to have episodes of some of Disney's most popular ABC shows, such as *Lost* and *Desperate Housewives*, made available for purchase through Apple's iTunes store.

This opened up a whole new world of potential revenue for the company from a young, tech-savvy generation. This move also showed the world that Iger meant business when it came to making Disney a key player in the company's use of new media.

Did You Know?
Disney CEO Bob Iger began his career at ABC in 1974, after first working as a TV weatherman in Ithaca, N.Y.

Pixar Animation Studios Deal

Around the same time Iger became CEO, Disney's contract with Pixar Animation Studios was set to expire. As a result of previous tension between Michael Eisner and Steve Jobs, the Disney/Pixar distribution agreement was in danger of not being renewed, which would have been a huge financial blow to Disney.

Iger resumed negotiations with Pixar and then shocked the Hollywood community with a major announcement in early 2006. Instead of renegotiating the contract with Pixar, Disney planned to acquire the company outright for $7.4 billion.

The deal afforded Pixar CEO Steve Jobs a 7% stake in Disney, making him the company's largest single stockholder and earning him a seat on the Disney board of directors. Pixar president Ed Catmull would become president of the Pixar and Disney Animation Studios. John Lasseter was given the position of Chief Creative Officer for Disney Animation. Iger pledged to allow Pixar to continue to operate its studio in northern California with little changes to the culture of the organization, a promise he has since upheld.[21]

Philippe Perebinossoff, associate professor in the Department of Radio-TV-Film at Cal State Fullerton, worked with Iger at ABC in the 1990s. He said the Pixar deal offered insight into Iger's management style.

> With Iger, it's forming better relationships. He waited patiently as the number two man to Eisner. He waited and waited and was able to negotiate more favorable things—he brought them back.[22]

Purchase of Marvel Entertainment

Iger made headlines again just a few years later with the announcement in 2009 that Disney would acquire Marvel Entertainment for $4 billion. The purchase included an assortment of properties with great potential for the future, explained reporter Richard Siklos.

> In addition to film, Marvel has television, digital, and merchandising arms—not to mention a surprisingly buoyant business of still printing and selling comic books—all of which can undoubtedly be enhanced by being funneled into Disney's far vaster platform.[23]

For Disney, the acquisition of Marvel opened a door of possibilities for capturing a greater share of the boys' market for its products, something that had eluded the company for many years.

Corporate Restructuring

On the management front, Iger instigated a major corporate shake-up in late 2009, when he reshuffled some of Disney's key personnel. Iger edged out long-time studio chief Dick Cook and replaced him with Rich Ross, who moved into the position after many years of building up the company's Disney Channel.

Iger also turned some heads when he had theme park chief Jay Rasulo trade jobs with chief financial officer Thomas Staggs, in what one reporter compared to "asking the guys who play Pluto and Donald Duck to change costume."[24] Iger maintained that the switch had the potential to bring new perspectives to each division that could ultimately result in future growth.

At the same time, Iger announced plans to cut back on the number of live action films produced each year by the studio and to concentrate primarily on some of the more successful movie brands such as the *Pirates of the Caribbean* franchise. Additional information about this will be provided in Chapter 5.

The Return of Oswald

Perhaps the most touching of all Iger's moves since assuming the CEO role occurred during his first year on the job. In early 2006, Iger negotiated a deal with NBC Universal that involved the transfer of veteran sportscaster

Al Michaels from ABC to NBC. In exchange, Disney would obtain from NBC cable television rights to coverage of several forthcoming sporting events.[25]

As part of the deal, Iger negotiated to have Universal give the Disney Company back the rights to Oswald the Rabbit, Walt Disney's original cartoon character. In a tip of the hat to the company's founder, Iger achieved something no one had been able to accomplish in nearly 80 years—he brought Oswald home.

Conclusion

In the years since Walt Disney's death, the Disney Company has experienced a myriad of changes that have led to its growth and expansion amidst a wide range of corporate challenges. Initial uncertainty within the company in the early years after Disney's death eventually led to the hiring of a strong leader in the persona of Michael Eisner.

In the 20+ years Eisner held the Disney CEO position, he transformed the organization from a medium-sized company into an entertainment powerhouse. Eisner's management style and focus on the bottom line was not without its drawbacks, however. Eventually, it was called into question by others within the organization and ultimately led to his replacement by current CEO Bob Iger, who brought his own approach to the company.

Today, Iger is working to lead the company in a new direction, upholding the commitment to quality and family values started by Walt Disney while at the same time embracing the rapidly changing landscape of the 21st century. Only time will tell whether or not the Disney Company story will continue to have a happy ending. ◆

Figure 3: Timeline—The Post-Walt Years

- 1971   Walt Disney World opens; Roy Disney dies
- 1972   Donn Tatum becomes Disney CEO
- 1976   Card Walker becomes Disney CEO
- 1982   Epcot opens
- 1983   Ron Miller becomes Disney CEO; Tokyo Disneyland opens; Disney Channel debuts
- 1984   Michael Eisner becomes Disney CEO; Frank Wells becomes president; Touchstone Pictures launches
- 1989   Disney-MGM Studios opens
- 1992   Euro Disney opens
- 1994   *Beauty and the Beast* premieres on Broadway; Frank Wells dies
- 1995   Disney buys Capital Cities/ABC
- 1998   Disney Cruise Line launches; Disney's Animal Kingdom opens
- 2001   Disney's California Adventure opens; Tokyo Disney Sea opens
- 2002   Walt Disney Studios (Paris) opens
- 2004   Disney acquires Muppets from Jim Henson Company
- 2005   Bob Iger becomes Disney CEO; Hong Kong Disneyland opens; Adventures by Disney launches
- 2006   Disney acquires Pixar Animation Studios; Oswald the Rabbit returns to Disney
- 2009   Disney acquires Marvel Entertainment; agreement for Disneyland Shanghai announced

Notes

1.   See Jon Lewis, "Disney After Disney: Family Business and the Business of Family," in Eric Smoodin, ed., *Disney Discourse* (New York: Routledge, 1994): 97.
2.   Ibid.
3.   Ibid., 99.
4.   See Douglas Gomery, "Disney's Business History: A Reinterpretation," in Eric Smoodin, ed., *Disney Discourse* (New York: Routledge, 1994): 78.
5.   Janet Wasko, *Understanding Disney* (Cambridge, England: Polity Press, 2001): 32.
6.   For detailed information about the backgrounds of Eisner and Wells, see Ron Grover, *The Disney Touch: How a Daring Management Team Revived an Entertainment Empire* (Homewood, IL: Business One Irwin, 1991).
7.   See Dawn C. Chmielewski and James Bates, "Roy E. Disney, 1930-2009; Nephew of Walt Revived Animation," *Los Angeles Times,* 17 December 2009, 1.
8.   See Julie Salamon, "Jeffrey Katzenberg: Disney's New Mogul," *The Wall Street Journal,* 12 May 1987, 1; and Aljean Harmetz, "Who Makes Disney Run?" *The New York Times,* 7 February 1988, A29.
9.   See Gomery, "Disney's Business History: A Reinterpretation," 80.
10. Chmielewski and Bates, "Roy E. Disney, 1930-2009; Nephew of Walt Revived Animation," 1.
11. Wendy Tanaka, "Eisner Had Huge Influence on U.S. Pop Culture Despite Current Woes," *The Philadelphia Inquirer,* 1 March 2004, 1.
12. See Meredith Downes, Gail S. Russ, and Patricia A. Ryan, "Michael Eisner and His Reign at Disney," *Journal of the International Academy for Case Studies* 13:3 (2007): 74.
13. See Tanaka, "Eisner Had Huge Influence on U.S. Pop Culture Despite Current Woes," 1.
14. For more details about Ovitz, see Kim Masters, *The Keys to the Kingdom: How Michael Eisner Lost His Grip* (New York: William Morrow, 2000): 351.
15. Wasko, *Understanding Disney,* 36.
16. Masters, *The Keys to the Kingdom: How Michael Eisner Lost His Grip,* 348.
17. "Pixar Animation Studios, Inc," *Hoovers Company Information,* Hoover's Inc., 2010.
18. See Chmielewski and Bates, "Roy E. Disney, 1930-2009; Nephew of Walt Revived Animation," 1.
19. See Downes, Russ, and Ryan, "Michael Eisner and His Reign at Disney," 74.
20. See "Robert A. Iger Named Chief Executive Officer of the Walt Disney Company," *Business Wire,* 13 March 2005, 1.
21. See Nick Wingfield and Merissa Marr, "Pixar Executive Played Key Role in Disney Deal," *Wall Street Journal,* 25 January 2006, B1.
22. Philippe Perebinossoff, in-person interview, July 29, 2010.
23. Richard Siklos, "Disney's Wonderful World of Marvel," *CNN/Money.com,* 15 September 2009. Also see Brian Steinberg, "Disney's New Superhuman Powers," *Advertising Age* 80:29 (September 7, 2009): 4.
24. Richard Siklos, "Big Changes in the Cast at Disney," *CNN/Money.com,* 13 November 2009.
25. See Gary Gentile, "Al Michaels Deal Reunites Disney with Original Animated Character," *Associated Press,* 10 February 2006.

4

Disney Characters

Walt Disney once said, "I only hope that we never lose sight of one thing—that it was all started by a mouse."[1] These words have come to be an integral part of Disney lore. For the Disney Company, however, the mouse was only the beginning.

Since the debut of Mickey Mouse in 1928, Walt Disney and the Disney Company have created and popularized a host of characters that are admired and embraced by children and adults throughout the world. The recognition of these characters has been perpetuated through Disney cartoons and television programs, as well as on merchandise bearing their likenesses. Even the U.S. Postal Service has acknowledged the appeal of certain Disney characters by featuring them on a series of commemorative postage stamps.[2]

Mickey Mouse himself has become a corporate icon, a symbol of the Disney Company recognized all over the world. His crusty sidekick, Donald Duck, has a history as one of the company's most popular characters and has entertained generations of audiences with his terrible temper and harebrained schemes.

One of Disney's most beloved characters is Winnie the Pooh, an animated bear whose roots stem from the creativity of an English author, but who has been easily adopted into the Disney character repertoire. In recent years, Disney has also developed character franchises, such as Disney Princesses and Disney Fairies. These characters have appealed to new generations of children and have been responsible for the creation and sales of billions of dollars in Disney merchandise.

Disney has also acquired some new characters in the last decade, The Muppets and the Marvel Entertainment superheroes, which the company is hoping to develop for the future.

This chapter will offer background on some of Disney's more popular characters and will provide insight into why and how they have attained their following. It will also discuss some of the marketing and promotional activities used by Disney to help these characters achieve universal recognition.

Mickey Mouse: A Disney Classic

As noted in Chapter 2, Walt Disney created Mickey Mouse in 1928, in response to his devastating loss of Oswald the Rabbit. Initially, Mickey's outward appearance was fairly simple—round black ears, spindly legs, roly-poly body, black nose, and a mischievous grin. In many ways, in fact, he resembled his predecessor Oswald.

He made his official screen debut in a short cartoon called *Steamboat Willie* on November 18, 1928, a date that is officially recognized by the Disney Company as Mickey's birthday. In actuality, Mickey had appeared in two previous shorts—*Plane Crazy* and *Gallopin' Gaucho*—that had not yet been released to the public. *Steamboat Willie* made people take notice of the animated mouse because the cartoon featured something moviegoers had not encountered before in animated films, explained reporter Daniel Chang.

> *Steamboat Willie* introduced the world to Mickey as the first cartoon synchronized with sound—specifically, squeaks, whistles and music. With new sound technology revolutionizing movies, Mickey's star ascended at about the same time Hollywood released the first truly successful 'talkie,' Al Jolson's *The Jazz Singer* in 1927.[3]

Walt Disney himself initially provided Mickey's voice and did so until 1947, when he was succeeded by Jim Macdonald and eventually Wayne Allwine in 1983.[4]

Remodeling the Mouse

The original Mickey Mouse was a bit of a rascal. He teased animals, aggressively pursued his love interest Minnie, and played practical jokes on other characters.[5] While the public responded positively to him, not everyone appreciated his naughty behavior, according to reporter Bruce Kauffmann, who noted that "A flood of angry letters convinced Disney that the movie-going public wanted a kinder and gentler mouse."[6]

So, Walt Disney toned him down—made him more polite, gracious, agreeable. Today, "he's everyone's good guy—friendly, charming, sophisticated, worldly," said Nancy Byrne, who portrayed Mickey Mouse at Disneyland for eight years in the 1980s. "If you think about it, he's almost like the perfect man—he can do no wrong," she said.[7]

Merchandising Mickey

The approach worked like a charm, and Mickey eventually evolved into a symbol for the company that created him, largely through some innovative merchandising strategies on the parts of Walt and Roy Disney. Mickey's first appearance on merchandise came in 1930, when his image was published on a writing tablet. Soon after, the Disney brothers contracted with advertising executive Herman "Kay" Kamen to handle the licensing rights for Mickey Mouse.[8] It wasn't long before images of the Mouse began popping up on everything and anything—candy bar wrappers, buttons, games, sheet music, pencil erasers, and toy trains, among other items.[9]

The first Mickey Mouse Club formed in 1929, and by 1932, there were more than one million members in chapters across the country. According to the Walt Disney Archives, "The Mouse Clubbers had a secret handshake, a special member greeting, a code of behavior and even a special club song, *Minnie's Yoo-Hoo*, a ditty with music by composer Carl Stalling and lyrics by Walt himself."[10]

These clubs were brought to life in 1955 with the debut of *The Mickey Mouse Club*, a televised tribute to the Mouse on ABC.[11] A series of Mickey Mouse comic strips was launched by King Features in the 1930s as well.[12]

An Impressive Résumé

Mickey continued to appear in more than 100 cartoons. His appearance as "The Sorcerer's Apprentice" in the feature film *Fantasia* in 1940 is perhaps his best-known movie role. Over the years, however, his importance as corporate icon has eclipsed his role as film star.

An article in the *Orange County Register* explained:

> Mickey has achieved career success in film, television, ice shows, theme-park entertainment, computer games and public relations. The perfect employee, he has evolved with the times, learned new skills, maintained a cheerful attitude and made millions for his company. All without gaining a wrinkle or a gray hair.[13]

Mickey Mouse celebrated his 80th birthday in 2008. Over the years, there has been talk of modernizing him to make him more appealing to a new generation of children who can relate more to the characters featured in interactive video games than those in short cartoons. Whether or not this transformation will be successful, one thing is certain. While Mickey Mouse may not have been Walt Disney's first cartoon character, he is certainly his most famous.

Donald Duck: The Feisty Fowl

With Mickey Mouse firmly established as the ultimate good guy, it was only natural that Walt Disney would come up with a counterpart for his famous mouse. The idea was to create a not-so-perfect character whose personality was the opposite of Mickey's calm, good natured manner—someone who was short-tempered, stubborn, a scrappy fighter at heart. Someone who was...Donald Duck.

Donald was the perfect antidote to Mickey Mouse. He made his first onscreen appearance as a bit player in *The Wise Little Hen* in 1934 and left an ever-lasting impression on moviegoers. He had a long yellow bill and was dressed in a blue and white sailor suit and cap. But, it was his quirky, slightly unintelligible voice that captivated the audience.

In short, when Donald spoke, he sounded like he was choking on a mouthful of marbles. This only added to his charm. Clarence "Ducky" Nash provided the original voice for Donald Duck for more than 50 years. He was succeeded after his death in 1985 by Tony Anselmo.[14]

Flexing His Feathers

Donald quickly became wildly popular with the public—even more so than Mickey Mouse.[15] Disney capitalized on this by placing him in more than 170 films over the years—more than any other Disney character. In many of these films, Donald displayed his hot temper, such as in the *Orphan's Benefit*, where he threw his first temper tantrum.[16]

One of Donald's trademarks was his fierce jealousy of Mickey Mouse and his constant determination to outwit, outclass, and outperform Mickey, which he inevitably failed to do every time, much to his own chagrin. He was first paired with Mickey in *The Band Concert* in 1935.

In *Don Donald* (1937), Disney introduced the alluring Donna Duck, who subsequently morphed into Daisy Duck—Donald's girlfriend—in *Mr. Duck Steps Out* (1940). Huey, Dewey, and Louie were added into the mix in *Donald's Nephews* (1938). Donald became the subject of a comic strip in 1938, and a series of comic books produced by animator Carl Barks in 1942.[17]

Because of the Duck's popularity, Disney featured him in a number of short films during World War II, which were used to promote patriotism. These included *Donald Duck Gets Drafted* (1942) and *Der Fuehrer's Face* (1943), which won an Academy Award for Best Cartoon Short Subject. He was also featured in the two films that resulted from Walt Disney's goodwill tour to South America in the early 1940s—*Saludos Amigos* (1943) and *The Three Caballeros* (1945).

Did You Know?

Walt Disney chose Clarence "Ducky" Nash to voice Donald Duck after hearing him recite "Mary Had a Little Lamb" on the radio in what later became known as his "duck" voice.

A Worldwide Sensation

Donald even had his own line of food products—orange juice, bread, rice, macaroni, etc. He was the only Disney character with this distinction.[18] "In the sphere of merchandising, the Duck was second only to the Mouse," according to *Orange County Register* reporter Linda Rosenkrantz.[19]

Like Mickey Mouse, Donald has longstanding international appeal. He is known as Paperino in Italy, Anders And in Denmark, and Donal Bebek in Indonesia. He has comic strip readers in 100 international newspapers, comic book fans in 47 countries, and television viewers in 29 countries.[20] "Over the years, he's been honored with a star on the Hollywood Walk of Fame, and impressions of his webbed feet grace the sidewalk near Hollywood's famed Grauman's Chinese Theater," noted one article.[21]

Although Donald Duck may be lacking Mickey Mouse's grace and style, he possesses a down-to-earth, earnest demeanor that resonates with people of all ages. It is this quality that helped establish his reputation early on and continues to endear him to the public.

Winnie the Pooh: The Beloved Bear

One of Disney's most beloved characters isn't even an original Disney creation. Winnie the Pooh was invented by A.A. Milne in England in 1924. Milne was an English poet and playwright who penned a series of poems and short stories based around the toys of his son, Christopher Robin Milne. At the center of these tales was a teddy bear, Edward Bear, more affectionately known as Winnie the Pooh.

Milne's stories revolved around Pooh and his friends—Rabbit, Piglet, Owl, Eeyore, Kanga, Roo, and Tigger—who all lived in the Hundred Acre Wood near Christopher Robin's house. Pooh's adventures were published in three books: *Winnie the Pooh* (1926), *Now We Are Six* (1927), and *The House at Pooh Corner* (1928). They were illustrated by Ernest H. Shepard.

The trials and tribulations of the "bear of very little brain" as Milne dubbed him,[22] touched the hearts of English schoolchildren and their parents. In 1930, "Milne sold the licensing rights to the entire Pooh franchise to a New Yorker named Stephen Slesinger. Years after publication, Winnie the Pooh toys finally began to pop up in small shops around the world," noted writer Louise Rosen.[23]

A New Brand of Bear

Walt Disney first learned about Winnie the Pooh through his daughter Diane.[24] After years of negotiations with Milne and his heirs (Milne died in 1956), he ultimately secured the licensing rights to Pooh in 1961. The negotiations for these rights included the payment of royalties to several organizations that had been named as beneficiaries in Milne's will, as well as royalty payments to Stephen Slesinger's heirs (Slesinger died in 1953).

Disney then developed an animated Winnie the Pooh character. He modified Shepard's original illustrations, making Pooh a bit more rotund, giving him a big, wide smile, and bestowing him with a voice provided by actor Sterling Holloway.

Disney first featured Pooh in a short film called *Winnie the Pooh and the Honey Tree* in 1966. The cartoon was based on Milne's original tales from his first book. It was followed by *Winnie the Pooh and the Blustery Day* (1968), which won an Academy Award for Best Cartoon Short Subject. Additional Pooh films followed over the years, as well as television programs for both network TV and the Disney Channel.

It was the merchandising of Pooh that really made him a star. Winnie the Pooh items were aimed at both children and adults, and the financial returns were staggering. In 2004, Winnie the Pooh ranked second on *Forbes* magazine's "Top Earning Fictional Character List," with $5.3 billion in retail sales, coming in behind number one, Mickey Mouse.[25] By 2010, he was earning the company approximately $6.9 billion in annual revenues.[26]

Pooh Goes to Court

In 2000, Disney bought out the beneficiaries of the Pooh estate for approximately $350 million, giving the company more flexibility with its merchandising efforts.[27] The thorn in Disney's side, however, has been the heirs of Stephen Slesinger, who still have a piece of the Pooh licensing pie.

Although the contract with the Slesingers was renegotiated several times over the years, in 1991, Stephen Slesinger's wife Shirley and daughter initiated a series of lawsuits, claiming Disney had cheated them out of royalties for certain products. At the heart of these lawsuits was a debate over the rights to the sale of videos and other electronic materials that hadn't existed when the initial licensing agreement was signed.

In 2004, a Los Angeles judge threw out one of the Slesinger lawsuits, citing unethical behavior on the part of the Slesingers.[28] A second suit was dismissed in 2009.[29] At the time of this writing, however, the Slesinger estate had vowed to carry on the fight against Disney.[30]

In the meantime, Disney continues to promote and market its lovable bear through a wide array of merchandise aimed at audiences of all ages. In addition, Winnie the Pooh lives on through a variety of entertainment media, including a new animated feature film starring the bear and slated for release in 2011.

Figure 4: Friends of Mickey Mouse and Donald Duck

While Mickey and Donald may be Disney's undisputed stars, other characters have accompanied them in a variety of cartoons over the years. They include:

• **Minnie Mouse**: The faithful girlfriend of Mickey Mouse, first seen with him in *Steamboat Willie* (1928). Minnie has her own style and spunk and is a bit of a flirt.

• **Pluto**: Mickey's devoted canine companion. He has been featured in cartoons alongside Mickey Mouse and has also had starring roles in some of his own.

• **Goofy**: A good-natured, happy-go-lucky friend of Mickey and Donald. Goofy has a habit of "goofing" up everything he tries, but he always maintains a cheerful attitude.

• **Daisy Duck**: Donald Duck's girlfriend, who knows how to deal with the feisty fowl's terrible temper. She also loves to be pampered by her guy.

• **Huey, Dewey, and Louie**: Donald Duck's nephews and a force to be reckoned with. They first joined their uncle onscreen in *Donald's Nephews* (1938).

• **Chip 'n Dale**: A pair of mischievous chipmunks who first appeared in *Private Pluto* (1943). They have antagonized both Pluto and Donald Duck in many Disney cartoon shorts.

Source: Walt Disney Archives Biographies of 10 Classic Disney Characters,
http://d23.disney.go.com/library/000000_WDA_AL_Bio10ClassicDisneyCharacters.html

Disney Princesses: The Classic Character Franchise

When *Snow White and the Seven Dwarfs* was released in 1937, Snow White became the first official Disney Princess. Over time, she was joined by two others who appeared in Disney versions of classic fairytales—Cinderella and Sleeping Beauty. Decades later, three more modern princesses appeared on the scene—Ariel from *The Little Mermaid*, Belle from *Beauty and the Beast*, and Jasmine from *Aladdin*.

For many years, these characters and the films in which they appeared were promoted and marketed to the public independently of each other. But in 2001, as a result of the brainchild of a Disney executive, all that changed. The result was a marketing phenomenon that has taken the public by storm—the creation of the Disney Princesses.

A Franchise Is Born

The idea for the Disney Princesses was dreamt up by Andy Mooney, who in 2000 had recently been appointed head of Disney Consumer Products. Mooney went to see a Disney on Ice show in Phoenix shortly after assuming his new role. At the show, he noticed there were throngs of little girls dressed like various Disney princesses.

"There was a little Snow White. And a Cinderella. And an Ariel. Everywhere Mooney looked, he saw little girls who had come to the figure-skating show dressed as their favorite Disney heroine," explained Greg Groeller of the *Orlando Sentinel*.[31]

Mooney realized the marketing potential of packaging the Princesses as a single brand and presenting them to the public. He worked with his staff to develop a line of Princess products that were likely to appeal to girls ages 3-6—dress-up costumes, tiaras, plastic jewelry, and the like.

The response was almost immediate. In 2001, the Princess line had annual sales revenues of approximately $300 million. By 2003, that number had increased to $1.3 billion, and by 2009, it was estimated at $4 billion.[32]

Mixed Messages

Although Princess products have been gobbled up by the little girls for whom they were intended, public response to the Princess phenomenon has been mixed. Some claim it is sending the wrong message to young females by encouraging them to focus on being beautiful and on waiting for Prince Charming to come and rescue them rather than learning to become strong and independent individuals. Others believe the Princess concept teaches young girls they can be anything they want—including a princess—and that being a princess is more about feeling empowered and attractive than it is about finding a prince.[33]

Regardless of these varied reactions, there is no denying the development of the Princess line seems to have no bounds. As Greg Groeller observed:

> One of Disney's smartest moves may have been to name the brand "Princess." The word provokes strong emotions in many little girls who grow up hearing stories—many of them created or popularized by Disney—about the magical lives led by princesses.[34]

The Princess brand gives them the opportunity to live the fantasy.

Dressing up like a favorite Disney princess is part of the magic and attraction for young girls.
Photo courtesy of Ann and Joe Holbrook.

Tinker Bell: Star of the Disney Fairies

One Disney character given recent star treatment is someone who has actually been in the public eye for many years. Disney's Tinker Bell first appeared on screen in the 1953 film *Peter Pan,* which was based on J.M. Barrie's 1911 novel. As Peter Pan's loyal fairy sidekick, she was silently devoted to and fiercely protective of him.

She eventually became the symbol of Disneyland and the ABC television show used to promote the park, as she sprinkled pixie dust with a touch of her wand at the start of each show. Actress Margaret Kerry was the model for the spunky sprite.[35]

Although Disney had long sold Tinker Bell merchandise in its theme parks, the company had not done much to develop the fairy's personality until recently. In an attempt to follow up on the success of its Princess franchise, Disney executives began looking for a new concept, one that would appeal to females ages 6-9. Disney elected to build a new product line around Tinker Bell. Called "Disney Fairies," it was to include books, DVDs, and an interactive website, "Pixie Hollow."

Did You Know?

The 2008 film *Tinker Bell* provided the popular pixie with a voice for the first time. In the original *Peter Pan* film, Tinker Bell did not speak.

According to reporter Scott Powers, Tinker Bell was a natural choice. "Tinker Bell is the anti-princess," he explained.[36] She has style, she has spunk, and she has attitude—the perfect combination for young girls who have outgrown the princess phase and are starting to come into their own.

The Muppets: Characters with Growth Potential

Kermit the Frog, Miss Piggy, Fozzie Bear, and an assortment of other Muppets became part of the Disney clan when Disney acquired them from the Jim Henson Company in 2004. The acquisition was the result of on and off negotiations that began in 1989, and finally concluded with a happy ending for Disney 15 years later.

Jim Henson was a puppeteer who rose to fame when he created a series of furry creatures that appeared to be a combination of marionettes and puppets and were aptly named "Muppets." He started using them in commercials and eventually made the move to children's television. When the Children's Television Workshop launched *Sesame Street* in 1969, Henson's Muppets were the undisputed stars of the show. The chief Muppet was Kermit the Frog.

Over the years, the Muppets caught on and went on to receive international acclaim. Kermit and his friends—Miss Piggy, Rowlf the Dog, Fozzie Bear, Gonzo, and many others—were known for their wacky antics and distinctive personalities. They made guest appearances on an assortment of TV variety shows, starred in several feature films, and in 1976, became the stars of their own television series, *The Muppet Show*.[37]

A Meeting of the Minds

Jim Henson first crossed paths with former Disney CEO Michael Eisner in 1967, when Eisner was a children's programming executive at ABC and was intrigued by Henson's menagerie. Twenty years later after assuming the role as Disney CEO, Eisner and Henson began talking about a possible Disney buyout of Henson's company.

In August of 1989, Disney announced that it would acquire the Jim Henson Company for $150 million.[38] According to the *Wall Street Journal*:

> Henson felt the Muppets would be guaranteed to live on under Disney management. Disney could make good use of the characters in movies, on television, in theme parks and retail merchandise.[39]

Henson died unexpectedly in spring of 1990, before the deal was finalized. He was only 53, and his five children, ranging in age from 19 to 30, inherited the company. Without Henson himself, the company was worth far less than $150 million to Disney. Unable to agree on a new price, talks between the two companies stalled, and the deal fizzled.[40] Henson's heirs did agree to allow Disney to license some of the Muppet characters for a show at Walt Disney World called, "Kermit the Frog Presents: MuppetVision 3-D," an attraction that had been developed before Henson died.[41]

Back in Business

Henson's children eventually sold their father's company to EM.TV & Merchandising AG, but they bought it back again in 2003.[42] The transaction provided an opportunity for the Disney Company to re-enter the picture with a new buyout plan. This time, the results were positive for Disney.

In 2004, Disney acquired the rights to the Muppets and to Bear in the Big Blue House, a character created by the Jim Henson Company after the initial 1989 talks. The transaction included "all Muppet assets, including the Kermit, Miss Piggy, Fozzie Bear, Gonzo and Animal characters, the Muppet film and television library, and all associated copyrights and trademarks."[43] The sale did not include the *Sesame Street* characters, as they had been sold to the Children's Television Workshop in 2001.

Marketing the Muppets

At the time of the purchase, Disney declared its intentions to "reinvigorate the Muppets franchise by giving them a fresh home on Disney TV venues such as the Disney Channel and the ABC broadcast network, and by expanding the characters' presence in Disney theme parks."[44]

Since 2004, Disney has made good on its promise, albeit slowly. For the first few years, the Muppets brand appeared to languish on the shelves. Then in 2008, Disney appointed Lylle Breier the general manager of Muppet Studios, and since then there has been significant movement on the Muppets front.

At the D23 Expo in 2009, Breier talked about some of the activities that had been set in motion for the Muppets to build visibility for the brand. Many of these involved the use of online and social media, including the debut of a website, Muppets.com, the release of Muppet viral videos on YouTube, and the creation of a Facebook page for each character.[45]

Breier discussed plans for several Muppet television specials, a new Muppet movie, and merchandising partnerships with a variety of companies including Supreme Skateboards, Steiff, and Macy's. The company also formed an alliance with F.A.O. Schwarz in New York and developed the Muppet Whatnot Workshop, where consumers could choose from an assortment of materials to build their own Muppets for about $130. The concept is similar to the customized doll program offered by American Girl Place stores.[46]

In 2010, Disney even added a Muppets float to its nightly parade at Disneyland.[47] The float appeared as a forerunner to the official start of the parade featuring the rest of Disney's characters, a subtle indication that the Henson creatures were still the new kids on the block, not yet fully part of the pack. Perhaps in a few years with the proper Disney handling, the Muppets will be fully integrated into the heart of the parade.

Marvel Comics Superheroes: Disney's Newest Characters

While Disney has had tremendous success reaching young girls with its characters in recent years, it has not done as well in attracting a young, male audience. At the end of 2009, however, when Disney acquired Marvel Entertainment for $4.2 billion, it was with the hope of broadening its male appeal. An article in *The Economist* pointed out the benefits of the sale.

> Disney will get access to both creative minds and—potentially far more valuable in an age where familiar stories rule the box office—an archive containing around 5,000 established characters, only a fraction of which have yet made the move from paper to the silver screen.[48]

The purchase included an assortment of superheroes such as Iron Man, Spider-Man, Captain America, X-Men, and The Incredible Hulk.

Marvel's characters are best known for their comic book presence, but in recent years the company has licensed some of its superheroes to Disney rival studios such as Sony Pictures (Spider-Man) and Universal (The Incredible Hulk).

At the time of this writing, it was unclear exactly how Disney planned to integrate the Marvel characters into its existing repertoire and work around these licensing agreements. However, industry observers agreed the purchase was likely to be just what Disney needed to reach its untapped male audience.[49]

Conclusion

When Walt Disney created Mickey Mouse in 1928, he launched what was to be the beginning of a legacy of memorable Disney characters. Since then, Mickey has been joined by others such as Donald Duck and Winnie the Pooh, who have charmed their ways into the hearts of millions and sold billions of dollars of merchandise for the Disney Company.

The creation of the Disney Princess and Disney Fairies lines in recent years has added to this collection of characters and has provided new franchise opportunities for the company. The acquisition of the Muppets and Marvel Entertainment superheroes has brought additional characters into the Disney fold. This will enable Disney to offer even more entertainment possibilities to its audiences in the future. ♦

Notes

1. Walt Disney, *Disneyland* television program, October 27, 1954.
2. "Mickey Mouse and Friends Honored on New Stamps Unveiled by U.S. Postal Service," *PR Newswire*, 30 December 2003, 1.
3. Daniel Chang, "At 75, Mickey Mouse Is Still a Worldwide Icon," *The San Diego Union-Tribune*, 19 November 2003, F5.
4. "Biographies of 10 Classic Disney Characters," *Walt Disney Archives*, http://d23.disney.go.com/wdarchives.html.
5. See Andy McSmith, "Funnier and More Mischievous–Mickey's Makeover," *The Independent*, 7 November 2009, 18.
6. Bruce Kauffmann, "The Animated Mouse that Roared," *Telegraph-Herald*, 16 September 2007, E3.
7. Nancy Byrne, in-person interview, November 3, 2009.
8. See David Bain and Bruce Harris, eds., *Mickey Mouse: Fifty Happy Years* (New York: Harmony Books, 1977): 15; and Bernard Shine, *Walt Disney's Mickey Mouse Memorabilia* (New York: Harry N. Abrams, 1986): 13.
9. Many of these early examples of Mickey Mouse merchandise are on display at the Walt Disney Family Museum in San Francisco.
10. "Biographies of 10 Classic Disney Characters," *Walt Disney Archives*, http://d23.disney.go.com/wdarchives.html.
11. Christine Laue, "World's Most Famous Mouse Is 75," *Omaha World*, 18 November 2003, 1a.
12. Bain and Harris, *Mickey Mouse: Fifty Happy Years*, 17.
13. Michele Himmelberg, "The Mouse that Scored," *Orange County Register*, 18 November 2003, A1.
14. See "Biographies of 10 Classic Disney Characters," *Walt Disney Archives*, http://d23.disney.go.com/wdarchives.html.
15. Ibid.
16. Jim Fanning, "Donald Duck: 75 Years of Mischief, Mayhem, & Mirth," *Disney Twenty-Three* 1:2 (Summer 2009): 42.
17. Marcia Blitz, *Donald Duck* (New York: Harmony Books, 1979): 186.
18. *Walt Disney's Donald Duck* (London: HP Books, 1984): 89.
19. Linda Rosenkrantz, "Donald Duck Is No Mouse When It Comes to Popularity," *Orange County Register*, 2 December 1989, E08.
20. "Biographies of 10 Classic Disney Characters," *Walt Disney Archives*, http://d23.disney.go.com/wdarchives.html.

21.   "Disney's Donald Duck to Mark 75th Birthday," *Alarabiya*, 8 June 2009.

22.   A.A. Milne, *Winnie the Pooh* (London: Methuen, 1926): 89.

23.   Louise Rosen, "Don't Pooh-Pooh the Pooh Bear," *Forbes*, 20 March 2000, 184.

24.   See Biographies of 10 Classic Disney Characters," *Walt Disney Archives*, http://d23.disney.go.com/wdarchives.html.

25.   "Forbes.com Names Disney Home to Three of Top Five Most Valuable Character Franchises in the World," *PR Newswire*, 21 October 2004.

26.   Disney Consumer Products, "Winnie the Pooh," https://www.disneyconsumerproducts.com/ Home/display.jsp?contentId=dcp_home_ourfranchises_winnie_the_pooh_us&forPri nt=false&language=en&preview=false&i mageShow=0&pressRoom=US&translationOf=null&region=0.

27.   "Disney Buys the Rights to Winnie the Pooh," *The New York Times*, 5 March 2001, C12.

28.   Bruce Orwall, "Disney Wins Bear-Knuckled, 13-Year Fight over Royalties," *Wall Street Journal*, 30 March 2004, B1.

29.   Dave Itzkoff, "Winnie-the-Pooh Suit Is Dismissed," *The New York Times*, 30 September 2009, C2.

30.   Rachel Lee Harris, "Winnie-the-Pooh Returns to Court," *The New York Times*, 16 November 2009, C2.

31.   Greg Groeller, "Royal Marketing; Walt Disney Co. Strikes Gold in the Branding of its Popular Film Heroines," *Orlando Sentinel*, 25 April 2004, H1.

32.   See "A Challenge to Barbie," *The Economist*, 19 April 2003, 54; Niz Proskocil, "Dressed to Rule: Has Glass Slippers? Loves to Wear Tiara and Carry a Wand? That Girl May Have Princess Syndrome," *Omaha World*, 13 March 2007, 1E; and "Disney Princess Power," *License! Global*, May 2009, 40.

33.   See, for example, Peggy Orenstein, "What's Wrong with Cinderella?" *New York Times Magazine*, 24 December 2006, 34; and Sarah Ebner, "The Princess and the Pay Gap," *The Times*, 4 August 2009, 6.

34.   Groeller, "Royal Marketing; Walt Disney Co. Strikes Gold in the Branding of Its Popular Film Heroines," H1.

35.   See Scott Powers, "Tinkering with Fairy's Image Leaves Innocence in the Pixie Dust," *Orlando Sentinel*, 18 August 2007, A1.

36.   Ibid.

37.   See The Jim Henson Legacy, www.jimhensonlegacy.org.

38.   Richard W. Stevenson, "Muppets Join Disney Menagerie," *The New York Times*, 29 August 1989, D1.

39.   See Richard Turner, "Disney, Muppets Find It's Not Easy Talking Green," *Wall Street Journal*, 14 December 1990, B1.

40.   Ibid.

41.   See Richard Turner, "Henson, Disney Settle Dispute over Muppets," *Wall Street Journal*, 1 May 1991, B8.

42.   Bruce Orwall and Neal E. Boudette, "Muppets Can Go Home Again after Sale Back to Henson Heirs," *Wall Street Journal*, 8 May 2003, B9.

43.   "The Walt Disney Company and the Jim Henson Company Sign Agreement for Disney to Buy the 'Muppets' and 'Bear in the Big Blue House,'" *Business Wire*, 17 February 2004, 1.

44.   Peter Grant and Bruce Orwall, "Leading the News: Disney Buys Henson's Muppets," *Wall Street Journal*, 18 February 2004, A3.

45.   Lylle Breier, public presentation at D23 Expo, Anaheim, Calif., September 13, 2009.

46.   See Brooks Barnes, "Fuzzy Renaissance," *The New York Times*, 21 September 2008; and "The Whatnots® Take Manhattan," *PR Newswire*, 13 November 2008.

47.   Eric Carpenter, "Miss Piggy, Kermit Team Up with Mickey," *Orange County Register*, 10 January 2010, Local 4.

48.   "Of Mouse and X-Men; Walt Disney Buys Marvel Entertainment," *The Economist*, 5 September 2009, 71.

49.   See Andrew Edgecliffe-Johnson and Matthew Garrahan, "Disney Plans to Strike with Marvel Muscle," *Financial Times*, 1 September 2009, 16; and Emily Claire Afan, "Disney Racks Up a Surplus of Superheroes," *KidScreen*, October 2009, 25.

5

Disney Films

Although the modern-day Disney Company is a multifaceted organization with many diverse holdings, the production of high-quality films has always been at the core of the organization. When many people think of animated films, the name Disney instantly comes to mind.

At the heart of every Disney film is a good story, one that combines colorful characters with an engaging plot. This was the driving force behind the early studio productions and still guides much of what is output by the company today.

Over the years, the focus of Disney films has expanded beyond animation to include live action movies that appeal to a wide range of audiences. The creation of Touchstone Pictures and Hollywood Pictures in the 1980s, and the addition of Miramax Films in the 1990s enabled Disney to move beyond its family-friendly G-rated fare and appeal to more mature audiences. At the same time, Disney has maintained its hold on quality without losing its grip on what is considered tasteful or appropriate for its audiences.

A partnership with Pixar Animation Studios in the 1990s moved the company in a new direction on the animation front. It prompted a shift from hand-drawn animation to computer-generated imagery, which had an impact on the company's approach to animated films. This relationship forced Disney to venture into new territory and ultimately led to the company's acquisition of Pixar in 2006.

This chapter will offer an overview of the film activities of the Disney Company by showing the evolution of the role film has played in the organization since its beginnings. It will examine some of the early films that initially put Disney on the map and will discuss the ventures the company has undertaken in recent years.

Early Days of Cartoon Shorts

The history of the Disney Company reveals the early challenges Walt Disney faced as he tried to find his way in a film industry that was still in its nascent stages. By focusing on animation, Disney was able to create a niche for himself and clear a path for others who followed him.

Even as a pioneer with minimal competition, however, he still struggled to gain his footing as he learned to develop his craft. His early work on the Alice Comedies and Oswald the Rabbit cartoons enabled him to experiment with drawing and animation techniques, which prepared him for the work he did on the early Mickey Mouse cartoons.

With the success of Mickey Mouse, Disney was able to develop a cast of characters to support him such as Donald Duck, Minnie Mouse, Pluto, and Goofy, who added a level of dimension to the antics of the cartoon mouse. What was most telling about these early cartoons, however, is that they were not merely a series of sight gags designed simply to make audiences laugh. At the heart of each cartoon was a story that was played out in the few short minutes it took for the cartoon to run its course.

It was this aspect of Disney's animated shorts that gave them great audience appeal. The ability to engage viewers with a story and evoke a wide range of emotions was a key factor to the success of Disney's early works. It also set the stage for the company's subsequent films. To this day, good storytelling is still considered the hallmark of a successful Disney film.

Silly Symphonies

The Silly Symphony cartoons were significant for Disney because they gave him and his animators an opportunity to develop their animation skills and to experiment with some of the technologies that were revolutionizing the film industry. Each Silly Symphony had a theme, and many were set to classical music, giving the series its name.

The Silly Symphonies acted as a training ground for many of the studio's employees. Authors Russell Merritt and J.B. Kaufman called Disney's Silly Symphonies:

> ...the series to which he routinely assigned his best artists and most versatile story people.... Everyone from the directors and chief animators to the composers and story directors on Disney's first features had cut their teeth on Silly Symphonies.[1]

Disney's first Silly Symphony was called *The Skeleton Dance* (1929). It was followed by others such as *Frolicking Fish* (1930), *Midnight in a Toy Shop* (1930), and *Mother Goose Melodies* (1931). All of these early cartoon shorts were filmed in black and white and featured music and sound effects.

While the early Silly Symphonies were innovative, they were not nearly as popular as the Mickey Mouse cartoons. According to Disney biographer Bob Thomas, Disney's distributor, United Artists, agreed to show them only if they were billed as "Mickey Mouse Presents a Walt Disney Silly Symphony."[2]

Flowers and Trees

In the early 1930s, a company called Technicolor developed a process that enabled cartoons to be filmed in color rather than black and white. Walt Disney realized this process could help him gain greater recognition for his Silly Symphony cartoons. He and his brother Roy negotiated a two-year exclusive contract with Technicolor, which gave them an edge over other studios still relying on black and white.

Disney and his animators had already started black and white production on *Flowers and Trees* when this contract was signed, but they switched to preparing the film in color to accommodate the new process. The result was worth the effort, noted Thomas.

> When *Flowers and Trees* opened at the Chinese [Theater], in July 1932, it created the sensation that Walt had hoped for. No longer was the Silly Symphony the neglected half of the Disney product; *Flowers and Trees* got as many bookings as the hottest Mickey Mouse cartoon. Walt decreed that all future Symphonies would be in color.[3]

Flowers and Trees also received Disney's first Academy Award for Best Cartoon in 1932.

The Old Mill

Another technological development Disney was able to test out with the Silly Symphonies was the use of the multiplane camera. This type of camera enabled cartoon cels to be layered and then filmed from above, creating a three-dimensional feel to the finished product. Disney first used this technique in a Silly Symphony called *The Old Mill*.

The Old Mill revolved around a single night in the life of a creaky windmill. As animals settled down inside the mill for the night, a storm brewed on the horizon, threatening the tranquility of the setting. The use of the multiplane camera in filming *The Old Mill* gave the cartoon an added level of realism that made the images of the animals and the mill itself seem almost tangible.

The Old Mill won an Academy Award for Best Cartoon Production in 1937. The multiplane camera was used in subsequent Silly Symphonies as well as in Disney's full-length animated features.

The Three Little Pigs

The most popular of all the Silly Symphonies was *The Three Little Pigs*. Based on an Aesop's fable, the story had an underlying message about the virtues of hard work and perseverance. It was released in 1933, in the midst of the Great Depression, and became an instant hit.

According to author Tom Tumbusch, the cartoon "resonated with Walt's audience like no other Disney film since *Steamboat Willie*.... People wanted to see it over and over again, resulting in more than four times the normal revenue for a cartoon short."[4]

The cartoon not only told the story of the three pigs' fight against the Big Bad Wolf but also featured a catchy tune by Frank Churchill called, *Who's Afraid of the Big Bad Wolf?* The melody became the Disney Company's first hit song. Tumbusch explained the appeal of the cartoon.

> In a sense, "The Three Little Pigs" was the first animated feature...just a mini-version. The film was uplifting to its audience. The story conveyed the idea the average guy did have a chance in a time when people needed to hear that message. "The Three Little Pigs" was the right film at the right time, providing a lift to the little guy on the street...and to the Disney Studio.[5]

Snow White and the Seven Dwarfs

Disney's first animated full-length feature, *Snow White and the Seven Dwarfs*, was a breakthrough film on several levels. For the Disney studio, it moved the company in a new direction and opened the doors for a whole new type of animated film production. For the movie-going public, it proved that if a cartoon had an engaging story and personable characters, it could hold the attention of an audience for more than just seven or eight minutes, just as live action films were able to do.

Attention to Detail

As discussed in Chapter 2, when Walt Disney first proposed the concept of *Snow White*, many at the studio were dubious, including his brother Roy. To ensure the project did not fail, Disney put meticulous detail into every aspect of the film, from the creation of its characters to the animated movements of its heroine.

Disney brought in live actors and filmed them acting out scenes, so his animators could try to recreate their movements on celluloid. One of these was Marge Belcher—later Marge Champion—who went on to become half of the famed dance team, Marge and Gower Champion.[6] This was a technique Disney was to repeat in later films.

A key element to the success of the film was the character development of the individual dwarfs. Each was given a distinct personality as well as drawn with distinguishing facial characteristics, mannerisms, and gestures. This added depth and color to the film and a sense of comic relief that counterbalanced the sometimes dark nature of the story.

The content and placement of the songs and the voices of the characters were also essential in helping audiences connect with the film. Frank Churchill wrote the movie's songs along with Leigh Harline and Paul Smith. For the role of Snow White, Disney selected Adriana Caselotti, whose operatic training was appropriate for the high-trilled nature of the songs written for the film's heroine.

Results Worth the Effort

In the end, all of Disney's attention to detail paid off at the film's premiere on December 21, 1937, at the Carthay Circle Theater in Los Angeles, explained author Christopher Finch.

> The audience was studded with celebrities. It was the kind of opening of which Disney had always dreamed. The reviews were sensational. *Snow White* was an overnight success, justifying all of Disney's hopes for it and impressing itself on the imagination of the Western World.[7]

Snow White and the Seven Dwarfs was the first of a long line of Disney films to be accompanied by a large-scale marketing and merchandising campaign. Drawing on his success in selling Mickey Mouse merchandise, Kay Kamen, the company's merchandising guru, arranged for the production of Snow White-related products from 70 different companies. These items included clothing, toys, phonograph records, and even "Snow White Soap Flakes," reflecting the film's washing scene.[8]

Overall, *Snow White and the Seven Dwarfs* was a personal coup for Disney, explained Finch, "a conscious effort on his part to advance the art of animation to a new level of sophistication—a level that everyone else had thought was beyond reach."[9]

Did You Know?
Walt Disney won 32 personal Academy Awards for his work. This earned him a place in the *Guinness Book of World Records*.

Film Distribution

One element that was crucial to the Disney studio's ability to grow its business was its relationship with its film distributors. Between 1929-1954, the organization used three different film companies to distribute its products: Columbia Pictures (1929-1931); United Artists (1931-1936); and RKO (1936-1954). The connections these studios had with movie theaters were invaluable, especially in the studio's early years when it was struggling to make a name for itself and stay financially solvent.[10]

It was not until 1954 that Disney established its own distribution arm, Buena Vista Distribution. This allowed the company to distribute not only its own films but also those of other companies, including Pixar Animation, which will be discussed later in this chapter.

Author Janet Wasko noted, "The move into distribution signaled the Disney company's transition from a marginal, independent film company to one of the Hollywood majors."[11] Today, the studio's distribution division is called Walt Disney Studios Motion Pictures International.

Fantasia

In the years following *Snow White and the Seven Dwarfs*, Walt Disney turned out several more full-length animated features—*Pinocchio* (1940), *Fantasia* (1940), *Dumbo* (1941), and *Bambi* (1942). As discussed in Chapter 2, a studio strike in 1941 and the onset of World War II hampered production as well as negatively affected profits during the 1940s. Both of these factors impacted Disney's plans to produce even more animated features over the course of the decade.

By far, the most unique of the features he was able to produce during this time period was *Fantasia*. Unlike the other films, which followed what has come to be known as the classic Disney fairytale formula, *Fantasia* had no set storyline. Instead, it was constructed almost as a collection of Silly Symphony segments packaged as a feature film. One of its purposes was to educate the public about the virtues of classical music.

The Sorcerer's Apprentice

The most famous of the vignettes from *Fantasia* was a Mickey Mouse segment called *The Sorcerer's Apprentice*, set to the music of French composer Paul Dukas. In fact, *Fantasia* originally came about because Walt Disney wanted to create a new vehicle for his cartoon mouse, who had gotten lost in the shuffle of Disney's other works over the years.[12]

Disney hoped to develop a longer piece for Mickey Mouse based on the Dukas music to be conducted by Philadelphia Orchestra conductor Leopold Stokowski. Ultimately, as a result of the collaboration with Stokowski, the segment grew in scope and scale beyond *The Sorcerer's Apprentice* into a full-length feature.

Stepped-Up Marketing

Fantasia was puzzling to Disney's audiences because it was so different from its predecessors, *Snow White* and *Pinocchio*. Consequently, the studio tried to be more creative in the marketing and promotion of the film, explained Tom Tumbusch.

> Many unique ways were attempted to market *Fantasia*. Study guides were made available through school music programs. Special promotions were offered through symphony orchestras and organizations. These extra efforts helped, but missed the mark with a large part of the traditional Disney audience.[13]

The Impact of the War Years

The films the Disney Studio produced for the U.S. government during World War II kept the business and its employees going and resulted in dozens of products. However, the inability to produce its regular fare took a financial toll on the company, one that took many years to recover from.

Donald Duck the Taxpayer

Although the majority of the government films produced during the war were for training and educational purposes, the studio also created a series of cartoon shorts featuring Donald Duck, Pluto, and Goofy. Because these characters were well known by the public, featuring them in cartoons designed to encourage patriotism diluted the fact that the films were essentially animated propaganda.

One Donald Duck cartoon, *The New Spirit*, was developed for the U.S. Treasury to explain to audiences the importance of paying their taxes. To promote the film, Walt Disney "ordered a full scale publicity campaign just as if *The New Spirit* were a feature film," noted Richard Shale, author of *Donald Duck Joins Up*.[14]

A financial saving grace for Disney during the war years was the decision to begin re-releasing films on a seven-year cycle, a process that became a long-term fixture for the company. The logic behind this decision was that after a sufficient period of time, Disney films had the potential to appeal to new generations of children and their parents.

"Several animated films they did are absolute classics that stand the test of time," said Brian Lowry, columnist and critic for *Variety*. "They were very smart in re-releasing and hitting new generations of kids with them."[15] The practice of re-releasing animated films on a timed cycle is one that continues to this day with Disney DVDs.

Live Action/Animation

During the 1940s, Disney was able to produce a few films that combined live action and animation. Two of these, *Saludos Amigos* (1943) and *The Three Caballeros* (1945), were a result of Disney's Goodwill tour to South America in 1941.

The animated sequences in *Saludos Amigos* featured Donald Duck and a Brazilian parrot named José Carioca. A third character, a Mexican rooster named Panchito, was added to round out the trio for *The Three Caballeros*. The live action segments of the films were taken from footage shot during the Goodwill tour and included scenes of the South American landscape.

Soon after the war, Disney also released *Song of the South* (1946). Based on the Uncle Remus tales by Joel Chandler Harris, the film centers on Uncle Remus, played by James Baskett, telling stories about Brer Rabbit, Brer Fox, and Brer Bear to a young boy named Johnny. Interwoven through his tales are animated segments featuring the animals.

Although *Song of the South* did well at the box office at the time of its release, in subsequent years, the film has been criticized as being racist because of its character portrayals. As a result, Disney has never released the film on video or DVD in the United States.

Post-War Package Films

During the post-war years, the Disney Company needed to straighten out its finances before undertaking production of new animated full-length features. To accomplish this, the company released several "package" films that contained a series of short cartoons—*Make Mine Music* (1946); *Fun and Fancy Free* (1947); *Melody Time* (1948); *and The Adventures of Ichabod and Mr. Toad* (1949). Some of the individual shorts from these releases, such as *Mickey and the Beanstalk* and *The Whale Who Wanted to Sing at the Met*, were packaged as individual cartoon shorts many years later when the company began releasing its films on home video.

Live Action Films

Although Disney had produced several live action/animation combination films in the 1940s, it was not until 1950 that the company produced its first completely live action feature. Part of this late entry into the field was Walt Disney's own resistance to the medium, as he believed the studio's focus on high quality animated films was what set it apart from others.

After the Second World War, however, as the company was looking for ways to rebuild itself financially, live action seemed like an easy fix. The films were less costly to produce and would not require the two to three years of preparation time typically demanded by a full-length animated feature.

Another factor that influenced the decision to start producing live action films was the economic aftermath of World War II. After the war, several European countries including England decreed that companies making a profit in Europe needed to spend the money they earned in Europe to help rebuild the economy. That meant any money Disney had made from the sale of its films during the war needed to be reinvested in the European market.

Treasure Island

With all these forces at play, Walt Disney decided to produce his first completely live action film, *Treasure Island*, in England. He assembled a largely English cast and crew, then went on location himself to oversee production of the film.

Ironically, despite his initial resistance, Disney was fascinated by the process of making a live action film and came back to the United States with a new enthusiasm for the medium. Box office results for *Treasure Island* may have influenced this as well, explained Disney biographer Neal Gabler. "The finished film...was both a critical and a financial success—the first in a long time. *Treasure Island* grossed $4 million, returning to the studio a profit of between $2.2 and $2.4 million."[16]

In the ensuing years, the studio continued its output of live action films. Disney made three additional features in England—*The Story of Robin Hood*

(1952), *The Sword and the Rose* (1953), and *Rob Roy* (1954). Soon after, he was able to relocate production back to his Burbank studio.

Other Hit Films

One of Disney's biggest hits from this period was *The Shaggy Dog* (1959), noted author Steven Watts. "*The Shaggy Dog* proved to be one of the most important films in the entire history of the Disney operation. It grossed an amazing $8 million in its initial release and became a roaring box office success."[17]

While many of the early live action films produced during the 1950s and 1960s have long since been forgotten, some have gone down in film history as Disney classics. These include *Old Yeller* (1957), *The Absent Minded Professor* (1961), and *The Parent Trap* (1961). Some of the classic live action films from the 1950s and 1960s have since been re-remade by the company with mixed box office success.[18]

Mary Poppins

Disney's most acclaimed live action film was actually a live action/animation combination, *Mary Poppins*, which was discussed in detail in Chapter 2. The film about an English nanny featured an engaging story, all-star cast, and award-winning songs by Richard M. and Robert B. Sherman.

For the making of *Mary Poppins*, Disney and company pulled out all the stops. As Walt Disney himself explained:

> After a long concentration on live action and cartoon films, we decided to try something that would deploy about every trick we had learned in the making of film. We decided to combine cartoon, live action and enormous fantasy into *Mary Poppins*.[19]

Critics agreed the results were nothing short of magical, and box office returns reflected this. *Mary Poppins* earned $31 million in the United States and $45 million worldwide.[20] Nearly 50 years after its release, *Mary Poppins* is still considered one of the best films ever produced by the Disney Company.

"*Mary Poppins* will be a great movie for every generation," said composer Joe Alfuso. "In a hundred years, people will still plop their kids down in front of *Mary Poppins* in whatever format it is, and it'll still be a great story."[21]

Figure 5: Animated Films Released Under Walt Disney

1937	Snow White and the Seven Dwarfs
1940	Pinocchio
1940	Fantasia
1941	Dumbo
1942	Bambi
1946	Make Mine Music
1947	Fun and Fancy Free
1948	Melody Time
1949	The Adventures of Ichabod and Mr. Toad
1950	Cinderella
1951	Alice in Wonderland
1953	Peter Pan
1955	Lady and the Tramp
1959	Sleeping Beauty
1961	101 Dalmatians
1963	The Sword in the Stone

Source: Walt Disney Archives: A Complete List of Disney Films,
http://d23.disney.go.com/library/000000_WDA_AL_ListOfDisneyFilms.html

True-Life Adventures

As discussed in Chapter 2, the True-Life Adventure series began almost on a whim. Inspired by a family trip to Alaska, Walt Disney saw potential in filming in that region with the possibility of developing a nature-oriented documentary film. He hired a husband and wife production team, Alfred and Elma Wilotte, to go to Alaska and film the wildlife they saw there.

With the footage they sent back, the studio put together a 30-minute nature film called *Seal Island* in 1948. As was to be expected, Disney's distributor, RKO, was reluctant to take on the film, as it was so unlike the studio's other works and too short to boot. Consequently, Disney persuaded a Pasadena theater owner to show the film for a week in December 1948, making it eligible for an Academy Award nomination.[22]

When *Seal Island* won the Academy Award for Best Two-Reel Short Subject in 1949, suddenly theaters all over the country were interested in showing it. This led to the start of what became known as the True-Life Adventure series. Many of these were short films—between 20-30 minutes. Six were produced as full-length features: *The Living Desert* (1953); *The Vanishing Prairie* (1954); *The African Lion* (1955); *Secrets of Life* (1956), *White Wilderness* (1958); and *Jungle Cat* (1959).

The editors putting these films together were trained in animation production and frequently looked for humorous footage that would be likely to appeal to audiences. Whimsical music was often used to accentuate the movements of the film subjects. As Walt Disney himself said, "At the very beginning, we discovered that old Mother Nature had rhythm. So, all our True-Life Adventures have musical interludes."[23]

Because these films were essentially "engineered" in the studio, they have been criticized by some who feel they are not authentic nature documentaries.[24] Nonetheless, explained Christopher Finch, "For all their defects, the True-Life Adventures pioneered a genre which was to become a staple of television programming in the form of shows like the *National Geographic* specials."[25]

Animation in Transition

By the 1950s, the Disney studio was actively involved in the production of full-length animated features once again at the same time it was gearing up its live action film division. Between 1950 and 1960, the studio released *Cinderella* (1950), *Alice in Wonderland* (1951), *Peter Pan* (1953), *Lady and the Tramp* (1955), and *Sleeping Beauty* (1959).

A decade later, however, the public's interest in animated features was in sharp decline, which influenced the focus of the studio. The sudden death of Walt Disney in 1966 had an impact on the studio's production of animated features as well. It was not until the late 1980s that the Disney Company would see a return to its former glory days as a leader in the production of high-quality animated films with the release of *The Little Mermaid* in 1989.

Did You Know?

Disney's first female animator was Retta Scott, who joined the company in 1938. Her work can be seen in *Dumbo* (1941), *Bambi* (1942), and *The Adventures of Ichabod and Mr. Toad* (1949).

The Resurgence of Disney Animation

The Little Mermaid brought the Disney Company back to its roots by embodying all that was the essence of Disney animation. Based on a story by Hans Christian Andersen, *The Little Mermaid* told the tale of a mermaid who longed to be human.

The film had all the makings of a successful Disney film—an engaging love story, an evil enchantress, and an array of humorous "sidekick" characters, including a Rastafarian crab named Sebastian. Songs by Alan Menken and Howard Ashman greatly contributed to the film's popularity. One of them, *Under the Sea,* won an Academy Award for Best Song in 1990.

The Little Mermaid earned $84 million when it was initially released in theaters and sold nine million copies when it was first released on video.[26] More importantly, *The Little Mermaid* set the stage for several more animated features produced during the 1990s that reminded the world that the Disney Company had not lost its touch as an animation superstar.

The Little Mermaid was followed by *Beauty and the Beast* (1991), *Aladdin* (1992), and *The Lion King* (1994), all of which were box office hits. In addition, their success led to the development of a new theatrical division within the Disney Company that began producing Broadway shows based on Disney animated films. More information about Disney's theater activities will be provided in Chapter 9.

The Effect of Computers on Disney Films

Computers began to play a role in Disney films in the early 1980s. *Tron* (1982) was a $20 million production that used computer technology to create the illusion of what one reporter called "a video game come to life."[27] While *Tron* was admired by critics for its special effects and received two Academy Award nominations, it did not hold the audience appeal the company had hoped for.

The studio began experimenting with computer-generated imagery in the mid-1990s to supplement the traditional hand-drawn animation cels that had been the cornerstone of the animation process for so many years. The development of a process called the Computer Animated Production System (CAPS) allowed "handmade animation drawings to be copied and colored electronically (eliminating the need for cels). It also [allowed] different elements of an image to be combined in elaborate ways that formerly would have been almost impossible."[28]

The use of CAPS was a significant time-saving technique and was to have a revolutionary impact on later animated feature films produced by the studio.

The Creation of Touchstone and Hollywood Pictures

Just as the animated feature had lost its audience in the 1970s, the live action family movie was headed in the same direction by the early 1980s. As audience tastes shifted, the Disney studio found itself behind the times by sticking with its family-friendly films while other studios were appealing to young adults with the production of racier and more sophisticated fare.

Not wanting to tarnish the Disney reputation as a producer of family-friendly movies, under the leadership of Ron Miller, the company created a new label called Touchstone Pictures. Its purpose was to release a brand of films aimed at more mature audiences. The creation of the line also enabled the studio to release films with PG-13 and R ratings for the first time in Disney history.

The first film released under the Touchstone banner was *Splash* (1984), starring Tom Hanks and Darryl Hannah. It was well received by both critics and audiences and earned $69 million in box office returns.[29] This boded well for the studio's new direction in live action films.

After Michael Eisner and Frank Wells took over the leadership of the Disney Company in 1984, the studio added a second production line of adult-oriented films called Hollywood Pictures. Both of these divisions were known for what author Ron Grover called "a simple formula: light, bright adult entertainment with finely honed story lines and ruthlessly tight budgets."[30]

According to Grover, part of the financial success of the early Touchstone and Hollywood Pictures films was the studio's ability to attract top-name talent whose Hollywood stars had been fading in recent years and hire them at reduced rates.[31] These included Bette Midler, Richard Dreyfuss, Goldie Hawn, and Angela Lansbury. All of these individuals saw their careers take an upturn as a result of their involvement in the Disney-produced films.

Some of the early Touchstone Pictures hits included *Down and Out in Beverly Hills* (1986); *The Color of Money* (1986); *Three Men and a Baby* (1987); *Who Framed Roger Rabbit* (1988); and *The Nightmare Before Christmas* (1993). Films released under the Hollywood Pictures label included *The Marrying Man* (1991); *Encino Man* (1992); *The Joy Luck Club* (1993); *Quiz Show* (1994); and *Mr. Holland's Opus* (1996).

Walt Disney Pictures

Disney has continued to produce its family-friendly live action films under the Walt Disney Pictures label. The most successful of the films produced by Walt Disney Pictures in recent years fall under the umbrella of what has become known as the *Pirates of the Caribbean* franchise. Based on the Pirates of the Caribbean Disneyland park ride, the original film, *Pirates of the Caribbean: The Curse of the Black Pearl,* was released in 2003. Directed by Jerry Bruckheimer, the movie starred Johnny Depp as swashbuckler Captain Jack Sparrow.

The film was a tremendous hit for Disney and grossed $305 million in domestic box office sales.[32] Two sequels have since been released—*Pirates of the Caribbean: Dead Man's Chest* (2006), and *Pirates of the Caribbean: At World's End* (2007). A third sequel, *Pirates of the Caribbean: On Stranger Tides,* is slated to be released in 2011.

Miramax Films

Disney also expanded its live action film options when it purchased Miramax Films. Miramax was founded by brothers Harvey and Bob Weinstein in 1979. The company had produced such films as *Sex, Lies and Videotape* (1989) and *The Crying Game* (1992) before Disney purchased it for $80 million in 1993. The Weinstein brothers were retained to manage the operation.

Under Disney's watch, the brothers churned out a string of successful films, including *Pulp Fiction* (1994), *The English Patient* (1996), *Shakespeare in Love* (1998), and *Chicago* (2002). However, disagreements over creative control between the Weinstein brothers and Michael Eisner led to a rift in relations.

In 2005, Disney severed its ties with the Weinsteins and replaced them with one of its own executives. The Weinsteins went on to form a new studio called The Weinstein Co.

Miramax continued to produce films, including *No Country for Old Men*, which won the 2007 Academy Award for Best Picture. Most of the studio's productions after 2005, however, paled in comparison financially to the films produced under the Weinstein brothers.

In late 2009, Disney shuttered Miramax's offices in New York and Los Angeles and put the company's film library up for sale for $700,000. Miramax was sold to investor group Filmyard Holding in 2010.[33]

The Impact of Pixar Animation

Perhaps the most significant influence on Disney films in the last two decades has been the company's relationship with Pixar Animation Studios. Pixar began as a computer graphics division of George Lucas's Industrial Light and Magic. Lucas sold the operation in 1986 for $10 million to Steve Jobs, co-founder and CEO of Apple Computer. Jobs renamed the company Pixar Animation Studios and moved it to Emeryville, Calif.

Pixar's Films

Pixar's first full-length feature, *Toy Story*, was directed by John Lasseter, a former Disney employee. He developed the movie as the industry's first fully computer-animated film, then contracted with Disney to have it distributed in 1995. *Toy Story* was an immediate hit and earned $192 million at the box office during its initial release.[34] The success of the film led to a partnership between the two companies that lasted until Disney bought Pixar in 2006, as discussed in Chapter 3.

Since *Toy Story* in 1995, Pixar has made 11 additional films. All have done extremely well at the box office as well as with subsequent DVD sales.

Pixar's Influence on Disney Animation

Not only did Disney profit from its arrangement with Pixar, it began changing its own animated film production as a result of the enthusiastic response of audiences to Pixar's films. While Disney had continued to produce animated films since the mid-1990s such as *Pocahontas* (1995), *The*

Hunchback of Notre Dame (1996), *Mulan* (1998), and *Lilo and Stitch* (2002), only a handful made a dent in the company's bottom line. Some such as *Atlantis: The Lost Empire* (2001) and *Treasure Planet* (2002) were box office failures.

As production costs were not being matched by profits, the company made the decision to stop producing traditional 2-D hand-drawn animated films in the early 2000s. The company closed its animation unit in Orlando, Fla., in 2004, and moved all the studio's animation operations to southern California. By the following year, Disney's animation unit stopped producing 2-D films altogether and began putting out only computer-generated (CG) films.[35]

Unfortunately for Disney, the company's subsequent CG releases, such as *Valiant* (2005) and *Chicken Little* (2005), did not come close to matching the box office success of Pixar's films. They were merely a blip on the animation radar screen.

As noted in Chapter 3, Disney almost lost its connection to Pixar as a result of conflict between Steve Jobs and Michael Eisner. Soon after Bob Iger assumed the reins of the Disney Company in 2005, however, it was announced that instead of separating from Disney, Jobs had agreed to sell Pixar to Disney for $7.4 billion.[36]

Figure 6: Disney/Pixar Films

1995	Toy Story
1998	A Bug's Life
1999	Toy Story 2
2001	Monsters, Inc.
2003	Finding Nemo
2004	The Incredibles
2006	Cars
2007	Ratatouille
2008	WALL-E
2009	Up
2010	Toy Story 3
2011	Cars 2

Source: Walt Disney Archives: A Complete List of Disney Films,
http://d23.disney.go.com/library/000000_WDA_AL_ListOfDisneyFilms.html

Return to Hand-Drawn Animation

Disney's purchase of Pixar opened the door for a multitude of animation possibilities. As part of the deal, John Lasseter assumed the position of Chief Creative Officer for the studio's animation division.

Steve Segal is an animation instructor at the Academy of Art University and the California College of the Arts who worked on *Toy Story* and *A Bug's Life* with Lasseter at Pixar. He believes Lasseter's appointment has been a boon to the studio.

"He's a true lover of animation—both 2-D and 3-D. He's very knowledgeable, somebody who's really passionate about it," Segal explained.[37]

While Lasseter himself helped pioneer the use of CG animation, he was still a big fan of the hand-drawn animation process. As one of his first tasks at Disney, he led the company back to its beginnings with the production of *The Princess and the Frog* in 2009. Based on the classic fairy tale *The Frog Prince*, the film was the Disney Company's first 2-D hand-drawn animated feature since 2004. More hand-drawn animated films are expected to follow, including a new rendering of A.A. Milne's *Winnie the Pooh* stories in 2011.

The Future of Disney Films

In the years since Bob Iger became CEO in 2005, the Disney Company's film division has seen its share of ups and downs. Certainly, the acquisition of Pixar has been a tremendous shot in the arm to the organization's animation division and is likely to help stabilize that area for the immediate future.

On the live action front, business has been a bit more volatile. The economic recession that began in the late 2000s has had an impact on people's entertainment spending patterns. This has affected money spent on trips to the movies as well as DVD sales.

The company's biggest challenge in recent years has been developing live action films with significant moneymaking potential. A 3-D version of *A Christmas Carol*, starring Jim Carrey and directed by Robert Zemeckis, opened in late 2009 with disappointing box office results. A second film, *Old Dogs*, starring Robin Williams and John Travolta, opened around the same time and barely caused a stir with the movie-going public. One ray of light was the Tim Burton film, *Alice in Wonderland*, which grossed nearly $334 million at the box office in early 2010 and helped generate merchandise sales as well.[38]

Studio Reorganization

As mentioned in Chapter 3, in late 2009, Bob Iger reorganized Disney's film division, replacing long-time Disney employee Dick Cook with Rich Ross, who moved over from a successful run with the Disney Channel. A preliminary analysis suggests that Ross and his team are hoping to create what the *Los Angeles Times* called "a new business model for Hollywood to address the sweeping changes that are roiling the industry, including slumping DVD sales and the growing role the Internet plays in movie marketing."[39]

In early 2010, Disney announced plans to focus on some of its film brands that can feed into the company's established marketing and merchandising efforts. An example of this is a new Muppets movie expected to be released in 2011. The film can be tied into the Muppets attractions at several of Disney's theme parks and promoted through the sale of Muppets merchandise at the parks and in Disney Stores. Future films based on the newly acquired Marvel Entertainment characters are expected to fit into this new model as well.

"The whole entertainment industry has changed," explained Philippe Perebinossoff, associate professor in the department of Radio-TV-Film at Cal State Fullerton. "Disney wants to develop projects that have the potential to become franchises like the *Pirates of the Caribbean*."[40]

Wall Street Journal reporter Ethan Smith suggested that the company's new direction "is trying to remake the studio as an ecosystem of three well-known divisions—Pixar, Marvel and Disney Studios proper. Each would produce its own flavor of movie."[41]

In some respects, this approach reflects a shift away from the more adult-oriented films that have characterized the studio's output in the last few decades. Instead, it represents a return to the family-friendly films the company started out with back in the days of Walt Disney.

Disney also struck an agreement with Steven Spielberg's Dreamworks Studio in 2009 to distribute four to six Dreamworks pictures each year. The agreement includes merchandising rights to any consumer products that result from these films.[42] This is likely to bring in some additional revenue for Disney.

Disneynature

Nearly 40 years after the last True-Life Adventure was produced, the Disney Company launched a new documentary production unit called

Disneynature. The purpose was to develop a new brand of nature films modeled after the concept of the originals. The company released its first Disneynature film, *Earth*, in 2009, followed by *Oceans* in 2010.

According to the *New York Times*, Disney hopes the series will appeal to its overseas as well as its domestic markets, explaining that while "the company's films have long been successful in foreign countries...nature documentaries, with film gathered from around the globe, cross borders much more easily."[43]

Conclusion

Though the Disney Company has become a force to be reckoned with in many different areas of today's entertainment industry, at the heart of the organization is its production of high quality films. Throughout the company's existence, the combination of engaging storytelling and innovative technique has been the driving force behind Disney's success. This was a practice developed and nurtured by Walt Disney and carried on by his successors.

Over the years, Disney has produced a string of blockbuster animated and live action films as well as films that have not hit their mark financially. Technological innovation and changing audience tastes have had an impact on the studio and affected the content and production of its films.

Structural changes set in motion by current CEO Bob Iger within the company's film division are likely to result in new developments and directions for the studio in upcoming years. Whatever may ensue, one fact will likely remain constant. The Disney Company will continue to produce family-friendly films for audiences of all ages, upholding a tradition put into place long ago by its founder Walt Disney. ◆

Notes

1. Russell Merritt and J.B. Kaufman, *Walt Disney's Silly Symphonies* (Gemona, Italy: La Cineteca del Friuli, 2006): 4.
2. Bob Thomas, *Walt Disney: An American Original* (New York: Disney Editions, 1994): 118.
3. Ibid., 115.
4. Tom Tumbusch, *Walt Disney the American Dreamer* (Dayton, OH: Tomart Publications, 2008): 37.
5. Ibid., 38.

6. See Christopher Finch, *The Art of Walt Disney: From Mickey Mouse to the Magic Kingdoms* (New York: Harry N. Abrams, 2004): 147.

7. Ibid., 151.

8. See Steven Watts, *The Magic Kingdom: Walt Disney and the American Way of Life* (Columbia, MO: University of Missouri Press, 1997): 161-162.

9. Finch, *The Art of Walt Disney: From Mickey Mouse to the Magic Kingdoms*, 152.

10. See Douglas Gomery, "Disney's Business History: A Reinterpretation," in Eric Smoodin, ed., *Disney Discourse* (New York: Routledge, 1994): 72.

11. Janet Wasko, *Understanding Disney* (Cambridge, England: Polity Press, 2001): 22.

12. See Thomas, *Walt Disney: An American Original*, 151.

13. Tumbusch, *Walt Disney the American Dreamer*, 50-51.

14. Richard Shale, *Donald Duck Joins Up: The Walt Disney Studio During World War II* (Ann Arbor, MI: UMI Research Press, 1982): 29.

15. Brian Lowry, telephone interview, July 30, 2010.

16. Neal Gabler, *Walt Disney: The Triumph of the American Imagination* (New York: Alfred A. Knopf, 2006): 471-472.

17. Watts, *The Magic Kingdom: Walt Disney and the American Way of Life*, 406.

18. These include *The Parent Trap* (1998), *Freaky Friday* (2003), and *The Shaggy Dog* (2006) among others.

19. Walt Disney as quoted in film clip about the making of *Mary Poppins*, Walt Disney Family Museum, San Francisco.

20. See Wasko, *Understanding Disney*, 22.

21. Joe Alfuso, telephone interview, June 21, 2010.

22. See Thomas, *Walt Disney: An American Original*, 208.

23. Walt Disney as quoted in film clip about the making of the True-Life Adventures, Walt Disney Family Museum, San Francisco.

24. See, for example, Richard Schickel, *The Disney Version: The Life, Times, Art and Commerce of Walt Disney* (Chicago: Irwin R. Dee, 1997): 289-291; and Janet Wasko, *Understanding Disney* (Cambridge, England: Polity Press, 2001): 148-149.

25. Finch, *The Art of Walt Disney: From Mickey Mouse to the Magic Kingdoms*, 391.

26. See Wasko, *Understanding Disney*, 133-134.

27. Charles Solomon, "Will the Real Walt Disney: Please Stand Up?" *Film Comment* 18:4 (July/August 1982): 49.

28. Finch, *The Art of Walt Disney: From Mickey Mouse to the Magic Kingdoms*, 293.

29. See Ron Grover, *Disney Touch: How a Daring Management Team Revived an Entertainment Empire* (Homewood, IL: Business One Irwin, 1991): 16.

30. Ibid., 222.

31. Ibid., 225.

32. See Box Office Mojo, http://www2.boxofficemojo.com/movies/?id=piratesof thecaribbean.htm.

33. See Claudia Eller and Dawn C. Chmielewski, "Disney Agrees to Sell Miramax Films to Investor Group Led by Ron Tutor," *Los Angeles Times*, 30 July 2010.

34. See Box Office Mojo, http://boxofficemojo.com/movies/?id=toystory.htm.

35. See Finch, *The Art of Walt Disney: From Mickey Mouse to the Magic Kingdoms*, 366.

36. "Pixar Animation Studios, Inc," *Hoovers Company Information*, Hoover's Inc., 2010.

37. Steve Segal, telephone interview, October 7, 2009.

38. See Box Office Mojo, http://boxofficemojo.com/movies/?id=alicein wonderland 10.htm.

39. Claudia Eller and Dawn Chmielewski, "Disney Drama Might Alter the Industry," *Los Angeles Times*, 23 November 2009, B1.

40. Philippe Perebinossoff, in-person interview, July 29, 2010.

41. Ethan Smith, "Disney Narrows Its Movie Focus, Building on Known Characters," *Wall Street Journal*, 12 March 2010, B1.

42. See Ronald Grover, "Disney Remakes the Movie Studio," *Business Week*, November 9, 2009, 50.

43. Brooks Barnes, "Disney Looks to Nature, and Creates a Film Division to Capture It," *The New York Times*, 22 April 2008.

6

Disney Television

By the 1940s, a new medium had appeared on the scene with the potential to completely change the entertainment habits of millions of Americans. Television offered consumers the opportunity to be entertained without leaving the comforts of their own homes.

For many in the film business, this newfangled invention proved a tremendous threat to the future of the industry. While some worried that television would alter the entertainment landscape for the worse, others hoped it was just a passing fad that would quickly go away.

Walt Disney regarded the new medium with a combination of vague interest and healthy intrigue. As a filmmaker, he recognized the potential damage it could do to the film industry. At the same time, he saw the enormous potential the new medium could offer in helping to promote his existing films as well as the project he was working on at the time—the creation of the Disneyland theme park.

Disney's interest in the future of television eventually led to a partnership with ABC. In exchange for the network's investment in Disney's fledgling park, the filmmaker agreed to produce two new television programs for ABC. One of these, *Disneyland*, would serve as a not-so-subtle promotional vehicle for the new park. The other, *The Mickey Mouse Club*, set a new standard for children's programming and to this day is remembered as one of the cultural icons of the 1950s.

In time, with the advent of cable television, the Disney Company would launch its own channel. The Disney Channel enabled the company the opportunity to take ownership of the medium by broadcasting its own brand of TV programs. Over time, it has become one of the most important aspects of the company's marketing and promotional activities and has extended its reach into the company's music and consumer products divisions.

The creation of Touchstone Television in the mid-1980s led to the development of a variety of Disney-produced shows that were available for viewing on both network and cable television. These included hits such as *The Golden Girls* and *Home Improvement.*

By 1996, the Disney Company had come full circle with the purchase of Capital Cities/ABC. This acquisition of the network that once gave Disney a start in the television business would allow Disney to become a major player in all aspects of the broadcast industry and enable it to add to its repertoire of entertainment offerings.

This chapter will discuss the evolution of Disney's involvement in television, beginning in the 1950s. It will explore the different aspects of the field the company has had a hand in and look at how Disney has been able to grow and develop some of these areas to become major parts of the company's success.

Getting Into the Business

Like many in the film industry at the time, Walt Disney was initially a bit dubious about making the transition into television. The cost and energy required to produce a weekly or daily television program could potentially outweigh the benefits since the medium was still in its beginning stages, and financial success was uncertain. Unlike some others in the industry, however, Disney recognized the powers that television could have to help him promote other aspects of his business—in particular, the theme park concept he was working on.

Testing the Waters

As an experiment, Disney produced a special called, *One Hour in Wonderland* for NBC, which aired on Christmas Day, 1950, and featured Walt Disney and Edgar Bergen as co-hosts. The show offered viewers a promotional glimpse of Disney's upcoming animated film *Alice in Wonderland* and his live action *Treasure Island*. It "provided Walt with a method of testing television's potential impact on his theatrical business," explained writer Bill Cotter.[1]

One Hour in Wonderland was a success and led to Disney's production of another Christmas Day show for CBS the following year called *The Walt Disney Christmas Show*. From these two ventures, Disney was able to see the value of using television to promote his other entertainment media.

In the early 1950s, there were four networks broadcasting on television—NBC, CBS, ABC, and Dumont. NBC and CBS were the major players with the most sponsors, while the other two networks ran a distant third and fourth. At the time, Disney was actively looking for a corporate partner to invest in his Disneyland theme park. After the success of his Christmas specials, he realized that a TV network might be the ideal choice for his plans.

Forming a Partnership

Walt Disney and his brother Roy began discussing with several of the networks the possibilities of developing a television program that would also help him promote his park. "From the outset, Walt and Roy made it clear that the Park was an integral part of the package they were pedaling—no support for Disneyland, no show," explained Cotter.[2]

While NBC and CBS were eager to acquire access to Disney's products, they were not terribly interested in allowing him to use a television program to promote the park. ABC, on the other hand, saw a partnership with Disney as an opportunity to improve its position in the television market.

In 1954, ABC agreed to partner with Disney by investing in Disneyland in exchange for a Disney-produced weekly television show. ABC invested $500,000 for a 35% share in the park and offered a line of credit of $4.5 million. The company also agreed to pay Disney $2 million for a weekly television anthology series to be called *Disneyland*. Walt Disney would then be able to use this series to promote the new theme park he was building.

The partnership generated considerable interest from the media at the time. *New York Times* reporter Thomas M. Pryor called it "the most important development to date in relations between the old and the new mass entertainment form."[3] He noted that Disney was "the first leading Hollywood producer to enter into formal alliance with television."[4]

Disneyland

The first episode of *Disneyland* debuted on ABC on October 27, 1954. From the start, Disney was quite frank with his audience that the show was to have a dual purpose: as an entertainment medium and as a promotional tool for his company.

Launching the Series

At the beginning of the premiere episode while explaining the purpose of the show, he pointed to a large map of plans for the theme park he was in the process of building. He said, "I want to tell you about it because later on in the show, you'll find that Disneyland the place and *Disneyland* the TV show are all part of the same."[5]

Disney explained that the series was to feature different segments each week that reflected the four lands of the Disneyland Park—Frontierland, Adventureland, Tomorrowland, and Fantasyland. Each week after that, he presented programs that reflected these themes. There were westerns representing Frontierland; tales of adventure for Adventureland; science fiction for Tomorrowland; and animated films for Fantasyland.

Disney also used the show as a way to keep viewers up-to-date on the construction progress of the Disneyland park. He said, "We hope that through our television shows that you will join us and take part in the building of Disneyland and that you'll find here a place of knowledge and happiness."[6] This worked as the ideal promotional tactic to spark the interests of a nationwide audience that was eager to see Disney's finished product when it finally opened on July 17, 1955.

At the urging of the network, Walt Disney served as the host of the *Disneyland* series and introduced each week's program. According to film critic Leonard Maltin, this "made him a familiar figure to viewers, young and old. He wasn't just a name on a movie title or a company logo. He was like a surrogate uncle with the keys to a magic kingdom."[7]

Disneyland was an immediate hit. By the end of the first season, it was the sixth-highest rated show on television. According to reporter Chuck Ross, "It was the first time a show on ABC had even made it into the top 20 regularly scheduled series for the year."[8] The show also received an Emmy for Best Variety Series.

Changing With the Times

Walt Disney originally wanted to air his series in color, but ABC executives rebuffed the idea since most of their affiliate stations didn't have the equipment needed to broadcast in color. Disney went ahead and filmed many of his episodes in color anyway, thinking they could possibly be reused at a later date when color television was more in vogue. This proved to be a smart decision in the long run.

Despite the show's success for ABC, a brewing legal battle led to an early parting of the ways between the studio and the network after the 1959–1960 season. Disney then moved the show to NBC in 1961, where he was finally able to broadcast in color. The show was renamed *Walt Disney's Wonderful World of Color* and moved to Sunday nights at 7:00 p.m.

The Disney anthology series became a staple of Sunday night television for many years. The format changed over time, and it eventually aired on all three networks and The Disney Channel. The show remained on the air until 1990, consequently introducing several generations of children and adults to Disney magic.

Did You Know?

The premiere episode of *Walt Disney's Wonderful World of Color* introduced the character of Professor Ludwig Von Drake. He provided viewers with a lesson about color.

The Marketing Power of Crockettmania

The biggest surprise of the first season of *Disneyland* was the overwhelming success of a Frontierland segment that aired in the show's early days. *Davy Crockett* was created as a three-part series starring Fess Parker, chronicling the life of the famed Texas frontiersman. The series became a national sensation and a merchandiser's dream as well, according to author David Tietyen.

"Crockettmania" swept the country by storm, launching an astonishing marketing phenomenon that Disney used to full advantage. Everywhere you went, there were coonskin hats, jeans, lunch buckets, and hundreds of Davy Crockett-imprinted items.[9]

A song created for the series, *The Ballad of Davy Crockett*, became an "off-the-charts" hit as well. More information about the song will be provided in Chapter 8.

The three television segments featuring Davy Crockett were so popular that Walt Disney edited them together and released them as a feature film in 1955 called, *Davy Crockett, King of the Wild Frontier*. According to Cotter, the film was "an outstanding financial success, raking in $25 million at the box office. This was an unprecedented feat, particularly considering that the television episodes had already been seen by 90 million television viewers."[10]

Disney later produced two additional episodes for the TV series that focused on Crockett's early adventures (similar to the "prequel" technique used by George Lucas after the success of the original *Star Wars* films). These were released as a second feature film, *Davy Crockett and the River Pirates*, in 1956.

The Mickey Mouse Club

The Mickey Mouse Club was the second television program Walt Disney's studio produced for ABC. The show debuted on October 3, 1955, just a year after *Disneyland*. Unlike its predecessor, *The Mickey Mouse Club* was created as a daily rather than a weekly show.

The Mickey Mouse Club was originally designed as a children's program but quickly amassed a following of both children and adults. As author J.P. Telotte noted, "Approximately three-quarters of the televisions in use during the 5:00–6:00 p.m. weekday viewing slot were tuned into the program during its first season."[11] This translated into approximately 14,000,000 viewers.[12]

The show used a variety format and featured song and dance segments, cartoons, newsreels, and serials. Each day of the week had a different theme such as "Guest Star Day" or "Circus Day." But, the highlight of *The Mickey Mouse Club* was the show's group of young performers who came to be known as the "Mouseketeers."

Choosing the Mouseketeers

Twenty-four children from around the country were selected to appear on the show, along with two adult leaders, Jimmie Dodd and Roy Williams. It was the combined innocence and assorted talents of these youngsters that made the show so appealing to viewers. Mouseketeers were primarily selected for the show based on their "kid next door" qualities, according to Cotter.

"Walt wanted to avoid using known show business professionals, as he knew the show had a better chance of success if audiences related to the Mouseketeers."[13]

The Mouseketeers were featured in a "roll call" segment at the beginning of the show where they announced their names. They also appeared in the theme of the day part of each program. However, according to author Lorraine Santoli, they are probably best remembered for the closing of the show:

> The Mouseketeers, seated under a Mickey Mouse banner, with Jimmie Dodd and Roy Williams standing beside them, slowly and reverently sang the song baby boomers and generations to follow will never forget: "Now it's time to say goodbye to all our company. M-I-C ['See ya real soon,' recited Jimmie Dodd], K-E-Y ['Why, because we like you,' he declared], M-O-U-S-E."[14]

Walt Disney's hunch about the relatability of the Mouseketeers paid off. Soon after the show's debut, the studio was flooded with fan mail for the young performers. The company capitalized on this by formally introducing the Mouseketeers to the world through its publicity department, explained Santoli.

"Their Disney-issued biographical and feature-story material was distributed to nationwide press with descriptive phrases of each child that echoed the simplicity of the era and was perfect fodder for media placement," she said.[15] The studio also sent a number of the Mouseketeers to make public appearances at shopping centers, local parades, hospitals, and charity events, where they would sing and dance, greet the public, and sign autographs.

The Magic of Annette

By far, the most popular of the Mouseketeers was a shy, dark-haired young girl from southern California named Annette Funicello. Author Jerry Bowles observed:

Annette had that certain magic something of which stars are made. Just what that something was, exactly, nobody ever quite figured out. But it quickly became obvious to all that Annette was *the* star of the show. Within a few weeks, she was getting close to four thousand letters a month, nearly one third of the total for the entire cast.[16]

Bob Wheeler, now in his sixties, remembers racing home from school on his bike every day to watch *The Mickey Mouse Club* on television with his friend Larry. "We'd go to my house, and we'd turn on the television and watch for Annette Funicello," he said.

Wheeler was 13, and his friend was 14. Like many teenage boys at the time, they were mesmerized by the young Mouseketeer. Although he admits that much of their interest had to do with Funicello's physical attractiveness, he said:

She was a good singer, she had presence, and she seemed to be a dominant character, in a positive way, on the show. Part of the fascination was that she was in the same age range as Larry and I. She could have been that pretty girl in English or math or geometry, so we truly could relate that way.[17]

For Wheeler, watching *The Mickey Mouse Club* was "an embedded part of my youth, one of the memorable times in adolescence."[18]

The Impact of *The Mickey Mouse Club*

As the show grew in popularity, so did the merchandising opportunities. By the second year of the show, 38 companies were selling Mickey Mouse Club merchandise including T-shirts, record players, puzzles, toothbrushes, roller skates, yo-yos, pajamas, and bubble bath, according to Santoli. The most popular item of all was a replica of the felt Mickey Mouse ears worn by the Mouseketeers on the show. "The original all-black version of the ears sold for 69¢ and after *The Mickey Mouse Club* had been on the air only twelve weeks, over 2,000,000 hats had been sold."[19]

The Mickey Mouse Club ran until 1959. A number of the original Mouseketeers were replaced in the second season, and by the third year, the show was reduced from one-hour to 30-minutes a day. It ended after its fourth season.

The show went into syndication from 1962–1965, and again from 1975–1977. *The New Mickey Mouse Club* was launched in 1977 to appeal to a new generation of fans and their parents, who had been children themselves during the original run of the show. However, it lasted only two seasons.

The company had better success with *The All New Mickey Mouse Club*, which ran on the Disney Channel from 1989–1996. That show was responsible for launching the careers of some of today's well-known performers such as Christina Aguilera, Keri Russell, Britney Spears, Justin Timberlake, and Ryan Gosling.[20]

Despite the popularity of the show's third incarnation, it is the original *Mickey Mouse Club* for which Disney is best known. As *Orange County Register* reporter Kimberly Edds explained, it was "a series that launched a television revolution, which combined entertainment and education, and the showbiz careers of several original Mouseketeers."[21]

Figure 7: Cast of The Mickey Mouse Club First Season, 1955–56

Nancy Abbate	Annette Funicello	Tim Rooney*
Sharon Baird	Darlene Gillespie	Mary Sartori
Billie Jean Beanblossom	Judy Harriet	Bronson Scott
Bobby Burgess	Dallas Johann*	Mike Smith
Lonnie Burr	John Lee Johnson	Ronnie Steiner
Tommy Cole	Bonnie Lou Kern	Mark Sutherland
Johnny Crawford	Cubby O'Brien	Doreen Tracey
Dennis Day	Karen Pendleton	Don Underhill
Dickie Dodd	Paul Petersen*	
Mary Espinosa	Mickey Rooney Jr.*	

Club Leaders: Jimmie Dodd, Roy Williams, Bob Amsberry

*Did not finish season
Source: The Original Mickey Mouse Club Show, http://www.originalmmc.com/cast.html

The Disney Channel

The Disney Channel has proven to be one of the hottest segments of the Disney Company. Initially launched as a vehicle for showcasing the company's entertainment programs, in recent years it has also been responsible for jumpstarting the careers of some of Disney's teen stars. As a result, it has imprinted the Disney brand onto the consciousness of millions and children and teens.

The channel debuted in 1983, in response to the burgeoning cable television industry. At the time, the *Los Angeles Times* called it "Hollywood's most ambitious effort yet in cable and pay-TV programming."[22]

In its early years, the Disney Channel was a premium cable channel and offered subscribers an all-Disney-all-the-time viewing experience. Programming included classic Disney cartoons, live action films, Disney park-related specials, and children's shows.

The Disney Channel does not use traditional commercial advertising. Instead, commercial breaks are used to promote the company's own products through "TV show promotions, music videos, news, 'behind-the-scenes' views of new theme parks or studios and highlights from upcoming film/video releases," explained reporter Jeffrey Zbar.[23]

In 1995, Disney changed the channel from a premium to a basic cable channel. Consequently, viewership increased significantly as the channel became available to more households. By the early 2000s, Disney began developing more original programming for the channel, particularly with shows aimed at 6–14-year-olds. This led to a string of hit shows for the channel and a new focus on the "tween" market.

Lizzie McGuire

One of these early hits was *Lizzie McGuire*, a show about "the comic perils of a seventh grader coping with boys, curfews and meddlesome parents," according to an article in *The New York Times*.[24] Not only was the show itself a favorite with audiences, but, like *The Mickey Mouse Club*, it resulted in a line of best-selling show-related merchandise—Lizzie clothes, accessories, books, dolls, school supplies, etc.

The star of the show, Hilary Duff, became a hit herself with the release of several Lizzie-related CDs, which ultimately led to a more expansive singing and acting career for the actress. *Lizzie McGuire* was, in fact, only the beginning of what has become an all-powerful, synergized TV-music-film-merchandise phenomenon involving Disney's teen stars.

The success of *Lizzie McGuire* and its star Hilary Duff inspired Disney executives to continue producing original programs for the Disney Channel designed to create teen sensations. Disney followed up with the sitcom, *That's So Raven*, starring actress Raven-Symone, and then cast Symone as part of the

Cheetah Girls singing group. Symone also went on to star in the Disney film *College Road Trip*, and released several CDs of her own.[25]

Did You Know?

Disney Channel's Raven-Symone began her television career on *The Cosby Show* in 1989. She portrayed Bill Cosby's granddaughter Olivia Kendall.

Hannah Montana

Perhaps the most successful example of these young Disney stars has been Miley Cyrus, whose sitcom, *Hannah Montana*, in 2006 "was the second most-watched TV program in the US (after *American Idol*)...among children aged six to 14," according to reporter Neil Shoebridge.[26] The show depicts the adventures of Miley Stewart, who lives a double life of normal teen by day and rock star by night.

Hannah Montana was such a winner for The Disney Channel that it essentially became its own brand. *Los Angeles Times* reporter Mary McNamara observed, "Miley Cyrus doesn't look like a mouse. Or a befuddled bear. Or even a princess. But make no mistake, like Mickey, Winnie the Pooh and Snow White before her, she is a Disney franchise."[27]

The popularity of Hannah Montana led Disney to create other, similar shows with home-grown stars such as *The Wizards of Waverly Place*, starring Selena Gomez; *The Suite Life on Deck*, starring Dylan and Cole Sprouse; *Sonny with a Chance*, starring Demi Lovato; and *Good Luck Charlie*, starring Bridgit Mendler.

Brian Lowry, columnist and critic for *Variety*, and Philippe Perebinossoff, associate professor of Radio-TV-Film at Cal State Fullerton, credit the producers and casting directors of these shows for their popularity.

"They really think they know who their core audience is and have gone after it in a tightly focused sort of way, finding and discovering young talent," Lowry said.[28]

"I think the people involved in casting decisions have an eye, they can tell," Perebinossoff explained. "They groom stars beautifully—Selena Gomez,

Zac Efron, Miley Cyrus. They look for potential," he said, more than just what they see "right at that moment."[29]

High School Musical

The synchronicity of Disney's marketing efforts was also apparent with the 2006 release of its original Disney Channel movie, *High School Musical.* The film focused on the auditions for a high school show and starred Zac Efron as basketball jock Troy, and Vanessa Anne Hudgens as geek Gabriella. An article in *Fortune* magazine dubbed it "part *Grease*, part *West Side Story*, only tamer."[30]

Disney promoted the show heavily on the Disney Channel for several weeks before it debuted on January 20, 2006. As a result, "the movie's premiere drew 7.7 million viewers in 5 million households, a record for their cable channel," explained *New York Times* reporter Ben Sisario.[31]

The movie was rerun on the channel several more times before the end of January. Disney concurrently released the soundtrack as well as several songs as single hits from the film, which quickly reached the Top 40 on the Billboard charts. The songs were also played extensively on Radio Disney. When the DVD was released a few months later, it included a sing-along version with on-screen lyrics to let viewers sing along with the stars—a sort of karaoke for the tween set.[32]

For many in the industry, the blockbuster success of *High School Musical* "came out of the blue," said Brian Lowry, forcing a lot of people in the industry to sit up and take notice. Prior to the film's debut, he said, many of the Disney Channel's shows hadn't even been reviewed by the press. After the movie took off, however, "the media community had to pay a good deal more attention to them," he said.[33]

Though it cost only $4.2 million to make, by 2007, Disney had already made more than $100 million from the film and its related merchandise sales.[34] *High School Musical 2* was shown on the Disney Channel on August 17, 2007, to an audience of 17.2 million viewers. In addition, Disney released *High School Musical 3* directly to theaters in 2008. The film took in $252 million at the box office.[35]

Toon Disney and Disney XD

Disney launched a second cable channel called Toon Disney in 1997. Its purpose was to feature Disney's animated titles and was aimed at the younger demographic of the Disney Channel's audience. Toon Disney ran some of Disney's classic films but also included more recent cartoon series that had been developed for the Disney Channel or for Saturday morning network cartoon viewing, such as *Darkwing Duck* and *The New Adventures of Winnie the Pooh*.[36]

Toon Disney did not generate nearly the audience the Disney Channel did, and by 2009, the company was ready to try a different approach. As part of its efforts to attract more boys between the ages of 6–14 to its product offerings, Disney retooled Toon Disney into a new entity, Disney XD. The channel was created with a concentration on programming specifically targeted toward boys in this coveted age group, with programs focused on action, adventure, sports, and videogames.

To generate interest in the channel, Disney went beyond the use of traditional media and incorporated a variety of digital platforms to promote its new enterprise—iTunes, cell phones, Sprint TV, and MobiTV, among others.[37] This was a natural approach in trying to attract what *Marketing Week* called, "the digitally aware children of Generation X. It is made up of children born between 1995 and 2001, who have never known a world without the internet."[38]

Figure 8: Disney Channel Teen Stars

Star	Show
Miley Cyrus	Hannah Montana
Hilary Duff	Lizzie McGuire
Zac Efron	High School Musical
Selena Gomez	The Wizards of Waverly Place
Vanessa Anne Hudgens	High School Musical
Demi Lovato	Sonny With a Chance
Bridgit Mendler	Good Luck Charlie
Cole Sprouse	The Suite Life on Deck
Dylan Sprouse	The Suite Life on Deck
Raven-Symone	That's So Raven!

Source: http://home.disney.go.com/tv

Touchstone Television and Buena Vista Television

While the Disney Channel offered the Disney Company opportunities on cable television, the organization had not had much of an impact on network television beyond the two programs it created for ABC in the 1950s. When Michael Eisner became CEO in 1984, he wanted the company to make stronger inroads into the network television market.

To accomplish this, in the mid-1980s, Disney started a television production division called Touchstone Television. Its purpose was to create original programming for the major networks and develop shows that could be sold for syndication, according to Telotte.[39]

Touchstone Television produced a wide range of shows, some of which became longstanding series, and others that lasted only a season or two. Among the more memorable programs were *The Golden Girls; Empty Nest; Live! With Regis and Kathie Lee; Boy Meets World; Home Improvement;* and *Ellen.*

Touchstone's programs were distributed through the company's Buena Vista Television division. Buena Vista was also responsible for the hit show, *Who Wants to Be a Millionaire?* Touchstone Television was merged into the ABC Entertainment Television Group in 1999. Buena Vista Television was re-branded as Disney-ABC Domestic Television in 2007.

Moving Into the Big Leagues With ABC

Disney scored the ultimate television coup in 1996, when the company returned to its TV roots and bought Capital Cities/ABC for $19 billion. This brought the company full circle, as it took ownership of the network that had helped introduce Disney to TV viewers back in the 1950s.

The purchase was the second largest corporate takeover in the history of the United States, according to Telotte, and "the result was the creation of what is arguably the world's largest media company, with its dominating presence in the rapidly converging fields of entertainment, information, and multimedia."[40]

The takeover allowed Disney to become a key player in network television entertainment in a variety of ways. Disney could continue to develop original programming for a network as well as for the Disney Channel. The company also inherited a news division that included programs such as *World News With Charles Gibson, 20/20,* and *Good Morning America.*

Disney also became the custodian of ABC Sports as well as ESPN, which was owned by Capital Cities/ABC at the time of the sale. More information about Disney sports programming will be discussed in Chapter 11.

Finally, the company became the owner of a network of ABC-affiliated television stations as well as radio stations throughout the United States. This ultimately contributed to the development and growth of Radio Disney. More information about Radio Disney will be provided in Chapter 8.

Making Creative Adjustments

In the decade and a half since Disney bought ABC, the company has experienced a roller coaster ride of peaks and valleys. After a sluggish start in the late 1980s and early 1990s, the television division began to show new signs of life after Disney executive Anne Sweeney moved from the Disney Channel to spearhead the ABC Television Group.

Sweeney felt a stronger emphasis on marketing and promotion was needed to jump-start the network. She enlisted the assistance of Stephen McPherson, who had earned his stripes as head of Touchstone Television, and who had recently overseen the development of two new ABC shows, *Desperate Housewives* and *Lost*.

An article in *Broadcasting & Cable* magazine reported:

> McPherson blew up ABC's creative and strategic marketing strategies overnight, replacing them with the now widely imitated formula of promoting a few key shows with innovative marketing techniques. *Housewives* and *Lost* exploded out of the gate, and Touchstone's *Grey's Anatomy* took off midseason.[41]

Disney also made a dent in the reality show craze with its debut of *Extreme Makeover: Home Edition* in 2003, and *Dancing With the Stars* in 2005. In an attempt to make the network more digitally savvy, Disney made headlines in 2006 when the company announced it would allow customers to purchase downloaded episodes of its ABC shows from iTunes through an agreement with Apple Computer. The company also allowed audiences to view shows on its website, ABC.com. In 2009, Disney invested in a 30% stake in the video aggregation site Hulu, along with NBC Universal and News Corporation, in order to make ABC shows available on the site.[42]

Coping With Hard Times

As the recession hit the television industry hard in 2008 and 2009, however, Disney was forced to make adjustments to its operations. In early 2009, the company combined its ABC television network with its ABC studio production unit. Shortly after that, Disney announced the elimination of hundreds of jobs.[43] Stephen McPherson left the company in 2010. At the time of this writing, the company is still assessing the long-term impact of these changes.

"Every network has its ups and downs," said Brian Lowry. "ABC has probably had bigger ups and bigger downs."

Lowry believes part of the challenge for Disney/ABC has been determining how to mesh the network with other Disney divisions. "The TV arm of the company has been less leveraged than was the intent," he said.

When the deal was made to buy ABC in the mid-1990s, he explained, it was expected there would be tremendous synergy between ABC and other aspects of the Disney Company. "There has been some of that. I don't think there's been quite as much of that as Disney thought there would be."[44]

Other Cable Television Ventures

Beyond the Disney Channel, Disney XD, and ESPN, Disney also has other cable TV outlets through its ABC Cable Networking Group. The most prominent of these is ABC Family, which, according to Hoovers, "targets the 18–34-year-old audience segment with programming that is mostly on the safe side."[45] The channel has aired original series like *The Secret Life of an American Teenager*, as well as reruns of shows such as *That '70s Show* and *Gilmore Girls*. ABC Family also runs family-friendly films previously shown in theaters as well as made-for-TV movies.

For 10 years, Disney operated a cable channel called SoapNet, which rebroadcast episodes of ABC daytime soap operas. In 2010, it was announced that SoapNet would be replaced by Disney Junior, created to compete with the Nickelodeon Channel's Nick Jr., in reaching the preschool audience.[46]

Disney also owns a 42% stake in A&E Television Network, which includes the History and Biography Channels. A joint venture with the Hearst Corporation and NBC Universal added the Lifetime Entertainment Service to the A&E repertoire in 2009.[47]

Conclusion

Disney's presence in the television industry has been intricate and complex throughout its evolution from its early beginnings in the 1950s to the present. Over the years, it has encompassed everything from the use of the television medium for promotional purposes to the strategic development and production of news, sports, and entertainment programming.

As new media become a more accepted part of the television landscape, it is conceivable this will factor into the future of Disney television as well. The possibilities remain to be seen. ◆

Notes

1. See Bill Cotter, *The Wonderful World of Disney Television* (New York: Hyperion, 1997): 3.
2. Ibid., 58.
3. Thomas M. Pryor, "Disney to Enter TV Field in Fall," *The New York Times*, 30 March 1954, 24.
4. Thomas M. Pryor, "Disney and A.B.C. Sign TV Contract," *The New York Times*, 3 April 1953, 19.
5. Walt Disney, *Disneyland* television show, October 27, 1954.
6. Ibid.
7. Leonard Maltin, quoted in the introduction to *Walt Disney Treasures–Disneyland USA* DVD, 2001.
8. Chuck Ross, "Recalling a Hit From TV's Frontier Days," *TelevisionWeek* 23:43 (October 25, 2004).
9. David Tietyen, *The Musical World of Walt Disney* (Milwaukee, WI: Hal Leonard Publishing, 1990): 114.
10. Cotter, *The Wonderful World of Disney Television*, 64.
11. J.P. Telotte, *Disney TV* (Detroit, MI: Wayne State University Press, 2004): 83.
12. See Cotter, *The Wonderful World of Disney Television*, 185.
13. Ibid., 183.
14. Lorraine Santoli, *The Official Mickey Mouse Club Book* (New York: Hyperion, 1995): 51.
15. Ibid., 60.
16. Jerry Bowles, *Forever Hold Your Banner High!* (New York: Doubleday, 1976): 27.
17. Bob Wheeler, in-person interview, May 25, 2010.
18. Ibid.
19. Santoli, *The Official Mickey Mouse Club Book*, 85.
20. See Joseph Dionisio, "Cool 2 Know: Ear They Are!" *Newsday*, 24 October 2007, B2.
21. Kimberly Edds, "Mouseketeers Celebrate 50th Anniversary," *Orange County Register*, 4 October 2005, A1.

22. David Crook, "The Disney Channel Does It Walt's Way," *Los Angeles Times*, 17 April 1983, T3.

23. Jeffrey D. Zbar, "Wishing Upon a Star Only the Beginning," *Advertising Age* 71:15 (April 10, 2000): S12.

24. Laura M. Holson, "*Lizzie McGuire* Has Become a Hot Disney Brand," *The New York Times*, 2 December 2002, C1.

25. See Julia Boorstin, "Disney's 'Tween Machine," *Fortune* 148:6 (September 29, 2003): 110.

26. Neil Shoebridge, "From Sensation to Sequel," *Business Review Weekly*, February 15, 2007, 26.

27. Mary McNamara, "Spun Gold: A Kid Show 'Find' Turns Pop Star, Then Film Ingenue," *Los Angeles Times*, 8 July 2007, E1.

28. Brian Lowry, telephone interview, July 30, 2010.

29. Philippe Perebinossoff, in-person interview, July 29, 2010.

30. Julie Schlosser, "Behind the *High School Musical* Sensation," *Fortune* 153:8 (May 1, 2006): 22.

31. Ben Sisario, "A Musical for Tweens Captures Its Audience," *The New York Times*, 8 February 2006, E1.

32. See Edna Gundersen, "'High School,' the Musical," *USA Today*, 28 February 2006, 4d.

33. Brian Lowry, telephone interview, July 30, 2010.

34. See "Magic Restored," *The Economist* 387:8576 (April 19, 2008): 73.

35. See Box Office Mojo, http://boxofficemojo.com/movies/?id=highschoolmusical3.htm.

36. See "Disney Is Launching a Cartoon Network Aimed at Digital Cable," *The Wall Street Journal*, 9 December 1997, 1; and Jim McConville, "Toon Disney Ready to Roll," *Electronic Media* 17:15 (April 6, 1998): 8.

37. See Ronald Grover, "A Digital Ad Blitz for Cable's Disney XD," *Business Week*, January 9, 2009, 17.

38. Branwell Johnson, "Generation XD Uses Internet for Better Social Interaction," *Marketing Week*, January 14, 2010, 7.

39. Telotte, *Disney TV*, 88.

40. Ibid., 89.

41. Jim Benson and Anne Becker, "Synergy: Easy as ABC," *Broadcasting & Cable* 135:41 (October 10, 2005): 10.

42. See Ryan Nakashima, "Disney Joins NBC and News Corp. With Hulu Stake," *Associated Press*, 1 May 2009; and "ABC, Inc.," *Hoovers Company Information*, Hoover's Inc., 2010.

43. See Sam Schechner and Peter Sanders, "Disney Set to Merge ABC Network, Studio," *The Wall Street Journal*, 23 January 2009, B3; and Peter Sanders, "ABC to Lay Off 200 Employees," *The Wall Street Journal*, 30 January 2009, B4.

44. Brian Lowry, telephone interview, July 30, 2010.

45. "ABC Family Worldwide," *Hoovers Company Information*, Hoover's Inc., 2010.

46. See Brooks Barnes, "Disney to Replace Soap Opera Channel With Programming for Preschoolers," *The New York Times*, 27 May 2010, B7.

47. See "Disney-ABC Television Group, Hearst Corporation & NBC Universal Announce Joining of A&E Television Networks and Lifetime Entertainment Services," press release, The Walt Disney Company, August 27, 2009.

7

Disney Theme Parks

When Walt Disney first conceived the concept of a family-friendly amusement park, no one imagined the impact it would have on the world of entertainment. Disney's idea was met with skepticism and criticism because it was so far removed from the core products of his film studio.

Ultimately, Disney was hailed for his forward-thinking ideas. Disneyland opened in Anaheim, Calif., in 1955, and is considered the paragon of the modern-day theme park. As the company's press materials state, "Disneyland introduced an entirely new concept in family entertainment and launched today's global theme park industry."[1] Since the park's opening, people have traveled from all over the world to enjoy the attractions at the park and experience the stories and characters behind them.

The success of Disneyland led the company to undertake a similar venture in central Florida but on a much grander scale. As a result, there are now four distinctly different parks in Florida, as well as a complex of hotels, shops, restaurants, and entertainment venues.

The first international Disney park opened in Japan in 1983. It was followed by others in France and Hong Kong, with another expected to be built in China within the next decade. All of the Disney parks have stories behind them. Some have been immediate hits with the public, while others have been slower to catch on, offering management challenges to the company.

Today there are 11 Disney theme parks in the United States and abroad. Disney parks are among the most popular tourist attractions in the world; eight of the 11 Disney parks rank in the world's top 10 most attended theme parks.[2]

This chapter will look at the evolution of Disney's theme parks, from Disneyland to the Disney Company's forthcoming park in Shanghai. The chapter will provide an overview of how each park has been developed over the years and will examine the impact each has had on the public and on the company itself.

Disneyland Resort

Disney's theme park business began with a single park called Disneyland, which opened its doors to the public in 1955, in Anaheim, Calif. Today, the Anaheim area is home to two Disney parks, as well as three Disney hotels and a shopping district called Downtown Disney. All fall under the umbrella of the Disneyland Resort.

Disneyland

As the first of the Disney theme parks, Disneyland is, for many, the standard against which all others are measured. Although not as big or elaborate as some of the parks that followed, Disneyland's claim of being the first gives it an air of enchantment and nostalgia.

As discussed in Chapter 2, Walt Disney conceived the idea for Disneyland at a time when his film studio was finally beginning to recover from the financial toll of the 1940s. Consequently, when he proposed the concept for Disneyland, those around him thought his ideas were irrational and unrealistic.

Disney subsequently put some of his own money into the project and sought funding through a partnership with ABC to finance his dream. This partnership allowed him to use the medium of television to reach out to millions of people in order to promote his park. When Disneyland finally opened, it had a built-in audience eager to walk through its gates.

The park's opening on July 17, 1955, is recalled as being somewhat of a public relations disaster, especially given all the advance hype, explained reporter Cynthia Gorney.

The water fountains weren't working, half the rides broke down, and Fantasyland sprang a gas leak. The lines were an hour long. The food stands couldn't handle the crowds. The asphalt on Main Street softened and sagged in the midday sun, and women in spike heels sank in as they stood there.[3]

The day would come to be known as "Black Sunday." To top it off, some of the day's disorganization was captured on television, as the park's opening was broadcast live on ABC by hosts Art Linkletter, Bob Cummings, and Ronald Reagan. While media reviews of Disneyland were dubious, they did not stop the crowds from coming to the park to see it for themselves.

By the end of seven weeks, one million guests had come to Disneyland, noted an article in the *Toronto Star*. "By the end of the year, 3.8 million parents and children had come to revel in what was now a smoothly running machine."[4]

At the time of its opening, Disneyland featured four lands: Fantasyland, Tomorrowland, Adventureland, and Frontierland. The park opened with 18 attractions, including some that still remain today, such as Jungle Cruise, Autopia, and Mr. Toad's Wild Ride.

This model on display at The Walt Disney Family Museum in San Francisco represents the Disneyland of Walt Disney's imagination and features attractions developed by Disney himself.
Photo by Cesar Rubio, Courtesy The Walt Disney Family Museum.

The park's first section was called Main Street U.S.A. and was modeled after Walt Disney's nostalgic recollection of the town of his youth, Marceline, Mo. Filled with old-fashioned shops, restaurants, and a plaza featuring entertainment such as barbershop quartets and Dixieland bands, it evokes a feeling of days gone by.

Main Street represents "all the good in us, the minute we walk into the park," explained Joe Alfuso, a composer who has written and arranged music for Disney's theme parks.[5] While subsequent Disney parks have varied the different lands they offer, every Disneyland park has a version of Main Street in the front.

When they were built, the attractions at Disneyland were designed to be different from typical rides of the day at other amusement parks. A team of Disney "Imagineers" such as Herb Ryman, Marty Sklar, Mary Blair, and others lent their expertise and creative talents to the development of these rides.

Some of the attractions such as It's a Small World, Pirates of the Caribbean, and the Haunted Mansion are now indelibly linked to the Disney brand. Even today, as new attractions are added to the park by modern-day Imagineers, they are constructed with features that continue to set them apart from rides at other theme park chains.

Walt Disney once said, "Disneyland will never be completed as long as there is imagination in the world."[6] This has been the catalyst for the growth and changes that have taken place in the park since it opened. Today, Disneyland is the second most popular theme park in the world, welcoming 15.9 million visitors in 2009.[7] Author Karal Ann Marling summed up the world's fascination with Disneyland:

> It is easy to understand why Disneyland was such a hit in 1955.... By the end of the first summer of operation, more than a million visitors would pass through the turnstiles and march down Main Street—and they have never stopped coming. They came because Disneyland embodied ideas, yearnings and half-remembered dreams buried deep in the heart of America.[8]

Disneyland was the first park, but it was certainly not to be the last. It served as a model for many more Disney parks to follow around the world. What makes the original park special for so many is that it has the stamp of Walt Disney all over it, explained author Tom Tumbusch. "This was Walt's park and no matter how many Magic Kingdoms eventually come to pass, there will still only be one Disneyland."[9]

Disney's California Adventure

The initial idea for a second Anaheim park to complement Disneyland was raised in the early 1990s, but it came to life nearly a decade later when Disney CEO Michael Eisner and his cohorts began planning a park that would focus on the wonders of California. The park would be completely different from the fantasy world of Disneyland, as it would be designed to highlight real places rather than fictitious characters and stories.

Behind the momentum for a second park was a desire to make Anaheim a vacation destination. Disneyland was primarily a local park, and visitors tended to come for a day rather than a weekend. Adding a second park would provide incentive for people to come from greater distances and stay longer.

Disney's California Adventure opened its gates on February 8, 2001. Built on what had been Disneyland's parking lot, the park was just a hop, skip, and a jump away from its older sister. A new shopping and dining area called "Downtown Disney," opened between the two parks at the same time.

In the beginning, California Adventure was quite different from Disneyland, as Eisner had intended, explained *Wall Street Journal* reporter Merissa Marr.

> He positioned the new park as a contemporary alternative to Disneyland. It included three main areas: the Hollywood Pictures back lot; the Golden State wharf, which included offbeat, decidedly sedate features like a vegetable garden and tortilla factory; and the carnival-style Paradise Pier, anchored by a big, traditional roller coaster.[10]

California Adventure featured more upscale eateries than Disneyland, where fast food reigned supreme. Traditional Disney characters like Mickey and Minnie Mouse were conspicuously absent from the park to set it apart from Disneyland.

The unique concept of California Adventure earned it a great deal of praise from the media, which initially drew in people eager to see what the park had to offer. Within a few months, however, the public began to grumble that it didn't offer enough.

Critics claimed the park was too adult-oriented, lacking sufficient attractions for children. The scarcity of Disney characters roaming the premises was bemoaned. In addition, people protested that admission to the park cost the same as Disneyland despite the fact the new park was just two-thirds the size of the original with fewer attractions. Within several months, it became clear to Disney executives that more was needed—much more.[11]

In the years since California Adventure opened, the Disney Company has gone to great lengths to reconfigure the park to meet the demands of the public, thereby increasing ticket sales. Within the first few years of the park's opening, Disney added a children's ride area called "Flik's Fun Fair," based on characters from Pixar's *A Bug's Life.*

Disney characters were soon seen strolling around California Adventure. The company even revived its Main Street Electrical Parade—once a staple at Disneyland but dormant since 1996—and imported it into the new park.[12]

Did You Know?

The Grand Californian Hotel and Spa at Disney's California Adventure was the first Disney hotel to be located inside one of the company's theme parks.

A few years later, in 2007, Disney revealed plans for even more. The company announced a forthcoming overhaul of California Adventure that was estimated to cost $1.1 billion—an amount nearly twice as much as the $600 million it had cost to build the park in the first place.

An interactive, 3-D ride called Toy Story Mania kicked off the upgrade in 2008. Then, in 2010, Disney unveiled a nighttime water show in its main lagoon called "Worlds of Color," featuring Disney characters from an assortment of the company's animated films. Other planned changes included the opening of a ride called The Little Mermaid: Ariel's Undersea Adventure in 2011, and a Cars Land attraction based on the Pixar film *Cars* in 2012.[13]

Clearly, the original intention to leave traditional Disney characters and attractions out of the mix of the park had been replaced by a plan to make California Adventure feel more familiar to fans of its sister park across the way. However, Disney executives hoped the changes would spark greater interest from families and boost attendance to the initial 7 million annual visitors they had predicted for the park back in 2001.

Within two years, the improvements seemed to be making a difference. Disney's California Adventure attracted slightly more than 6 million visitors in 2009, a 9.5% increase over 2008.[14] Things were definitely looking up.

Walt Disney World Resort

Unlike Disneyland, which was built as an individual park and grew into something more, Disney's Florida property was always intended to be a resort. As discussed in Chapter 2, Walt Disney's original vision encompassed a site that included a Disneyland-type theme park as well as a futuristic community where people could live and work.

To this end, in the 1960s, the Disney Company bought up 43 acres of Florida land—the approximate size of the city of San Francisco—in order to have the space to build and grow. Today, the Walt Disney World Resort consists of four theme parks, a large network of hotels, two water parks, and a shopping and entertainment district.

Disney's Magic Kingdom

The Magic Kingdom was the first of the four Disney parks to debut in Florida. The park's opening on October 1, 1971, was the culmination of a journey that had begun nearly 10 years earlier.

As discussed in Chapter 2, in the early 1960s, Walt Disney began hatching plans to expand his Disneyland theme park success into something more. His initial idea was to offer those living in the Eastern and Midwestern areas of the United States an entertainment experience similar to what those on the West Coast had been able to enjoy with Disneyland. He also wanted his new enterprise to be bigger and better.

The Disney Company identified central Florida as the ideal location for Walt's latest dream. Unbeknownst to many, the company began purchasing parcels of land in the area, ultimately accumulating 28,000 acres. Another 2,000 acres were added later.

The company also convinced the Florida government to allow it to set up its own utilities district and administer its own zoning laws within the newly purchased property. This afforded the Disney Company a great deal of political muscle. As one article published in the *New York Times* during this period explained, "The state has given the company, in effect, the powers of a county."[15]

Walt Disney died in 1966, before he could get very far with the new project. His brother Roy continued Walt's work, focusing on the theme park piece of his plans. On October 1, 1971, Roy Disney dedicated Walt Disney

World, a theme park five times the size of Disneyland that had cost $400 million to build.

The park was similar in its design to Disneyland but with additional attractions and much more room to grow. Eventually, as more parks were added to the property, Walt Disney World became the name of the overall Florida resort, and the park became known as the Magic Kingdom.

The park caught on almost immediately. In the early days, the company relied heavily on media coverage to generate public interest. It was not until the 1980s that Disney began relying more on advertising to bring in visitors, not only from the United States but from all over the world.[16]

Sasha Rademakers grew up in Perth, Australia. She first became aware of Walt Disney World in the mid-1980s when she was 10 years old and saw advertisements for the park on television.

"I was nagging my parents for a good six months" to take her to the park, she said. "When you're a kid, you don't understand about the distance—you've got to get there."

Rademakers was 30 years old when she finally made her first visit to the Florida park. The reality measured up to her childhood fantasy, and she has since been to four other U.S. Disney parks. "I loved the fact that it was so organized. They can house, feed, clothe and entertain all these people, keep everybody happy.... They've got the best rides. It's always innovative," she said.[17]

In the 40 years since the Magic Kingdom's opening, the park has entertained millions of visitors. In 2009 alone, it hosted 17.2 million people, making it the number one theme park destination in the world.[18] Florida's Magic Kingdom has been modernized and expanded several times, adding attractions and even lands to its initial design.

Disney announced plans for a $1.1 billion expansion in 2009, the largest in the park's history. Among the planned renovations are new attractions in the parks that will highlight two Disney franchises—the Disney Princesses and the Disney Fairies.[19]

Disney's Magic Kingdom was only the tip of the iceberg of the company's Florida venture. It was soon joined by other parks and attractions that have helped Disney become a leader in the theme park industry.

Epcot

Disney's second Florida park was loosely based on some of the ideas Walt Disney had developed for his Experimental Prototype Community of Tomorrow back in the 1960s. Disney's original plans called for a residential community where people would have easy access to shopping, entertainment, and an assortment of international cuisines. They would be able to live, work, and play in one area and would be transported by people movers and monorails.

Epcot opened on October 1, 1982, on the Florida property, built at a cost of $900 million.[20] It was connected by monorail to the Magic Kingdom, and, like its sister park, caught on immediately with the public.

The park was divided into two sections separated by a large lagoon. Future World highlighted the world of tomorrow and included attractions based on science, technology, and oceanography. The World Showcase featured individual pavilions dedicated to different countries around the world, complete with shops and restaurants selling products from those countries. In some respects, it was a modified version of the international aspect of the original prototype community Walt Disney had envisioned.

A big part of the original Epcot was its reliance on corporate sponsors for some of the park's attractions. Companies such as General Motors, Kraft, and Exxon made up some of the original sponsors. As time has passed, corporate sponsorship has dwindled due to higher costs and a sluggish economy.

Epcot has been modified and renovated over the years. More interactive exhibits have been added to Future World to capitalize on the keen interest in hands-on technology favored by today's youth. Two new countries have been added to the original nine found in the World Showcase. In 2009, 10.9 million people visited the park, making it the sixth most popular theme park worldwide.[21]

Disney's Hollywood Studios

Disney followed up the success of its two Florida theme parks by adding a third with a focus on the film industry. Disney-MGM Studios opened on May 1, 1989. According to the *Orlando Sentinel*, "The original lineup of attractions was tilted heavily toward images and themes drawn from Hollywood's 'golden age' of the 1920s, '30s, and '40s."[22]

Disney licensed the right to use the name "MGM" in the park's title, as well as some images from the legendary studio's film library. These were incorporated into some of the park's attractions like The Great Movie Ride. For the most part, though, the park retained a Disney focus and included features such as a backstage studio tour and a behind-the-scenes look at the process of Disney animation.

Disney-MGM Studios was an instant hit when it opened, causing then-Disney CEO Michael Eisner to announce a planned park expansion less than six months after the park's opening.[23] Business has continued to boom at the park—9.7 million visitors passed through its gates in 2009, making it the world's seventh most visited theme park.[24]

As times changed and Disney's own world began to expand to encompass the Disney Channel, ABC television, and Pixar Animation, the focus of the studio park shifted as well. The company added more attractions based on its films and television programs.

Disney officially changed the name of the park to Disney's Hollywood Studios in 2007, dropping the MGM reference altogether. This was partly a result of some legal sparring that had taken place between the two companies during the 1990s over licensing rights to the use of the MGM name.[25] Disney officials said the name change also reflected the adjustments the company had made to the park in the nearly 20 years since its opening.[26]

Disney's Animal Kingdom

The fourth park at the Walt Disney World Resort is substantially different from its three siblings, as it celebrates reality rather than fantasy. Disney's Animal Kingdom opened on April 22, 1998, with a theme of wildlife education and conservation. The park blends elements of a typical theme park with a large-scale zoo or animal preserve, similar in nature to the San Diego Wild Animal Park.

Animal Kingdom is Disney's largest park to date, covering an area of 500 acres, five times the size of Florida's Magic Kingdom.[27] Some of the park's lands are solely devoted to animals, while others include typical Disneyesque attractions such as roller coasters and character-greeting areas. The primary attraction is the Kilimanjaro Safari ride, where visitors are transported by tram through an area designed to look like the African plains. Real animals—lions, giraffes, elephants, zebras, etc.—roam the plains, offering Disney visitors close-up views and photo opportunities.

While the initial focus of Animal Kingdom was to be its animals, over the years, Disney has slowly introduced more and more rides at the request of park patrons.[28] The biggest of these is Expedition Everest, a 200-foot-high roller coaster in the park's Asia section.[29]

Animal Kingdom draws from some of the company's animal-oriented animated features such as *The Jungle Book* and *The Lion King*. At the center of the park is a Tree of Life, a tribute to the latter film. An article in *U.S. News & World Report* noted, "The massive Tree of Life...is to the Animal Kingdom what Cinderella's Castle is to the Magic Kingdom, its trunk carved with more than 350 animals and its hollow base home to a 430-seat theater."[30]

Before Animal Kingdom opened in 1998, Disney encountered some initial criticism after several animals died while the park was being readied to open. Groups such as People for the Ethical Treatment of Animals and Animal Rights Foundation of Florida staged protests and urged boycotts of the park.[31] In the years since the park's opening, however, objections from these groups have subsided.

Disney worked hard to market Animal Kingdom, especially at the beginning stages of the park. The company developed relationships with travel agents and established a sponsorship program with McDonald's. The sponsorship applied to the park's DinoLand U.S.A. area and lasted until Disney ended its ties to the fast-food chain at the end of 2006.[32]

Attendance for Disney's Animal Kingdom during its first year was 8.6 million, well below the company's other Florida parks. As Disney has added attractions over the years, that number has steadily increased. Although Animal Kingdom remains the least popular of the four Walt Disney World Resort parks, it still ranks as the 8th most popular theme park in the world. In 2009, the park attracted 9.5 million visitors.[33]

Tokyo Disney Resort

In the early 1980s, the Disney Company began to venture abroad with the construction of its theme parks, beginning with its first international park in Japan. The Tokyo Disney Resort is home to two Disney parks, Tokyo Disneyland and Tokyo Disney Sea, as well as three resort hotels and a shopping/entertainment complex called Ikspiari. Both parks have added significantly to Disney's bottom line, and, unlike the company's other international theme parks, have operated with relatively little hassle for the corporation.

Tokyo Disneyland

Tokyo Disneyland was the first international Disney theme park, and to date, it has been the most successful. In 2001, the park had approximately 13.6 million visitors, making it the third most popular theme park in the world behind Florida's Magic Kingdom and California's Disneyland.[34]

What is interesting about Tokyo Disneyland is that it is not directly owned by the Disney Company. Instead, it is licensed and operated by Japan's Oriental Land Company (OLC) in an arrangement that earns Disney management and licensing fees.

In the 1970s, with the success of the three American parks—Disneyland, Walt Disney World's Magic Kingdom, and Epcot—Disney management agreed to allow OLC to construct a park outside Tokyo in the Chiba Prefecture, an area of reclaimed land from the Tokyo Bay. At the time, given the uncertainty of the Disney Company's finances, Disney managers were reluctant to take on the financial responsibility of building and running the park themselves.

Instead, they agreed to lease the rights to OLC, while providing management consultation for a fee. In addition, the arrangement with OLC stipulated that Disney would earn 10% royalties on park admissions and another 5% on merchandise, food, and beverages sold at the park.[35] The park was ultimately funded by a joint consortium consisting of OLC, the Mitsui Real Estate Development Company, and the Kesei Electric Railway. It cost $650 million to build.

Tokyo Disneyland opened on April 15, 1983, and has been a thriving success ever since. The park is essentially a copy of the Florida Magic Kingdom park, with similar lands, shows, shops, and eateries. The Japanese public has embraced Tokyo Disneyland by making repeat visits and soaking up the Disney magic and all that comes with it during a theme park visit.

When the park was built, the decision was made to import a replica of the U.S. Disney parks' formula into Japan, right down to English-language signage and American style foods served at the park's restaurants. Over the years, this hard-and-fast rule has been modified somewhat. Signage for the park is now printed in both English and Japanese, and some Japanese food is sold onsite. For the most part, however, the park looks very much like its American cousins.

When southern Californian Milt Thurman visited Tokyo Disneyland in 2007, he was struck by the similarities to the Disneyland he was familiar with in Anaheim, Calif. Although he knew the park was not Disney owned, he couldn't tell from what he saw. "If there was a different control, it wasn't evident. It still felt like Disney," he said.[36]

The layout of the park was much like what he knew from California's Disneyland and the Magic Kingdom in Florida. The main differences, he explained, were the accommodations for Japan's colder climate. Main Street has a glass covering over the street, for example, and It's a Small World is a completely indoor ride—unlike its counterpart in California, where park patrons board their boats outdoors.

Mostly, Thurman was impressed by how much park visitors seemed to be enjoying themselves. "There were a few Americans there, but there were mostly Japanese. The people all seemed to be having a very good time. They are very much into Disney," he said.[37]

The majority of Tokyo Disneyland's visitors are locals. Nearly 96% of guests come from Japan, with others arriving primarily from southeast Asian countries such as Taiwan and South Korea. A large percentage of park patrons are female.[38]

Unlike some of Disney's other properties, Tokyo Disneyland has managed to weather the storm of a worldwide economic recession. During its 25th anniversary year in 2008, the park broke attendance records, ushering more than 14 million through its gates. Even a year after the anniversary festivities, attendance was down just slightly compared to other theme parks around the world.[39]

Tokyo Disney Sea

With the success of Tokyo Disneyland, Oriental Land Company elected to build a second Disney park adjacent to its first park. Tokyo Disney Sea opened on September 4, 2001, and is unlike any other Disney theme park.

Instead of "lands," the park features "ports of call" such as Mediterranean Harbor, Arabian Coast, and an American Waterfront depicting scenes of a Cape Cod fishing village. Disney Sea also has unique rides not seen at any other Disney park, including a thrill ride called Journey to the Center of the Earth and a boat ride called Sinbad's Storybook Voyage, similar in its design to It's a Small World.

The project cost the Oriental Land Company $4 million to build and included the construction of an onsite hotel. A monorail designed to connect the two parks was added as well. The Disney Company contributed $10 million toward the design of the project with the expectation that it would earn approximately $80 to $100 million in annual licensing fees.[40]

Disney Sea has proven to be nearly as popular as its neighbor, Tokyo Disneyland. In 2009, it attracted 12 million visitors, making it the 5th most popular theme park in the world.[41]

Disneyland Resort Paris

The Disney Company operates two theme parks in France under the umbrella of the Disneyland Resort Paris—Disneyland Paris and Walt Disney Studios. The resort also includes seven Disney hotels and a retail and entertainment area. While popular with the public, the Disneyland Resort Paris has proven financially challenging for the Disney Company.

Disneyland Paris

Once Tokyo Disneyland proved to be worth more than its initial investment, Disney executives began contemplating the feasibility of opening a second international park in Europe. This time, they intended to be involved in the park's ownership as well as management.

Ultimately, financial concessions offered by the French government resulted in the decision to build the park in Marne-la-Valle, approximately 20 miles outside Paris. The French government offered Disney a low-interest loan and a reduction on sales taxes on park admission tickets. It also agreed to extend a local commuter train from Paris to the gates of the new park.

Unlike the Tokyo Disneyland arrangement, which provided only licensing fees to the Disney Company, the agreement with the French government stipulated that Disney would have a 49% ownership stake in the new park, which was to be called Euro Disney. In exchange, the Disney Company would provide approximately 30,000 jobs for French citizens.[42]

Although the deal seemed like a win-win situation, initial reaction to the project by local citizens was lukewarm. To increase the likelihood of favorable reception from the public and press, for the park's opening on April 12, 1992, the Disney Company launched a massive public relations and marketing campaign to promote the park. Nearly 2,500 members of the media attended the park's opening, resulting in hundreds of news stories about Euro Disney.[43]

While press reception to the park was positive, the public's reaction was less enthusiastic. As with Tokyo Disneyland, Disney had imported its American theme park formula into an international setting. While this had worked in Japan, the same approach was not well received by the French. As an article in the *Wall Street Journal* explained:

> The American executives Disney first sent to Paris priced tickets too high and decided not to serve alcohol in a country accustomed to wine with meals. French labor inspectors bridled at the company's strict dress code, which regulated perfume and makeup while banning beards and mustaches.[44]

Part of the problem was also in the Disney Company's approach to its marketing efforts. Disney used a single marketing campaign across all of Europe rather than tailoring different marketing approaches to individual countries. An initial advertising campaign highlighting the "grandeur" of the park was interpreted by some as an example of an American company flaunting its riches. That did not go over well, particularly with French audiences.[45]

Did You Know?

The Disney family name originated in a French village called Isigny-sur-mer. The family's coat of arms is depicted near Le Chateau de la Belle au Bois Dormant at Disneyland Paris.

The numbers reflected a grim reality: Euro Disney posed a $921 million loss at the end of its first year. Compared to the profits earned by the other three Disney theme parks, this did not bode well for the future of the park.

Almost immediately, Disney began to regroup in an attempt to salvage the park. An investment of $300 million from a Saudi Arabian prince, Alwaleed bin Talal, provided a needed infusion of capital and readjusted the company's holdings in the park to 39%.[46] Revamped marketing and advertising strategies helped the company do a better job of reaching out to a European audience. Disney also began working with travel agents to offer more attractive vacation packages to tourists.[47]

The ultimate adjustment was a name change for the park from Euro Disney to Disneyland Paris, which was partly intended to highlight the park's location. As one reporter noted at the time, "The name change was also meant to help the facility shed a moniker that has come to be associated with the negative business news."[48] The retooling efforts proved sufficient, at least for the moment. By the end of 1995, Disneyland Paris showed a profit for the first time.[49]

Over the years, however, Disneyland Paris has had its share of fiscal ups and downs. While park attendance and profits improved for a few years, by the early 2000s, the park was again in financial trouble. A second restructuring occurred in 2004, which ultimately increased the Disney Company's stake in the park to 51%.[50]

Today, the crowds are finally flowing through the park's gates. In 2009, Disneyland Paris attracted 12.7 million visitors, making it the world's fourth most visited theme park and the most popular tourist destination in Europe.[51] Nevertheless, despite the increase in numbers, Disneyland Paris still struggles to recover from the financial woes of its earlier years.

Walt Disney Studios

Even with the uneven performance of Disneyland Paris, in the mid-1990s, Disney executives made the decision to open a second gate on the Paris property. Walt Disney Studios opened on March 16, 2002. Costing approximately $530 million to build, the park was modeled after Disney's Hollywood Studios in Florida, offering a tribute to the film and animation industries. As with California Adventure in Anaheim, Calif., the purpose of adding a second park was to encourage guests at Disneyland Paris to make a vacation of their visit rather than just a one-day excursion from Paris.

In an attempt to reach out to its audience, Disney tweaked the formula used in the Florida studios park and added in more European touches. Despite these efforts, the park has not really caught on with the public. This has hurt the overall returns of the Disneyland Resort Paris. The company is hoping the eventual end of the recession will put both parks on a more even footing and ultimately lead them out of the red and into the black.

Hong Kong Disneyland

With a well-established presence in Japan and a consistent if somewhat unsure footing in Europe, Disney set out to conquer a tourism market poised on the brink of explosion: China. With an eye on the burgeoning mainland China tourism market, the Disney Company tested the waters of possibilities by opening its first Chinese park in Hong Kong in 2005.

Once under British rule, Hong Kong was returned to the People's Republic of China in 1997, but it still maintains many elements of Western culture. At the same time, its proximity to the southern part of mainland China made it an ideal place for the Disney Company to explore the potential for a Chinese theme park audience.

Disney began negotiations with the government of the Hong Kong Special Administrative Region in the late 1990s to build a park on Hong Kong's Lantau Island, just 30 minutes by train from downtown Hong Kong. The park was to be a joint venture between Disney and the Hong Kong government.

Disney negotiated what was seen as a sweet deal for the company, explained an article in *Fortune* magazine.

> Disney drove a hard bargain in Hong Kong, demanding a fat stake for a next-to-nothing investment. Desperate to bring jobs and tourists to their then-beleaguered economy, Hong Kong officials capitulated, agreeing to put up $2.9 billion in taxpayer money, donate land, and build a network of access roads and railways in exchange for a 57% share. Disney got 43% for just $314 million.[52]

The company also negotiated royalty fees for park operations and management as part of the deal.

Hong Kong Disneyland is the smallest of the Disney parks because of the limited space available on the island. It is modeled after the original 1955 Disneyland with four lands: Main Street, Fantasyland, Adventureland, and Tomorrowland.

In developing the park, Disney executives were determined to make the most of the lessons they'd learned about cultural correctness from the Euro Disney experience. This time, they intended to take cultural considerations into account when planning the construction, operations, and marketing of the new park.

Disney executives hired a feng shui master to advise them on the layout of the park. This resulted in a slight adjustment of the angle of the front gate to ensure prosperity for the new venture. The opening date of September 12, 2005, was selected because it was deemed "an auspicious date for opening a business in the Chinese almanac," according to an article in the *China Business Review*.[53]

While the food at Disney's other international parks was mostly typical American fare, Hong Kong Disneyland was to offer a mix of American and Asian cuisine. Signage for the park was designed to be in both English and Chinese, as were some of the park's shows and attractions.

After the rocky start Disney had experienced with the opening of Euro Disney, company officials were determined to do as much as possible to try to anticipate the needs and expectations of Hong Kong Disneyland's Chinese audience. At first, the approach seemed to work. Initial response to the park was positive, and Disney hoped to meet a first-year target of 5.6 million.

Within several months, however, Hong Kong Disneyland encountered several problems that had an impact on public perception of the new park. A ticketing snafu led to hundreds of people being shut out of the park during the Chinese New Year holiday break in early 2006. Complaints that Hong Kong Disneyland was too small and offered little in the way of attractions led to a lack of repeat visitors. Perhaps the biggest problem was the fact that many Hong Kong residents and mainland Chinese guests were simply not familiar with the Disney characters and couldn't relate to what the park had to offer.

By 2008, the company began making adjustments to the park. Andrew Kam, managing director of Hong Kong Disneyland, told a *Japan Times* reporter that the company planned to implement a new strategy for the park's future: "focus more on young adults, keep introducing new attractions to lure the people of Hong Kong and not depend too much on the legacy of Disney stories, which many Chinese are not necessarily familiar with."[54]

Although these initiatives may have helped somewhat, Disney has yet to meet its original attendance goal of 5.6 million annual visitors. In 2009, the park hosted only 4.6 million and was operating at a loss.

Help may be forthcoming in the way of a new plan. In mid-2009, Disney announced a restructuring of its financial arrangement with the Hong Kong government as well as plans for a major expansion of Hong Kong Disneyland. Disney agreed to pay $450 million for the construction of three new lands at the park—Grizzly Trail, Mystic Point, and Toy Story Land. The expansion would increase the park's size by 23%, adding 30 new attractions over a period of five years.[55] Under the new arrangement, Disney's stake in the park would increase from 43% to 48%.

The expansion announcement was met with cautious optimism by those who were beginning to doubt the long-term feasibility of Hong Kong Disneyland. It was especially timely in light of Disney's plans for the company's future growth in China, which would be made public just a few months later.

Future Plans: Disneyland Shanghai

With Hong Kong Disneyland in the process of getting back on track, Disney was able to move ahead with its next theme park agenda item. In November 2009, the Disney Company announced it had reached an agreement with the central government of China to construct its 12th theme park in Shanghai's Pudong district.[56] Initial plans called for the construction of a Magic Kingdom park similar to those in Florida and Tokyo.

An article in the *Financial Times* noted the project would pave the way for Disney to:

> ...establish a foothold in mainland China.... With an estimated cost of $3.5 billion, the park would be one of the biggest investments in China by an international company.... A Shanghai park would raise the company's profile in China, increasing its ability to cross promote and sell TV programming, films and consumer products that are based on its library of characters.[57]

At the time of this writing, plans for the Shanghai park were just beginning to get under way. It was estimated that the park would likely open to the public in 2014.

Celebration: A Themed Living Environment

Although not a theme park, Disney's Celebration housing community is worth including in this chapter because it embodies some of the original ideas developed by Walt Disney in his concept for the Experimental Prototype Community of Tomorrow.

A Model Community

The Disney Company built the town of Celebration in the mid-1990s, on 4,900 acres just a few miles from its Florida parks. The idea was to create a self-contained community that was fashioned after the small-town values and ideals that Walt Disney often spoke of when he recalled his childhood in Missouri. At the same time, it would embrace some of the more modern ideas Disney had proposed for his experimental community by giving people access to everything they needed at their fingertips.

Articles written about the property at the time talked about the features that would be included in Celebration such as:

> ...the lakeside town centre, complete with town hall, post office, library, deli, restaurants, bookstore-cafe, grocery store, dry cleaner and...a 500-seat cinema. The town centre is meant to be a sociable place, with people living above the shops and streets designed for strolling. For more energetic types...miles of jogging and bike trails, tennis courts and a public golf course.[58]

The houses themselves were designed to capture a sense of old-fashioned, small-town charm with front porches and expansive sidewalks. Having the Disney name associated with the town piqued the curiosity of the public. When Disney initially announced a lottery and invited people to toss their names into a pool for a chance to buy one of the 350 Celebration homes being built, more than 4,500 responded.[59]

In the beginning, the town was firmly controlled by Disney. Residents had to agree to abide by rules that regulated the appearances of their yards or the types of window coverings they could hang. Nevertheless, the concept proved extremely popular with those who were already fans of Disney and didn't object to the company's strict sense of order.

Not Quite the Disney Dream

While Celebration was promoted as an innovative experiment for Disney, in the end, as author Janet Wasko noted, it was essentially a real estate venture. "The company paid about $200 per acre in the 1960s for land that was sold for Celebration in quarter-acre lots at $80,000 each," she explained.[60]

Disney began to extricate itself from Celebration in the early 2000s. The company sold the golf course to C.S. Golf Partners in 2003. The town center was sold to Lexin Capital, a New York-based real estate firm, in 2004.[61]

Around the same time, noted reporter Cynthia Barnett, "The company shifted majority membership of the homeowners association board to residents,"[62] leaving them to make their own rules.

Celebration still exists today with approximately 8,000 residents, but the original Disney sign proclaiming "Disney's Town of Celebration" no longer appears over the town's entrance. It is now up to the residents themselves to carry on Walt Disney's vision of a self-contained, prototype community.

Conclusion

When Walt Disney opened Disneyland in 1955, he not only led his company in a new direction but also changed the landscape of the amusement park business. Since then, the Disney Company has opened 10 additional theme parks in the United States, Asia, and Europe, which have attracted millions of visitors every year. While some of these parks have been steady moneymakers, others have proven to be financially challenging for the company.

Disney continues to expand its network of theme park with plans in the works to open another Disneyland in China in the next few years. As long as people continue to flow through the gates of the various Disney parks, it is expected that this segment of the Disney Company will keep growing. ♦

Figure 9: World's Top 10 Most Attended Theme Parks

Park	Visitors
1. Magic Kingdom, Walt Disney World	17.2 million
2. Disneyland	15.9 million
3. Tokyo Disneyland	13.6 million
4. Disneyland Paris	12.7 million
5. Tokyo Disney Sea	12.0 million
6. Epcot	10.9 million
7. Disney's Hollywood Studios	9.7 million
8. Disney's Animal Kingdom	9.5 million
9. Universal Studios Japan	8.0 million
10. Everland (South Korea)	6.1 million

Source: Themed Entertainment Association/AECOM, 2009 *Themed Index: The Global Attractions Attendance Report*, 2009

Notes

1. "Disneyland Resort Fact Sheet," The Walt Disney Company, www.disneylandnews.com.
2. See Themed Entertainment Association/AECOM, 2009 *Themed Index: The Global Attractions Attendance Report*, 2009, 11-12.
3. Cynthia Gorney, "The Mightiest Mouse! Disneyland Enters Its 4th Decade Guarding the Magic of Dreams Come True," *Washington Post*, 15 July 1985, D1.
4. Richard Ouzounian, "The House a Mouse Built," *Toronto Star*, 17 July 2005, C4.
5. Joe Alfuso, telephone interview, June 21, 2010.
6. See "Disneyland Resort Fact Sheet," The Walt Disney Company, www.disneylandnews.com.
7. See Themed Entertainment Association/AECOM, 2009 *Themed Index: The Global Attractions Attendance Report*, 2009, 11-12.
8. Karal Ann Marling, *Behind the Magic: 50 Years of Disneyland* (Dearborn, MI: The Henry Ford, 2005): 103.
9. Tom Tumbusch, *Walt Disney the American Dreamer* (Dayton, OH: Tomart Publications, 2008): 100.
10. Merissa Marr, "Disney's $1 Billion Adventure," *Wall Street Journal*, 17 October 2007, B1.
11. See Marr, "Disney's $1 Billion Adventure," B1.
12. See Bruce Orwall, "Disney Makes Plans to Spur Attendance at New Theme Park," *Wall Street Journal*, 4 May 2001, B8.
13. See Alex Pulaski, "Disney Magic Remakes California Adventure," *OregonLive.com*, 16 May 2010.
14. See Themed Entertainment Association/AECOM, 2009 *Themed Index: The Global Attractions Attendance Report*, 2009, 11-12.
15. Robert A. Wright, "Disney: A World of Show," *The New York Times*, 21 February 1971, F1. See also Wayne Ellwood, "Inside the Disney Dream Machine," *New Internationalist* (December 1998): 7.
16. See Stephen M. Fjellman, *Vinyl Leaves: Walt Disney World and America* (Boulder, CO: Westview Press, 1992): 160.
17. Sasha Rademakers, in-person interview, July 6, 2010.
18. See Themed Entertainment Association/AECOM, 2009 *Themed Index: The Global Attractions Attendance Report*, 2009, 11-12.
19. See Dawn C. Chmielewski, "Disney Announces Upgrades in Anaheim, Orlando," *Los Angeles Times*, 13 September 2009, A50; and Brooks Barnes and Andrew J. Martin, "Disney Plans 'Interactive' Updates in Theme Parks," *The New York Times*, 14 September 2009, B3.
20. See Thomas C. Hayes, "Fanfare as Disney Opens Park," *The New York Times*, 2 October 1982, 1.
21. See Themed Entertainment Association/AECOM, 2009 *Themed Index: The Global Attractions Attendance Report*, 2009, 11-12.
22. Scott Powers, "Mickey, MGM to Part Ways," *Orlando Sentinel*, 10 August 2007, C1.
23. See David J. Jefferson, "Disney Plans to Double Size of Florida Park—MGM Studios Crowds Top Capacity," *Wall Street Journal*, 2 August 1989, 1.

24. See Themed Entertainment Association/AECOM, *2009 Themed Index: The Global Attractions Attendance Report*, 2009, 11-12.
25. See Powers, "Mickey, MGM to Part Ways," C1.
26. See Jason Garcia, "Disney Park Grows Up," *Orlando Sentinel*, 1 June 2009, M3.
27. Dewayne Bevil, "Disney's Animal Kingdom Celebrates 10-Year Anniversary," *Orlando Sentinel*, 20 April 2008.
28. See Robert Johnson, "Disney Looks to Boost Animal Park Attendance With Mechanical Attractions," *Orlando Sentinel*, 20 April 2003, 1.
29. See Elinor Tatum, "High Adventure in the Himalayas," *New York Amsterdam News* 97:19 (May 4, 2006): 28.
30. Norie Quintos Danyliw and Margaret Loftus, "The Kingdom Comes," *U.S. News & World Report* 124:13 (April 6, 1998): 64.
31. Mireya Navarro, "New Disney Kingdom Comes With Real-Life Obstacles," *The New York Times*, 16 April 1998, A14.
32. Polina Shklyanoy, "Before Its First Visitor, Kingdom Exec Primes Pool," *Advertising Age* 70:5 (February 1, 1999): 4.
33. See Themed Entertainment Association/AECOM, *2009 Themed Index: The Global Attractions Attendance Report*, 2009, 11-12.
34. Ibid.
35. See Tracy Dahlby, "Tokyo Disneyland Bets on Mikki Mausu," *Washington Post*, 10 April 1983, F1.
36. Milt Thurman, telephone interview, August 2, 2010.
37. Ibid.
38. See Yoko Kubota, "At 25, Tokyo Disney Hobbled by Aging Population," *International Herald Tribune*, 16 April 2008, 13; and Nicholas D. Kristof, "Disney's Tokyo Kingdom," *The New York Times*, 27 August 1995, 5.
39. See "Tokyo Disney Resort Operator Logs Record Earnings," *Jiji Press English News Service*, May 7, 2009; "Tokyo Disney Park Visitors Fall, But 2nd Highest in FY 2009," *Jiji Press English News Service*, April 1, 2010; and Themed Entertainment Association/AECOM, *2009 Themed Index: The Global Attractions Attendance Report*, 2009, 11-12.
40. See "Japanese Park Becomes Land of the Rising Sum," *Orlando Sentinel*, 13 December 2000, B1; and Richard Verrier and Mark Magnier, "DisneySea Is Joining Wave of Theme Parks Rolling Abroad," *Los Angeles Times*, 30 June 2001, C1.
41. See Themed Entertainment Association/AECOM, *2009 Themed Index: The Global Attractions Attendance Report*, 2009, 11-12.
42. See "Introducing Walt d'Isigny," *The Economist* 323:7754 (April 11, 1992): 53; and Shawn Tully, "The Real Estate Coup at Euro Disneyland," *Fortune* 113:9 (April 28, 1986): 172.
43. See Karen Fawcett, "The (PR) Mouse That Roared in Six Languages," *Communication World* 9:12 (December 1992): 13.
44. Jo Wrighton and Bruce Orwall, "Mutual Attraction: Despite Losses and Bailouts, France Stays Devoted to Disney," *Wall Street Journal*, 26 January 2005, A1.
45. See Bruce Crumley and Christy Fisher, "Euro Disney Tries to End Evil Spell," *Advertising Age* 65:6 (February 7, 1994): 39.
46. See Richard Verrier, "For Struggling Euro Disney, Help From Across the Pond," *Los Angeles Times*, 10 June 2004, C1.

47.   See Bruce Crumley, "Disneyland Paris Hawks Adult Appeal," *Advertising Age* 65:45 (October 24, 1994): 2; and Angela Walker, "Disneyland Paris Nears Stability," *Hotel & Motel Management* 210:6 (April 3, 1995): 4.

48.   Nadine Godwin, "Disneyland Paris Is New Address in France for Mickey and Minnie," *Travel Weekly* 53:84 (October 24, 1994): 1.

49.   See Wrighton and Orwall, "Mutual Attraction: Despite Losses and Bailouts, France Stays Devoted to Disney," A1.

50.   See Wrighton and Orwall, "Mutual Attraction: Despite Losses and Bailouts, France Stays Devoted to Disney," A1; and Verrier, "For Struggling Euro Disney, Help From Across the Pond," C1.

51.   See Themed Entertainment Association/AECOM, *2009 Themed Index: The Global Attractions Attendance Report*, 2009, 11-12.

52.   Clay Chandler, "Mickey Mao," *Fortune* 151:8   (April 18, 2005): 170. See also Jonathan Landreth and James Zoltak, "Mouse Meets Mao," *Amusement Business* 117:9 (September 2005): 6.

53.   Paula M. Miller, "Disneyland in Hong Kong," *The China Business Review* 34:1 (January/February 2007): 31. See also Laura M. Holson, "The Feng Shui Kingdom," *The New York Times*, 25 April 2005, C1.

54.   Andrew Kam quoted in Reiji Yoshida, "Mojo Eludes Disney in Hong Kong," *Japan Times*, 4 February 2010.

55.   See David Pierson, "Disney Reaches Deal to Expand Struggling Hong Kong Theme Park," *Los Angeles Times*, 1 July 2009, B3; and Chester Yung and Jeffrey Ng, "In Asia, Disney's World Will Get Bigger—Hong Kong Theme Park to Increase Attractions; Government Converts Loans," *Wall Street Journal*, 1 July 2009, B5.

56.   See "The Walt Disney Company Reaches Another Major Milestone on Shanghai Theme Park Project," press release, The Walt Disney Company, November 3, 2009.

57.   Matthew Garrahan, "Green Light for Disney's Shanghai Park," *Financial Times*, 3 November 2009.

58.   "It's a Small Town After All," *The Economist* 337:7942 (November 25, 1995): 27.

59.   Ibid.

60.   Janet Wasko, *Understanding Disney* (Cambridge, England: Polity Press, 2001): 179.

61.   See Abby Goodnough, "Disney Is Selling a Town It Built to Reflect the Past," *The New York Times*, 16 January 2004, A10; and April Hunt, "Disney Sells Orlando, Fla., Downtown Development to New York Investment Firm," *Orlando Sentinel*, 22 January 2004.

62.   Cynthia Barnett, "A Decade of Celebration," *Florida Trend* 48:7 (November 1, 2005): 54.

8

Disney Music

Music has long been an integral part of Disney's heritage. From the musical sound effects featured in early Mickey Mouse cartoons to the trendy pop tunes performed by up-and-coming artists on Radio Disney, music has permeated the development of the Disney Company.

From the beginning, Walt Disney realized the importance of incorporating just the right blend of music into his animated films and using this music to advance the storytelling process. This was evident in the early Silly Symphony cartoons as well as in longer features such as *Fantasia*.

The creation of Walt Disney Records in 1956 enabled the Disney studio to capitalize on its use of music through the sale of records and CDs featuring some of the company's biggest hit songs.

Music has also been an essential ingredient of a visit to a Disney theme park. It is routinely performed live by both professional and amateur musicians, as well as piped through loudspeakers to create the proper mood and atmosphere.

In recent years, the establishment of Radio Disney has introduced music to a new demographic—the "tweens." It has also helped launch the careers of some of Disney's current musical stars such as Miley Cyrus—aka Hannah Montana—and the Jonas Brothers.

This chapter will discuss the role music has played in the development of the Disney Company. It will show how Disney has used music to advance the stories it creates and the franchises it has developed.

Music in Disney Films

Right from the start, there was music. Sometimes it came in the form of a song that moved a plot along. Other times it was used as background to depict a feeling of romance in the air or to create an aura of fear. As early as *Steamboat Willie* in 1928, Walt Disney realized the impact the right choice of music could have on the success of a film. Consequently, some of Disney's greatest films are just as easily remembered for their songs as for their plotlines.

As David Tietyen explained of Disney in his book, *The Musical World of Walt Disney*:

> The music and songs that flowed from his studio have become a part of our American heritage. These are songs that evoke fond childhood memories—memories of being caught up in the magical fantasies created by Disney.[1]

Early Cartoons

The first evidence of the importance of music to a Disney film came in the Mickey Mouse cartoon, *Steamboat Willie*. The film featured the initial use of synchronized sound in an animated short and included several musical sight gags. In one instance, Mickey Mouse played the "xylophone" on a cow's teeth. In another, he cranked the tail of a goat that had swallowed the sheet music to *Turkey in the Straw* to coax the notes out of the animal's mouth. While animal rights activists never would have approved, the results, nonetheless, showed audiences the power of combining melody with humor.

Disney hired Carl Stalling, the first of many musical directors for the company, and together they wrote the studio's first song, *Minnie's Yoo-Hoo*, in 1930. Stalling was partially responsible for the development of the Silly Symphony cartoons produced by the studio between 1929–1939. In these cartoons, music became a driving force in the storytelling process, according to Tietyen.

This emphasis on music set a new precedent for how music and animation would interact within a film, a precedent that would influence how later features would be developed. This commitment to building films around music greatly contributed to the enormous overall success of Disney studio productions.[2]

The first hit song to emerge from the studio was *Who's Afraid of the Big Bad Wolf?* by Frank Churchill from the Silly Symphony cartoon, *The Three Little Pigs* (1933). Walt Disney once noted that the tune "showed us the value of telling a story through a song."[3]

Churchill and Leigh Harline were two composers who exerted great influence over the studio's early animated full-length features and helped shape the musical direction of Disney films.[4] Churchill wrote and arranged the music for *Snow White and the Seven Dwarfs*. Three songs from this film became studio hits: *Someday My Prince Will Come; Whistle While You Work;* and *Heigh Ho*.

Harline wrote the music for *Pinocchio*, including the film's most well-known tune, *When You Wish Upon a Star*, on which he collaborated with lyricist Ned Washington. The song "was popular at the time of the film's release—then was resurrected in 1954 as the theme song of the *Disneyland* television series, and became even more widely known. In time it would be established as the studio's signature song," according to writer J.B. Kaufman.[5] *When You Wish Upon a Star* was the first Disney song to win an Academy Award in 1940.

The Music of *Fantasia*

Fantasia marked a new musical direction for Disney, as it exposed the company's animation fans to the storytelling powers of classical music. *Fantasia* began with the idea for a single cartoon—*The Sorcerer's Apprentice*—based on the music of composer Paul Dukas and featuring Mickey Mouse as a magician wannabe gone awry.

When Walt Disney happened to run into Philadelphia Orchestra conductor Leopold Stokowski at a Hollywood restaurant, he asked the famed musician if he would be interested in conducting the music for the sequence. Stokowski agreed.

After the piece was completed, Disney and Stokowski came up with a plan to create an entire feature film based on animated vignettes set to classical music with *The Sorcerer's Apprentice* as its centerpiece.

The result was a blend of color, artistry, storytelling, humor, and rhapsodic music. *Fantasia* is considered a Disney classic unlike any other animated film produced by the Disney studio because the film's music is as powerful and impressive as its animation.

To showcase the music in its best light, Disney, in conjunction with RCA sound engineers, created a new sound system for *Fantasia* dubbed "Fantasound," which, Tietyen explained, "would revolutionize the industry's approach to sound recording."[6] Disney and RCA received a special award from the Motion Picture Academy in 1941 for the Fantasound system.

Live Action Film Music

In the 1940s, as Disney began producing live action films, music continued to be a key part of movies like *Song of the South* (1946) and *So Dear to My Heart* (1949). The films resulted in popular hit songs such as *Zip-a-Dee-Doo-Dah* and *Lavender Blue (Dilly Dilly)*.

One of Disney's biggest hits came from a three part television series produced about Davy Crockett for the *Disneyland* television show in 1954. Walt Disney asked composer George Bruns to come up with a song to help connect the three segments of the series by telling a musical story about the famous frontiersman. The result exceeded even Disney's expectations, according to Tietyen.

"*The Ballad of Davy Crockett* spent more than six months on the Hit Parade, was recorded on more than two hundred record labels around the world, and sold more than ten million records."[7] It was performed by at least 20 different artists in a variety of musical genres—country/western, jazz, pop, etc. Even Fess Parker, the star of the series, recorded a version of the song, which sold 7,000,000 copies.

The Sherman Brothers

In 1960, the studio hired two songwriters who were to have tremendous influence on the musical output of the company. Richard M. and Robert B. Sherman—also known as The Sherman Brothers—wrote songs for nearly 30 feature films released between 1960-1971, including *The Parent Trap*, *Mary Poppins*, *Winnie the Pooh*, and *Bedknobs and Broomsticks*. They contributed pop songs for Annette Funicello as well as for the *Disneyland* and *The Wonderful World of Color* television programs.

Their most lasting contribution to the Disney musical legacy is a tune that is known by schoolchildren around the world—*It's a Small World*. Originally written for the 1964 New York World's Fair, the song took on a life of its own and is now played on a daily basis at the attraction bearing its same name at five of the 11 Disney theme parks.

"*It's a Small World* went on to become the most popular of any Disney song. It has been recorded more times and in more languages, has sold more records than any Disney song, and has been used by virtually every major entertainer at one time or another," noted Tietyen.[8]

Did You Know?

The Mike Curb Congregation recorded a version of *It's a Small World* in 1973. Today, Mike Curb is best known as the founder and chairman of Curb Records.

A New Generation of Disney Composers

The resurgence of animated Disney films in the late 1980s and 1990s introduced a new slate of Disney composers and lyricists into the mix. Alan Menken and Howard Ashman wrote the songs for *The Little Mermaid* in 1989, and *Beauty and the Beast* in 1991. Menken has also written songs for numerous other Disney films, including *Aladdin* and *Pocahontas*.

Elton John and Tim Rice composed the music for *The Lion King* in 1994. Other noted artists who have produced music for Disney films in the last two decades include Phil Collins, Randy Newman, Stephen Schwartz, and Glenn Slater.

Disney Songs

Music continues to play a crucial role in Disney films even though the public's interest in movie musicals has diminished since the company first produced some of its animated features. "The music supports the action, whether it's comedic or dramatic," explained Joe Alfuso, an independent composer who writes music for Disney's theme parks.

The songs, in particular, are often what people connect with when they watch a Disney film, he said.

> We certainly remember Disney movies because of the songs. The songs forward the drama. They're the things that make us feel love, feel laughter, transport us. Undoubtedly, the great contribution of Disney music in general is the songs.[9]

Figure 10: Academy Award–Winning Songs From Disney Films

Year	Song	Film
1940	When You Wish Upon a Star	Pinocchio
1947	Zip-a-Dee-Doo-Dah	Song of the South
1964	Chim Chim Cheree	Mary Poppins
1989	Under the Sea	The Little Mermaid
1990	Sooner or Later	Dick Tracy
1991	Beauty and the Beast	Beauty and the Beast
1992	A Whole New World	Aladdin
1994	Can You Feel the Love Tonight?	The Lion King
1995	Colors of the Wind	Pocahontas
1999	You'll Be in My Heart	Tarzan
2001	If I Didn't Have You	Monsters, Inc.

Source: AcousticMusic.org, www.acousticmusic.org

Walt Disney Records

While the Disney studio had been producing music almost from the beginning, it wasn't until the mid-1950s that the company established its own record label. Until that point, much of the musical hits produced by Disney had been recorded and distributed through agreements with outside record companies such as RCA and Cadence.

After the Davy Crockett craze, however, it became apparent that it was time to add a music label to the company's repertoire of products. In 1956, Disneyland Records was established. (It was renamed Walt Disney Records in 1989.) Writer Greg Ehrbar explained:

Disneyland Records released Disney film soundtracks, of course, but also classical, jazz, country/western, Dixieland and Broadway music albums on the label. The record company also created a second label, Buena Vista, for non-Disney music and records aimed at older audiences, particularly teens.[10]

Early Recording Success

One of the record division's early success stories through the Buena Vista label was Annette Funicello. The darling of the Mouseketeers, she made her record debut on the label in 1958, and subsequently released a number of songs written by the Sherman Brothers, including *Tall Paul* and *Pineapple Princess*.

According to authors Tim Hollis and Greg Ehrbar:

Annette was the first nonfictitious entity that the Disney Studio extensively marketed and merchandised. There were paper dolls, mystery novels, and other Funicello items, but her records had the most important impact on the company fortune.[11]

Part of the financial success of Walt Disney Records came from the creation of a product line called the "Disneyland Storyteller LP" record series. Each Storyteller LP featured a narrator telling the story of a Disney movie and playing the songs from the film. A color booklet containing scenes from the film accompanied each LP. Storyteller records were also produced to showcase Disneyland attractions such as *It's a Small World.*

Later Hits

With the release of *The Little Mermaid* in 1989 introducing classic Disney animation to a new generation of film-goers, Walt Disney Records experienced a significant growth spurt. By that time, vinyl LP records had become relics of the past, and the company switched to producing CDs for films that followed, such as *Beauty and the Beast, Aladdin,* and *The Lion King.* Walt Disney Records also began repackaging many of its previous LPs in CD format. This proved quite profitable for the company.[12]

Today, Disney's recorded music and music publishing division is called the Disney Music Group. It includes Walt Disney Records as well as Lyric Street Records (country), Hollywood Records (pop), and Walt Disney Publishing.

Theme Park Music

In addition to being a staple of Disney films and recordings, music takes center stage at the company's theme parks. Many of the park rides feature background music from the Disney films they are based on. High school marching bands, barbershop quartets, and Disneyland jazz bands frequently populate the sidewalks and streets of Main Street U.S.A. Music is also a regular part of the daily parades and nightly fireworks displays.

Background Music

Background music helps contribute to the fantasy element of the Disney experience, explained composer Joe Alfuso. "It makes you feel as though you're in a different world. Part of it's visual, and part of it's the music."

Alfuso believes people respond positively to the music in the park because "we're a society that lives with soundtracks," he said, whether they be in shopping centers, elevators, airports, or theme parks. Background music helps park visitors feel good about being transformed into a magical world. "It's all about eliciting an emotional response," he explained.[13]

Live Music

Live music is probably the most diverse of the types of park music and can be found in all areas of the Disney parks. One musical act with longevity is the "Dapper Dans," a barbershop quartet that performs daily along Main Street at Disneyland. The original quartet was formed in 1957, and while the individual singers have changed over the years, the current quartet still holds onto its roots, according to the group's website.

> The Dapper Dans today seek to build upon the great tradition of Dapper Dan quartets of the past, while making their own mark for the future. They have taken on the roles of men that live and work on Main Street, U.S.A. who come together to form the Dapper Dans barbershop quartet: the town barber, the grocery store owner, the Constable and the banker.[14]

Disney also has a long history of showcasing the musical talents of high school and college students at its parks, particularly Disneyland and the Magic Kingdom at Walt Disney World. Bands and choruses are routinely invited to perform at these parks. Walt Disney World also sponsors musical special events such as the Disney Jazz Celebration and Festival Disney, where teams of students are invited to compete and participate in instructional music master classes and workshops.[15]

Did You Know?

The original music for the Disneyland Main Street Electrical Parade was based on a piece called *Baroque Hoedown* by synthesizer pioneers Jean-Jacques Perrey and Gershon Kingsley.

Parade and Show Music

Every Disney theme park features a number of shows and parades that highlight Disney characters, songs, and storylines from the company's films. Some of these are permanent fixtures at the park, while others are rotated on a regular basis to keep repeat visitors entertained.

Composer Joe Alfuso has spent much of his career composing and arranging music for Disney's park productions in California, Florida, Tokyo, and Hong Kong. Alfuso starts with the Disney songs and works closely with a show's director to put together a production that includes medleys and dance numbers. The result, he said, is "splashes of visuals and music—you can't have one without the other."

For park audiences, he said, the shows and parades are generally a positive experience. "It's incredibly wonderful family entertainment where people can come to feel really good about themselves," he explained.[16]

In keeping with the company's merchandising practices, those who want to take home a souvenir of the varieties of musical entertainment featured at the Disney parks are given an opportunity to do so. Disney produces an assortment of CDs featuring songs from its rides, parades, shows, and special events and sells them at park stores.

Pop Music Magic

In recent years, pop music aimed at children and tweens has become a critical component of Disney's musical offerings. The establishment of Radio Disney and the launching of young musical talent through the Disney Music Group's Hollywood Records label has had significant influence on the pop music market at large and on Disney's ability to penetrate this market.

Radio Disney

In 1996, the Disney Company decided to reach out to a segment of the radio market that had been largely ignored by entertainment mass marketers—those between the ages of 6–14. The company created a new brand of radio, according to an article in *American Demographics* magazine, with its initial programming "designed to appeal to kids and their moms, with a mix of hits, oldies, and movie soundtracks, as well as news and ESPN sports for kids."[17] The content was "spun by tyke-friendly deejays, who keep the energy high with lots of call-ins and special promotions."[18]

With its headquarters in Dallas, TX, Radio Disney was an immediate success with its target market. In 2000, it was broadcasting on 44 stations around the country and had a weekly audience of 1.5 million; by 2010 that number had grown to 49 stations with a weekly audience of 22.2 million.[19]

Over the years, Radio Disney has reached out to its young audience with a combination of tailored programming and targeted promotions and marketing. The station features a call-in request format that is extremely popular with young listeners. It sponsors a continuous stream of on-air promotions and contests, as well as community special events.

Mall promotions like this "3 Minute Game Show" are a routine part of Radio Disney activities.

Family-Friendly Fare

Parent Liz Regan became quite familiar with Radio Disney when her son and daughter were 8 and 10, respectively. "They listened to the station every morning going to school. Every time we got into the car, it was set to Disney on the AM dial. At home, it was always on the radio. They had CDs they would play that played music from Radio Disney," she said.

Regan said she felt comfortable letting her children tune in to Radio Disney on a regular basis because "it was just safe music for them to be listening to," she explained.

"The DJs never spoke any wrong way. The commercials followed the same order. You never had to worry about an off-color commercial or anything off-color. All the songs are usually upbeat and fun and positive. A lot of times they're very easy to sing along with. It leaves you with a good feeling," she said.[20]

Since its inception in 1996, Radio Disney has expanded its audience reach beyond the traditional commercial airwaves. It currently broadcasts on Sirius and XM satellite radio, XM/DIRECTV, iTunes Radio Tuner, through the Radio Disney iPhone App, and on RadioDisney.com.[21]

Music for the Tween Scene

In 2007, Radio Disney became part of the Disney Channel operation and subsequently relocated from Dallas to Burbank, Calif. In the last few years, it has played a significant role in helping to launch some of the channel's stars into pop music sensations. This partnership has also breathed new life into the Disney Music Group's Hollywood Records label, which produces much of the recorded music of these performers.

Promoting Hilary Duff

In a *Los Angeles Times* article, Bob Cavallo, chairman of the Disney Music Group, explained how Disney's music division first realized the power of joining forces with the Disney Channel in order to boost music sales for the record label. This transformation actually began in 2002 with actress Hilary Duff, the star of the Disney Channel show *Lizzie McGuire*.

When Duff expressed an interest in adding singing to her résumé, she was given the opportunity to record the *Lizzie McGuire TV Soundtrack, Lizzie*

McGuire Movie Soundtrack, and several other CDs, which ultimately launched her career as a pop star and solo performer. Her CDs, released on the Buena Vista label, sold more than 10 million copies.

Los Angeles Times reporter Dawn Chmiewlewski explained:

> Duff was the first artist for which the Disney Channel served as the creative incubator and a promotional slingshot. It developed a knack for propelling sales of budding artists who struggled to be heard beyond Radio Disney. It was a Disney cycle in which television, radio and, occasionally, the film studio reinforced one another with an almost inescapable buzz.[22]

Since then, the powerhouse combination of the Disney Channel, Radio Disney, and the Disney Music Group has successfully launched and marketed talent to the tween market (10–14-year-olds) with artists such as the Cheetah Girls, Miley Cyrus (Hannah Montana), the Jonas Brothers, and the cast members of the Disney Channel hit *High School Musical.* These young performers have not only brought their music to audiences via television, radio, and CD and digital recordings but through worldwide concert tours that attract crowds of thousands.[23]

Jonas Brothers

The Jonas Brothers are a classic example of the well-oiled marketing efforts of this collaboration. Kevin, Joe, and Nick Jonas were initially signed by Columbia Records and released their first CD, *It's About Time,* in 2006. When the album sold just 65,000 copies, the group was on the brink of being obliterated by the label.

After Columbia dropped them in early 2007, Cavallo signed the brothers to the Hollywood Records label.[24] They began recording their second album, *Jonas Brothers,* and the Disney marketing machine went to work.

In 2007, the Jonas Brothers appeared as the opening act for Miley Cyrus. By 2008, they were headliners. They starred in the Disney Channel movie *Camp Rock* in the summer of 2008 and were featured in a reality show called *The Jonas Brothers: Living the Dream* that same year. Their film, *Jonas Brothers: The 3D Concert Experience* opened in February 2009 and grossed approximately $19 million.[25] And in May 2009, their television series, *JONAS,* premiered on the Disney Channel.

Since signing with Hollywood Records in 2007, their four albums have sold approximately 8 million copies—a far cry from their initial Columbia run of 65,000, and a case in point of the powers of Disney's collaborative marketing efforts.

Conclusion

Music has always been part of the Disney legacy, and the company's use of music in its products has evolved over the years. Disney films are often remembered as much for their songs as their storylines. Music is also an integral part of the Disney theme park experience.

The tremendous success Disney has had making inroads into the pop music scene in recent years signifies a new direction for the company. As an article in *USA Today* noted, "Where the Disney songbook of previous eras came from the films of *Snow White* and *Beauty and the Beast*, fare that appealed to kids and adults alike, these new songs almost exclusively target children between 6 and 14."[26] Only time will tell how much of an impact this concentrated focus on a younger market will have on the Disney music of the future. ◆

Notes

1. David Tietyen, *The Musical World of Walt Disney* (Milwaukee, WI: Hal Leonard Publishing, 1990): 9.
2. Ibid., 23.
3. Film clip of Walt Disney discussing *The Three Little Pigs*, on display at Walt Disney Family Museum, San Francisco.
4. See Ross Care, "Disney Music During the Classic Era: An Overview," *The Cue Sheet* 18:3-4 (October 2002): 4.
5. J.B. Kaufman, "Walt's Musical World," handout from Walt Disney Family Museum, 2009.
6. Tietyen, *The Musical World of Walt Disney*, 49.
7. Ibid., 114.
8. Ibid., 128.
9. Joe Alfuso, telephone interview, June 21, 2010.
10. Greg Ehrbar, "How Walt Got His Groove Back," *D23: The Official Community for Online Fans*, http://d23.disney.go.com/articles/102309_NF_FS_JimmyJohnson.html.
11. Tim Hollis and Greg Ehrbar, *Mouse Tracks: The Story of Walt Disney Records* (Jackson, MS: University Press of Mississippi, 2006): 50.
12. Ibid., 187.
13. Joe Alfuso, telephone interview, June 21, 2010.
14. Dapper Dans, www.harmonize.com/dapperdans.

15. See Walt Disney Youth Groups, http://disneyyouthgroups.disney.go.com/wdyp/home.
16. Joe Alfuso, telephone interview, June 21, 2010.
17. Rachel X. Weissman, "Mouse in the House," *American Demographics* 21:2 (February 1999): 30.
18. Ibid.
19. See Jeff Silberman, "Children's Radio: It's a Small World, After All," *Billboard* 112:8 (February 19, 2000): 67; Michael Maney, "Radio Disney Raises the Volume," *Disney Newsreel*, January 30, 2009, 9; and Radio Disney Fact Sheet, www.disneyabctv.com/division/pdf/radio.pdf.
20. Liz Regan, in-person interview, July 22, 2010.
21. Radio Disney Fact Sheet, www.disneyabctv.com/division/pdf/radio.pdf.
22. See Dawn C. Chmielewski, "A Cinderella Story for Disney Music Group," *Los Angeles Times*, 9 July 2007, C1.
23. See Ethan Smith, "How Disney Is Reviving a Band Still in Its Teens," *The Wall Street Journal*, 19 July 2007, B1.
24. See Ann Donahue, "The Jonas Brothers Dominate a Multimedia World," *Billboard* 120:25 (June 21, 2008): 25.
25. Box Office Mojo.com, http://boxofficemojo.com/movies/?id=jonasbros3dconcert.htm.
26. Brian Mansfield, "Disney Music Machine Runs at Top Speed," *USA Today*, 5 April 2007.

9

Disney Theater and Live Entertainment

After many years of storytelling success on both the large and small screen, Disney was ready to venture into another genre of entertainment—live Broadway theater.

Disney established itself as a key player in the revitalization of New York's Times Square/42nd Street area—the heart of Broadway—in the late 1980s, while under the leadership of Michael Eisner. The company agreed to renovate the dilapidated New Amsterdam Theatre to create a space where it could showcase its own Broadway productions.

In the process, however, Disney succeeded in jumpstarting a badly needed urban renewal project. This led to increased foot traffic to the Times Square neighborhood as well as increased attendance at Broadway shows.

In conjunction with the theater renovation project, the company created a new division, Disney Theatrical Productions, and began developing a stage version of its animated film *Beauty and the Beast*. The popularity of this show, which opened on Broadway in 1994, led to the development of others. Some, like *The Lion King* and *Mary Poppins*, have been very successful, while others, like *Tarzan* and *The Little Mermaid*, have operated at a loss for the company.

Disney Theatrical Productions has also been involved in the licensing of some of its musicals to high schools, colleges, and community theater groups. The most popular of these has been a stage version of *High School Musical*, based on the 2006 Disney Channel film.

A secondary area of Disney's theater division is Disney Live! This segment of the company partners with Feld Entertainment to produce the *Disney on Ice* shows, as well as family-friendly touring productions such as *Playhouse Disney Live!* and *Mickey's Magic Show.*

This chapter will examine the impact Disney's move into theater has had on Broadway audiences. It will look at some of the shows Disney has produced in the last two decades and discuss how these shows have fared. An overview of the productions put on by Disney Live! will also be included.

Disney's Impact on the New Broadway

In its heyday in the 1930s and '40s, New York's Broadway was a vibrant and magical place. Neon theater marquees in dazzling colors announced hit plays and musicals. Theater patrons from all over the globe knew that seeing a show on Broadway was a special experience.

By the 1970s and '80s, however, the public's interest in live theater had diminished. The 42nd Street/Times Square area, the heart of Broadway, had become a seedy and dangerous place. Once-thriving theaters had been shuttered and left to rot. Trendy restaurants were replaced by porn theaters, pawn shops, and peep shows.

An organization called The 42nd Street Development Project (42DP) was formed to clean up Times Square and try to restore the New York neighborhood to a semblance of its former self. One possible solution was to find a corporate partner willing to invest in the restoration effort by renovating the New Amsterdam Theatre, once home to the Ziegfeld Follies.

To those at 42DP, the Disney Company, at the time under the leadership of CEO Michael Eisner, was a logical choice. Disney's brand was well known, and the company had the financial muscle needed to invest in such a renovation.

The organization floated the idea by Eisner in the late 1980s but was initially met with strong resistance. Eisner was reluctant to sign on for the theater restoration project because he thought the idea was "too risky, and not the core business," according to an article in *Fortune* magazine.[1]

Around the same time, the Disney Company was considering making its first move into live musical theater. The success of the 1992 animated film *Beauty and the Beast* had led to discussions about a possible Broadway musical version of the show. One of Eisner's concerns was where to find a venue large enough to house such a production. Suddenly, the idea of owning a Broadway theater was starting to make good business sense.

Taking on the New Amsterdam Theatre

Eisner finally agreed to take a tour of the New Amsterdam Theatre in 1993. Once inside, his attitude shifted, according to author Anthony Bianco. Eisner was quoted as saying:

> The interior was badly gutted. Still, the theater's remarkable detailing remained in ghostlike form—its Art Noveau décor, Wagnerian friezes, and allegorical murals. The once-lavish grandeur of this building was easy to visualize, even in its dilapidated state. By the time we left, I felt excited.[2]

Disney was in. But, the company's negotiations with 42DP took several years. Eisner and his team initially hoped to be able to create a Disney space around the New Amsterdam Theatre by putting a gate around it to control the crowds and keep out unwanted traffic. As Bianco explained:

> The city—especially the big city—was foreign territory to Walt Disney Co. Its forte was the creation of insular utopias of leisure and fantasy—think Disney World—that occupied the urban periphery and offered escape from the city's messy realities.[3]

In actuality, the proximity of New York's Port Authority Bus Terminal made this request unrealistic and almost ludicrous. Disney also wanted an exit option as part of the deal unless at least two other reputable entertainment companies agreed to invest in nearby property. In addition, the company hoped to be able to purchase the New Amsterdam Theatre outright rather than lease it.

In the end, the state of New York invested $26 million in the theater through a subsidized loan to the Disney Company. Disney's overall investment in the project totaled approximately $8 million.[4] Two other entertainment companies, AMC and the Tussaud's Group, agreed to join forces to build a retail and entertainment center near the New Amsterdam Theatre. Disney was unable to purchase the theater, however; instead, the company received a 49-year lease on the property.

Did You Know?

The New Amsterdam Theatre was the largest theater in New York when it opened in 1903. It was home to the Ziegfeld Follies from 1913–1936 and later served as a movie house.

Revitalization Pays Off

Initially, news that Disney planned to try to resuscitate the ailing Times Square neighborhood was greeted with skepticism and amusement by the public and the media. Ultimately, however, Disney's investment in the restoration of the New Amsterdam Theatre led to the revival of Times Square.

In 1997, the Ford Motor Co. invested in the renovation of the Apollo and Lyric theaters by combining them into one new theater, the Ford Center for the Performing Arts. Other buildings brought to life again by this resurgence of interest in Broadway were the Empire Theatre and the Selwyn Theater, which was remodeled and renamed the American Airlines Theater after an investment by the airline.

According to the *Broadway: The American Musical* website:

> Retail outlets began to sign leases in the Times Square area, new bright and elaborate electronic signage began appearing in the theater district for the first time since the beginning of World War II, and several business and communications firms announced plans to build new offices on or adjacent to West 42nd Street.[5]

Even Disney itself opened a Disney Store next door to the New Amsterdam Theatre.

Broadway was back, and Disney was partly responsible for its reawakening. Now the company was ready to make the next move of bringing some of its beloved animated films to the Great White Way.

Disney Theatrical Productions

The credit for Disney's venture onto the Broadway stage has been attributed to *New York Times* critic Frank Rich. In 1992, while reviewing the Tony Award candidates for Best Musical, Rich facetiously noted that the year's best musical was, in fact, Disney's animated film *Beauty and the Beast*. That got Michael Eisner and his associates thinking about the possibilities of bringing the film to Broadway.[6]

The following year, Eisner sanctioned the formation of Walt Disney Theatrical Productions to develop a stage version of *Beauty and the Beast*. This coincided with the activity surrounding the restoration of the New Amsterdam Theatre, as discussed in the previous section.

The eventual success of *Beauty and the Beast* led to the production of additional shows that have been performed on Broadway as well as around the world—*The Lion King, Aida, Tarzan, Mary Poppins,* and *The Little Mermaid*—largely under the tutelage of Disney's Thomas Schumacher.

Making a Splash on Broadway

According to Paul Hodgins, theater and dance critic for the *Orange County Register*, Disney's venture onto the Broadway stage has "upped the ante in many respects, brought an end to the era of Sir Andrew and the big effects musicals—*Sunset Boulevard, Phantom*, etc.—and placed more of an effort on story, character, and theatrical effects."[7]

Today, Disney Theatrical Productions falls under the Disney Theatrical Group (DTG) umbrella, headed up by Schumacher. According to Disney's 2009 annual financial report, "Disney Theatrical Productions develops, produces and licenses live entertainment events.... In addition, the Company licenses musicals for local school and community theatre productions."[8] DTG also includes Disney Live Family Entertainment, which will be discussed later in this chapter.

Following is a look at the Broadway shows that have resulted from Disney's venture onto the live stage and an explanation of how some of these shows have impacted today's Broadway entertainment experience.

Beauty and the Beast

After the decision was made to tread the boards of Broadway, Disney turned to Houston's Theater Under the Stars director Frank Young for assistance in developing its first production. Young was instrumental in helping Disney translate the animated fantasy about a young woman who falls in love with a prince-turned-beast into a plausible stage show that would keep the essence of the film but work well with human characters.[9]

To make the film more appropriate for the stage, six new songs were added to complement the existing score by Alan Menken and Howard Ashman. Five were written by Menken and Tim Rice. (Ashman died in 1991, before the creation of the stage show.) The stage version of *Beauty and the Beast* also encompassed lavish sets and special effects, including pyrotechnics.

The show ran for a month in Houston at the end of 1993, before opening on Broadway on April 18, 1994. Because the New Amsterdam Theatre was still being renovated, the show debuted at the Palace Theater and was eventually relocated to the Lunt-Fontanne Theatre in 1999.

When *Beauty and the Beast* opened on Broadway, it was greeted with mixed reviews. While critics gave the show a lukewarm reception, the public embraced it wholeheartedly.[10]

Beauty and the Beast remained on Broadway for 13 years and 5,464 performances, until it closed on July 29, 2007. In the interim, the show resulted in two national U.S. tours and 13 worldwide productions in 115 countries. It was also licensed to numerous high schools, colleges, and community theaters, according to *Variety*.[11]

More importantly, *Beauty and the Beast* proved to Disney executives that there was a promising future in live theater. The success of Disney's initial Broadway production opened the door to a new genre for the company, one that would generate Disney awareness on the part of theater enthusiasts and help create an appreciation of Broadway on the part of children and teens.

The Lion King

Unbeknownst to Disney and its audiences, the best was yet to come. *The Lion King* was the company's second Broadway show and its first to appear in the newly-restored New Amsterdam Theatre. When the show opened with a roar on November 13, 1997, it announced to the world that Disney's entrée into live theater was more than just a passing fad.

The Lion King was based on the animated film of the same name and featured music by Elton John and Tim Rice. What set the show apart, though, was its innovative use of costuming—a blend of exotic fabrics, masks, and sculptured figures designed by the show's director, Julie Taymor, which transformed actors into animals.

Reviews for *The Lion King* far surpassed those of *Beauty and the Beast*, and the praise for Taymor's influence on the show was unending. A review in the *New York Daily News* proclaimed:

Broadway has long known how to take real people and turn them into flat, two-dimensional cartoons. Taymor has done it the other way round. She has taken cartoon characters and filled them with real humanity. In the process, she has restored the meaning of the word 'animation.' The musical has been brought to joyous life.[12]

Audiences and theater buffs responded in kind. *The Lion King* won six Tony Awards in 1998, including Taymor's award for Best Director of a Musical. Taymor was the first woman in Broadway history to receive that award. The show also earned a 1998 Grammy for Best Musical Show Album.[13] *The Lion King* went on the road in 1998, both nationally and internationally.

By the end of 2010, the show had begun its 13th year on Broadway and had played in more than 60 cities in 14 countries. Productions in London and Tokyo had been running for 10+ years. Since its debut in 1997, *The Lion King* has grossed more than $3.8 billion.[14] It has been seen by 50 million people worldwide, more than any other American musical.[15]

The Lion King was followed by other Disney Broadway shows, but none so far has been able to equal its unprecedented success, explained *Orange County Register* theater critic Paul Hodgins. "I think that was the high water mark for them. They've always been trying to recreate *The Lion King* experience and not quite making it."[16]

Did You Know?

Costumes from the Broadway production of *The Lion King* were donated to the Smithsonian Institution's National Museum of American History.

Aida

For their next act, executives at Disney Theatrical Productions elected to take a giant step onto a theatrical limb. Instead of sticking with what was now a tried-and-true formula of turning popular animated films into Broadway productions, the company ventured off in a more daring direction.

Building on the success of the Elton John/Tim Rice partnership, Disney hired the duo to write a musical theater version of Giuseppe Verdi's 1871 opera, *Aida*. The stage show would continue Disney's use of lavish costumes and elaborate sets, including a giant pyramid that opened and closed on stage.

Aida, however, was plagued with problems from the beginning. At first-run tryouts in Atlanta in 1998, mechanical failure led to disastrous results with the pyramid. Local critics panned the show and compared it to comedian Steve Martin's famous "King Tut" routine, according to the *Wall Street Journal*.[17]

After a major overhaul, *Aida* finally opened at the Palace Theatre on Broadway on March 23, 2000. Given the negative publicity following the tryouts, Disney execs made a concerted effort to promote the show long before the Broadway curtain went up on opening night. Part of this promotional strategy involved the posturing of the show to its potential audiences, explained *Advertising Age* reporter Larry Dobrow.

"The decision was made early in the marketing process to position *Aida* as sophisticated adult entertainment, suitable for children but certainly not for 5-year-olds still clutching their Simba toys."[18]

In advance of the show's opening, Disney staged a preview presentation for organizers of group ticket sales, featuring excerpts from the show. Five months ahead of opening night, the company also purchased eight pages of advertising in the *New Yorker* magazine, "one of the magazine's biggest advertisements ever for a Broadway show, let alone one that wouldn't be opening for months," noted an article in the *Wall Street Journal*.[19]

Electronic media was also used to reach potential customers. Disney execs sent out personal emails that included a message from Elton John and audio clips of the show's music.[20]

The strategy worked. Although critics never really warmed to *Aida* even after a strong and relatively problem-free opening, the public was curious enough to investigate the latest Disney production. By 2001, a year after it opened, the show was ranked second in ticket sales behind *The Lion King*.[21]

Aida closed on September 5, 2004, after 1,852 performances and a 4-1/2 year run on Broadway. It was the first of Disney's three Broadway musicals to close, but it had lasted several years longer than some of its early critics had predicted.

Mary Poppins

Mary Poppins was probably Disney's most anticipated Broadway musical, largely because of the backstage drama involved in bringing the classic film to the stage.

As noted in Chapter 5, the 1964 release of *Mary Poppins* is considered by many to be Walt Disney's finest film, combining elements of live action, animation, and special effects with colorful characters and memorable music by Richard M. and Robert B. Sherman. For Walt Disney, the triumph was made even sweeter because of the tremendous difficulties he'd had in obtaining the rights to the *Mary Poppins* stories from their author, P.L. Travers.[22]

Unfortunately for Disney, Travers's ultimate dissatisfaction with the finished film led to her steadfast refusal to sell him the stage rights to the tales of her famous character. In fact, for many years, Travers refused to let anyone have those rights.

In 1993, after more than 20 years of his own negotiations for the stage rights to *Mary Poppins*, British producer Cameron Mackintosh (*Phantom of the Opera, Cats, Les Misérables*) was able to persuade Travers to sell them to him. He then tried to no avail to convince the Disney Company to grant him access to the Sherman Brothers' songs from the 1964 film to use in a musical theater production.[23]

Talks between Mackintosh and the Disney Company were stalled for years until 2001, when Thomas Schumacher flew to London to meet with Mackintosh. In discussing their individual visions for a stage musical version of *Mary Poppins* based on Travers's stories, Schumacher and Mackintosh realized they were actually on the same page.[24] Mackintosh and the Disney Company reached an agreement to co-produce the show, and work on a stage version of *Mary Poppins* was finally able to begin.

Two British composers, George Stiles and Anthony Drewe, were brought in to add seven new songs to the Sherman Brothers' existing repertoire. Although he did not produce any new work for the stage version of *Mary Poppins*, Richard Sherman remained actively involved in the development of the show as a consultant.[25]

Unlike Disney's previous musicals, *Mary Poppins* made its debut in London's West End rather than on Broadway on December 15, 2004. Some critics felt the show had a dark quality to it, much darker than the "spoonful of sugar" sweetness made famous by actress Julie Andrews in the Disney film. Part of the dark nature of the show was that it drew as much on Travers's original stories as on Disney's screen interpretation of these tales.

By the time *Mary Poppins* opened at Broadway's New Amsterdam Theatre on November 16, 2006, the show had been tweaked a bit to make it more appealing to American audiences. This worked to appease the critics. As *New York Times* reviewer Ben Brantley explained:

> The show's producers seem to have figured out that gray is not the favorite color of Americans. So cake-frosting pinks, greens, lilacs and yellows have, for the most part, pushed away sootier tones.[26]

The London production played for more than three years until it closed on January 12, 2008. The show then went on tour throughout the United Kingdom for the year following its closing. Other international productions of *Mary Poppins* have been performed in Scandinavia, the Netherlands, Hungary, and Australia. In the United States, a traveling production of the show went on the road in 2009, and continues to make stops in cities throughout the country.

Tarzan

For Disney, even the magic couldn't last forever. The company's two most recent Broadway productions, *Tarzan* and *The Little Mermaid*, have each lasted just slightly over a year on Broadway, despite much hype and promise.

Tarzan featured music and lyrics by Phil Collins and a book by David Henry Hwang, who had also written *Aida*. The show opened on May 10, 2006, at the Richard Rodgers Theater to mixed reviews and a bit of bewilderment on the part of critics. Most of the show's plot about an English boy raised by apes into an ape-man adult took place in the jungle. Most of the show's characters were animals.

To simulate jungle conditions, *Tarzan's* set designers concocted a production that involved lots of swinging on "vines" from place to place on stage. According to critics, the overzealous acrobatics made the show feel more like a circus than the combination of story and spectacle that theater-goers had come to expect from a Disney production.[27]

Despite the initial expectations of its creators for a longer run, *Tarzan* closed on July 8, 2007, after 486 performances. International productions in the Netherlands and Germany fared slightly better than the Broadway run. For the most part, however, *Tarzan* didn't come close to living up to the hopes of Disney executives and fans.

The Little Mermaid

Disney closed its Broadway production of *Beauty and the Beast* at the end of 2007, after a 13-year run, to make way for another Disney Princess—one that had a special place in the hearts of Disney fans.

The Little Mermaid was the first animated film released by Disney after a long absence of high-quality, classic animation. At the time of its release in 1989, the film had been a breath of fresh air for audiences and paved the way for Disney's production of others like it such as *Aladdin, Beauty and the Beast,* and *The Lion King.*

As a result, the Broadway version of the popular film was eagerly anticipated by the public when it opened at the Lunt-Fontanne Theatre on January 10, 2008. The show featured the original music by Alan Menken and Howard Ashman, as well as new songs by Menken and lyricist Glenn Slater.

The challenge for the show's set designers was to create a stage universe that alternated between above and below the sea. For costume designers, there was the added challenge of equipping sea creatures with tails and fins while still allowing the actors portraying them to be ambulatory while on stage. This was accomplished with what a *New York Times* article called, "wheel-heeled footwear known as merblades,"[28] similar to the popular children's sneaker/skate shoe called Heelys.

Despite the creative attempt at simulating the undersea world, something appeared to be missing from the show, as critics were quick to point out. While reviews for *Tarzan* had been mixed, reviews for *The Little Mermaid* were dubbed "scathing."[29]

Adding in the effects of an economic recession and the high cost of tickets, show sales did not meet expectations. By August 30, 2009, after just 685 performances, the show closed, leaving only *The Lion King* and *Mary Poppins* remaining on Broadway.

Figure 11: Disney Theatrical Productions

Broadway Shows

Beauty and the Beast	1994-2007
The Lion King	1997-present
Aida	2000-2004
Mary Poppins	2006-present
Tarzan	2006-2007
The Little Mermaid	2008-2009

Other Productions

Der Glockner von Notre Dame	1999-2002 (Berlin)
On the Record	2004-2005 (national)
High School Musical on Tour	2007-2008 (national)
Peter and the Starcatchers	2009 (La Jolla, Calif.)

Other Disney Theater Productions

In the years since the initial establishment of Disney Theatrical Productions, the company's theater division has experimented with other musicals beyond those staged on Broadway.

Der Glockner von Notre Dame was the first of these and was a stage version of Disney's animated film *The Hunchback of Notre Dame*. The show opened June 5, 1999, in the Musical Theater Berlin at Potsdamer Platz and ran for three years.

On the Record was a musical revue that included a variety of classic Disney songs from the company's animated and live action films. The show opened in Cleveland on November 9, 2004, and played in 24 different cities during a nine-month run.[30] What was most noteworthy about this show was that it featured actress Ashley Brown, who eventually went on to star on Broadway as Belle in *Beauty and the Beast* and in the title role in *Mary Poppins*.

A production of *Peter and the Starcatchers* debuted at the La Jolla Playhouse on February 13, 2009, in conjunction with Disney Theatrical Productions.

The show was billed as a "prequel" to *Peter Pan* and is based on the book by Dave Barry and Ridley Pearson. It tells the story of Peter and the Lost Boys before they arrived in Never Never Land.[31]

High School Musical on Stage

Following the success of the 2006 Disney Channel movie *High School Musical*, Disney execs realized there was great potential for turning the hit film into a real live high school musical. Given the show's content, the work didn't seem sophisticated enough for Broadway audiences. However, it was deemed a natural for schools and community groups to put on through licensing agreements with Disney.[32]

In the fall of 2006, the company posted an announcement about the licensing availability of *High School Musical* on the website of Musical Theatre International, the organization that handles licenses for Disney shows. Disney received 15,000 email requests in response to the post.[33]

Schools and community groups throughout the country began mounting productions of *High School Musical*, and in some cases, ticket demand for the show was fierce.[34] Disney soon realized it would be profitable to put together its own touring production of the show as well. On August 1, 2007, the company's theatrical division opened a version of the show called, *High School Musical on Tour* at the LaSalle Bank Theatre in Chicago and then sent it on the road to 42 U.S. cities.[35]

One of the great attractions of the stage version of *High School Musical* was its familiarity to its audiences because of the 2006 film. As Thomas Schumacher was quoted as saying in an article in the *Chicago Tribune*:

> This really is a chance for us to build a new audience for the theater. If you go and see *High School Musical* when you're 9, maybe you'll come back and see *Lion King* when you're 18.[36]

Marketing a Disney Musical

Generating audiences is a constant challenge for any theater organization and is one that has been a steady issue for the Disney Company, especially during the recent recession years. As Disney has experienced the trials and tribulations of balancing its Broadway hits with its less successful productions, the company has constantly needed to re-invent its marketing and promotional strategies along the way.

As previously noted, for *Aida,* the company identified adults rather than children as its target market and devised promotional strategies to appeal to their interests. Going after the tween market has proven successful for the company with several of its shows like *The Little Mermaid* and *High School Musical,* not only through the show's marketing efforts but also with the promotional merchandise that is generated to accompany each production.

Mary Poppins has been dubbed by *Variety* as "a nostalgia trip for baby boomers looking to relive one of the most beloved kiddie movie musicals ever."[37] As a result, some of the show's advertisements and merchandise have been designed to appeal to this demographic.[38]

If Disney continues to launch new shows on Broadway as well as on the road, the company will need to keep developing innovative marketing strategies like these to encourage theater patrons to support them.

Disney Live Family Entertainment

As noted earlier in the chapter, a second segment of the Disney Theatrical Group is Disney Live Family Entertainment, which produces the *Disney on Ice* and *Disney Live!* touring shows in conjunction with Virginia-based Feld Entertainment. Although the division was formed in 2003, the *Disney on Ice* shows have actually been around for 30 years.[39] Disney and Feld Entertainment started with *Walt Disney's World on Ice* in 1981, and have since produced 30 different ice skating shows.

To complement the success of the ice shows, Disney and Feld Entertainment developed a series of non-ice programs designed to appeal to young children and their families under the heading Disney Live! These have included *Winnie the Pooh, Mickey's Magic Show, Disney Live! Rockin' Road Show, Three Classic Fairytales,* and *Playhouse Disney Live!*[40]

Disney Live! productions have been performed throughout the United States as well as in 40 different countries, according to Disney's 2009 annual report.[41] This has worked well to build greater global awareness of Disney.

Conclusion

Since venturing into the theater business in the early 1990s, the Disney Company has made quite an impression on Broadway and its audiences. Disney helped revitalize New York's Times Square area with its redevelopment of the New Amsterdam Theatre in the 1990s. The company has also had success with a variety of shows based on its animated films. While not all have been blockbuster hits, most have resonated with audiences who can relate to the story or characters because of their familiarity with them.

As theater critic Paul Hodgins explained:

> If people already know the story, that acts as a multiplier at the box office. Disney has a great variety of properties. They are better equipped than almost every entertainment company to produce money-making musicals to the horizon.[42]

Disney's theatrical division is still relatively young compared to its film and television counterparts. During its 20-year existence, however, it has added another level to the company by providing a new dimension of quality entertainment for Disney audiences. As the economy recovers and attendance improves, Disney is expected to continue to generate new shows designed to draw many more people to its live entertainment productions. ◆

Notes

1. Frank Rose, "Can Disney Tame 42nd Street?" *Fortune* 133:12 (June 24, 1996): 94.
2. Michael Eisner quoted in Anthony Bianco, *Ghosts of 42nd Street* (New York: Harper Perennial, 2004): 279.
3. Ibid., 280.
4. See *Broadway: The American Musical,* www.pbs.org/wnet/broadway.
5. Ibid.
6. See Everett Evans, "Disney Debut: First Stage Musical, 'Beauty,' Will Test Waters in Houston," *Houston Chronicle,* 28 November 1993, 8.
7. Paul Hodgins, in-person interview, May 20, 2010.
8. The Walt Disney Company, *Walt Disney Fiscal Year 2009 Annual Financial Report and Shareholder Letter,* 15.
9. Evans, "Disney Debut: First Stage Musical, 'Beauty,' Will Test Waters in Houston," 8.
10. See Hap Erstein, "Despite Poor Reviews, Broadway Goes Beast Crazy," *Journal Record,* 27 May 1994.
11. David Rooney, "'Little' Moves Are Part of Disney's Big Plan," *Variety* 405:10 (January 22-28, 2007): 38.

12. Fintan O'Toole, "Mane Event Is Spectacular; Adaptation of Disney Film Reigns Supreme as Musical Theater," *New York Daily News*, 14 November 1997, 4.

13. See "Disney's *The Lion King* Celebrates 10th Anniversary on Broadway," *PR Newswire*, November 6, 2007.

14. See "*The Lion King* Celebrates 5,000 Performances on Broadway," *The Walt Disney Company News From Investor Relations*, December 2009, 4.

15 . See "Smithsonian's National Museum of American History; *The Lion King* Roars Into the Smithsonian," *Entertainment Newsweekly*, October 9, 2009, 171.

16. Paul Hodgins, in-person interview, May 20, 2010.

17. Lisa Gubernick, "Triumphal March for a New Aida?" *Wall Street Journal*, 9 December 1999, B1.

18. Larry Dobrow, "Yes, Disney Proves It Can Do an Opera, Too," *Advertising Age* 72:13 (March 26, 2001): 10.

19. Gubernick, "Triumphal March for a New Aida?" B1.

20. See Dobrow, "Yes, Disney Proves It Can Do an Opera, Too," 10.

21. Ibid.

22. See Caitlin Flanagan, "Becoming Mary Poppins: P.L. Travers, Walt Disney, and the Making of a Myth," *The New Yorker* 81:41 (December 19, 2005): 40.

23. See Cathleen Mcguigan, "There's Something About Mary," *Newsweek* 148:20 (November 27, 2006): 54.

24. See Cameron Mackintosh, "P.L. Travers From the Page to the Stage," *Mary Poppins the Musical–The Making Of*, www.marypoppinsthemusical.co.uk.

25. See Irene Lacher, "Helping in a Most Delightful Way," *Los Angeles Times*, 8 November 2009, E6.

26. Ben Brantley, "Meddler on the Roof," *The New York Times*, 17 November 2006, E1.

27. See Ben Brantley, "Broadway and Vine: Ape-Man Hits Town," *The New York Times*, 11 May 2006, E1.

28. Ben Brantley, "Fish Out of Water in the Deep Blue Sea," *The New York Times*, 11 January 2008," E1.

29. See "Last Dive for Broadway's *The Little Mermaid* Set for Aug. 30," *Los Angeles Times*, 30 June 2009.

30. See Andrew Gans, "Disney's *On the Record* Ends National Tour July 31," *Playbill.com*, 31 July 2005.

31. See James Herbert, "The Great Adventure Is Life Itself," *San Diego Union-Tribune*, 12 February 2009, 13.

32. See Chris Jones, "How Disney Almost Dropped the Ball on a 'Musical' Megahit," *Chicago Tribune*, 29 July 2007, 1.

33. See Michael Kuchwara, "Musical's Phenomenal Success Catches Disney Off-Guard," *Providence Journal*, 18 November 2007, I.4.

34. See Kevin Pang, "When Actual High Schoolers Perform *High School Musical*, Chaos Ensues and a Small-Time Production Becomes...Big," *Chicago Tribune*, 2 February 2007, 1.

35. See "Live Productions of *High School Musical* Fill Stages and Arenas Around the World," *PR Newswire*, 28 January 2008.

36. Thomas Schumacher quoted in Jones, "How Disney Almost Dropped the Ball on a 'Musical' Megahit," 1.

37.   Robert Hofler, "B'way Alters Family Values," *Variety* 415:10 (July 27-August 2, 2009): 26.

38.   See, for example, Patricia Cohen, "Marketing Broadway: Selling Hope for a Song," *The New York Times*, 10 December 2008, C1.

39.   See William B. Hall, "Tanbark Topics," *The White Tops* 79:4 (July-August 2006): 24.

40.   See Jim Steinmeyer, "Making Mickey Magic," *Genii* 70:1 (January 2007): 59; and "Playhouse Disney Live! Brings Disney Channel Favorites Together on Stage to 70 U.S. Cities in Their First Live Touring Production," *PR Newswire*, 7 May 2007.

41.   The Walt Disney Company, *2009 Year in Review*, 2009, 12.

42.   Paul Hodgins, in-person interview, May 20, 2010.

10

Disney Travel and Tourism

With the success of its theme parks, the Disney Company established itself as a major player in the travel and tourism industry. According to the U.S. Travel Association, however, theme parks comprise only 6% of vacations, leaving plenty of untapped potential for growth.[1]

By the 1990s, Disney was ready to move into other areas of the travel and tourism business. Since then, the company has made headway into three major areas of travel: cruises, escorted tours, and time-share vacations.

Disney Cruise Line was launched in 1998, with two ships, *Disney Magic* and *Disney Wonder*. By 2011, the cruise line was operating itineraries in the Caribbean, Mexico, Europe, and Alaska. The Adventures by Disney escorted tour program began with trips to two destinations in 2005, and less than five years later had itineraries running in 17 countries.

In the last two decades, Disney has also developed one of the most successful time-share accommodation programs in the world—Disney Vacation Club—by using its existing fan base as its customers. The program was started in 1991 and is going strong with 400,000+ members.

The establishment of the Disney Cruise Line and Adventures by Disney tours as well as the company's Disney Vacation Club program has thrust the Disney Company into three major segments of the tourism market. This has enabled Disney to compete with companies that have been in these businesses for many years.

This chapter will look at Disney's impact on these three areas of the tourism industry. It will explain how the Disney Company has applied its own brand of pixie dust to them in order to expand its travel and tourism offerings to those interested in more than just a day at a Disney park.

Disney Cruise Line

Disney originally initiated its cruise line in 1998, in an attempt to increase attendance at its Florida theme parks. The idea was to attract repeat visitors looking for a new way to experience Disney, as opposed to individuals who were cruise enthusiasts.[2] Within a few years, the cruise line concept took hold, largely because of the focus on applying the company's family-friendly approach to the high seas.

Launching the Line

The launch of the Disney Cruise Line was accompanied by an aggressive marketing campaign that began about two years before the first ship left port. It included direct mail, print advertising, "trailers on Disney videos, and promotions and commercials on the Disney Channel, ABC and ESPN," according to an article in *Advertising Age*.[3]

Disney Cruise Line started with two ships. The *Disney Magic* had its maiden voyage in July 1998, and was soon followed by the *Disney Wonder*, which set sail in October of the same year. Initially, the ships sailed from Port Canaveral, Fla., to the Bahamas. Eventually, itineraries in the eastern and western Caribbean were added. During the 50th anniversary of Disneyland in 2005, the *Disney Magic* was briefly relocated to Los Angeles for cruises to the Mexican Riviera as well.[4]

A Private Getaway Spot

The Bahamas and Caribbean sailings include port stops on Disney's private Bahamian island. Disney purchased the island formerly known as Gorda Cay in 1996, equipped it to accommodate cruise ship traffic, and renamed it Castaway Cay.[5]

The island itself is not unique. Other cruise lines such as Holland America, Princess, and Carnival also make similar stops on their own private islands. What Disney promotes with Castaway Cay is the Disney magic that accompanies a visit to *this* island.

"Walt Disney Imagineers designed Castaway Cay with one-of-a-kind areas and activities for every member of the family, while celebrating the natural beauty of the 1,000-acre island," noted an article in *Leisure & Travel Week*.[6] A replica of a pirate ship rests in the water near the entrance to the island, and Disney characters greet passengers as they disembark from the ship.

Figure 12: Facts About Castaway Cay

- Formerly named Gorda Cay

- Located in the Commonwealth of the Bahamas

- 1,000 acres; only 55 acres developed

- Took 18 months to renovate to accommodate passengers

- Has its own post office

- 60 crew members live and work on the island

- Pirate ship moored offshore was featured in *Pirates of the Caribbean: Dead Man's Chest*

- Recycled cooking oil from cruise ships is used to run island machinery

Source: Disney Cruise Line News, http://disneycruise.disney.go.com/cruises-destinations/bahamas/ports/castaway-cay; Disney Cruise Line Fun Facts, http://www.disneycruisenews.com/AssetDetail.aspx?AssetId=d953bf1d-fea5-4fbe-b555-d434d25e2353

Something for Everyone

Disney has tried to set itself apart from other cruise lines by promoting the family-oriented cruising experience. "Our focus is on families and fun," explained Karl Holz, president, Disney Cruise Line and New Vacation

Operations, during a presentation at the D23 Expo. "We establish a cruise vacation tailored for every member of the family."[7] As a result, each cruise attracts many variations of travelers.

Approximately half of the passengers on a Disney cruise are children and teens. The company has created an assortment of programs and activities that cater to the interests of these youngsters and alleviate the worries of their parents. Each ship features two play areas where parents can leave their children in the care of Disney counselors. A nursery is also available onboard for children under 3.

A separate area of the ship is designated for teens and features activities tailored to their interests. There is also a teen lounge for those who just want to hang out or play video games. In keeping with Holz's comments about the tailored vacation, Disney has gone to great lengths to provide something that is likely to appeal to everyone under the age of 18, a feature most other cruise lines don't offer. This approach works well as a marketing tool for parents looking for a family vacation to meet the needs of both children and adults.

Family-Friendly Cruising

When Elaine Dunn began thinking about a vacation she and her then 5-year-old son Adam could enjoy together, she was drawn to the idea of a Disney cruise. Although she had sailed on other cruise lines with friends, the promise of a family-focused cruise seemed much more appropriate with a child in tow.

Dunn, a physical therapist from Washington, N.C., was so impressed with the Disney cruise that two years later, she and Adam went on another one. She liked the fact that she could let him go and hang out with other children and not have to worry about him. This allowed her the opportunity to relax as well.

"With a child, they're so accommodating, so you can have adult time," she said. On her second cruise when Adam was seven-years-old, she estimated that she spent about 60% of her time doing things with Adam and 40% on her own while Adam was busy with his activities. The cruise line supplied her with a pager, so that if Adam needed to reach her, she could easily be contacted.[8]

With such an emphasis on families with children, it would seem that Disney cruises would be less appealing to couples without children or individuals traveling on their own. To compensate for this, Disney has made a concerted effort to create areas of the ship and activities that are meant to appeal specifically to adults.

One swimming pool on each ship is designated for those over 18, as are several quiet cafés and sunbathing areas. Some of the onboard events are also deemed "adults only." This provides an opportunity for those Disney fans who are kids at heart but not necessarily kid friendly to have their own Disney cruise experience.

"There are so many different activities for adults," said Beth Gieseking of St. Peters, Mo. "If you don't want to be around [kids], you don't have to be."

Gieseking and her friend, Holly Favazza, were first introduced to Disney Cruise Line a number of years ago when Beth's brother worked for Disney. Even though he no longer works for the company, they have continued to cruise with Disney. Beth has been on nine Disney cruises, and Holly has been on seven.

What brings them back every year is Disney's emphasis on customer service, explained Gieseking. "Every single person that you encounter here asks, 'How's your day? Is there anything else I could do for you?'"[9]

"It's all about the service," added Favazza, "because of the attention you get, because of how they treat you."[10]

Did You Know?

When Disney Cruise Line ships blow their horns,
the sound heard is the first seven notes of
When You Wish Upon a Star.

Maintaining the Disney Magic

To ensure that cruisers never lose sight of the fact they are on a Disney cruise ship, the company peppers its activity agendas with regular reminders. Disney characters make daily appearances for photos and autograph signings. Disney movies are shown throughout the day in various locations on the ship as well as on televisions in each stateroom.

The shops on board sell everything Disney: toys, clothing, jewelry—even designer handbags with Disney motifs. In keeping with the tradition of the company's theme parks, a Disney cruise even features a fireworks display to culminate one of its evening social activities.

What is conspicuously absent from a Disney cruise is an onboard casino, something that is a staple on most other major cruise line ships. While bingo is featured as an onboard activity and could technically be considered a form of gambling, casinos do not fit well into the wholesome family image concept that Disney tries so hard to promote. As a result, they have been deliberately omitted from the roster of onboard entertainment offerings.

Expanding the Fleet

Given the popularity of its two existing cruise ships, in 2009, the Disney Company began construction of two additional ships—the *Disney Dream* and *Disney Fantasy*. The *Dream* is expected to set sail in 2011, and the *Fantasy* in 2012. The ships are 50% larger than the two existing ships, according to Karl Holz, holding approximately 4,000 passengers apiece as opposed to the 2,700 that the *Disney Magic* and *Disney Wonder* can accommodate.[11]

During a presentation at the D23 Expo, Holz also announced the proposed itineraries for the Disney fleet once the two new ships joined their seafaring sisters. The *Disney Dream* was to dock at Port Canaveral, replacing the *Disney Wonder*, which would relocate its home port to Los Angeles. The *Wonder* would then be used for Mexican Riviera cruises in the winter and temporarily move its base to Vancouver for Alaska sailings in the summer.[12]

Once completed, the *Disney Fantasy* was also to be based in Port Canaveral, and the *Disney Magic* to be relocated to a site to be announced at a later date. To accommodate the additional number of passengers brought to Castaway Cay by the two larger ships, Disney also expanded the facilities on its private island in 2010, adding water slides, beach cabanas, and new bathing areas to the site.[13]

Although the Disney Cruise Line was originally started as a complement to the company's theme parks, it has developed into a tourism attraction in its own right. Disney may not achieve the same level of business experienced by competing cruise lines because of the small size of its fleet. However, the company has carved out a niche for itself by focusing on family-friendly cruising, This makes it ideal for those wanting to combine a vacation at sea with the familiarity of the Disney brand.

Adventures by Disney

Less than a decade after the debut of its cruise line, the Disney Company took on another segment of the tourism industry by starting its own brand of escorted tours. Adventures by Disney began in 2005 with a pilot program to two destinations, Hawaii and Wyoming. By 2009, the enterprise was in full swing with 22 itineraries in 17 countries.

Hassle-Free Travel

As with Disney Cruise Line, the company emphasizes the concept of family-friendly travel. Disney promises to take the hassle out of travel by applying its famous customer service to the escorted tour market. Disney advertises that it will take care of all the details of each trip. This is particularly appealing for those families wanting to try more challenging itineraries they might not typically consider when planning a vacation with children.

Disney promotes its guided tours by emphasizing the company's longstanding tradition of storytelling. Sightseeing stops encourage participants to become characters in their own stories as they include places such as the castle in southern Germany used as the model for Sleeping Beauty's castle at Disneyland. Added special touches are included in each tour to set them apart from other escorted tour companies, explained reporter Brooks Barnes.

> A tour of California stops in Hollywood for an exploration of Jim Henson's studio, home to 'The Muppets' and otherwise off limits to the public. In London, guests go backstage at the West End production of *The Lion King*.[14]

Unlike the Disney cruise, there are no Disney characters along for the ride on an Adventures by Disney tour. However, travelers might encounter local actors dressed like historical characters appropriate to a tour's locale. Benjamin Franklin has been known to suddenly appear during a stop in Philadelphia, for example, and the Grimm Brothers have shown up on the "Once Upon a Fairytale" itinerary in Germany.[15]

While many other escorted tour companies often employ local guides to lead their tours, only some of Disney's tour leaders are locally trained guides. "Many are from the company's theme parks, resorts and cruise ships. They are trained in Disney rhyme and rules, as well as field experience in their location," according to reporter Jodi Mailander Farrell.[16]

A Wide Range of Options

Each Adventures by Disney tour includes plenty of hands-on activities to appeal to the wide-ranging ages of children on each trip. These might include trying on 18th-century costumes at Schoenbrunn Palace in Vienna or making scones at an Irish farmhouse.[17] As with the Disney cruises, the tours also build in supervised activities just for kids, leaving the adults an opportunity for some alone time.

Adventures by Disney trips are considered premium guided tours and, "on average, Disney packages cost roughly 10% more than other similarly posh family tours," noted Matthew Link in a *Time* magazine article.[18] Consequently, while the Adventures by Disney tours have been extremely popular since their inception, even the company's Disney magic couldn't ward off the effects of an international economic downturn, which led to a decrease in worldwide travel by the end of 2009.

Downsizing During Recession

In 2010, Disney scaled back its Adventures by Disney tours, trimming the number of trips it offered and eliminating several European destinations from its itineraries. As an incentive to attract new business, at the end of 2009, Disney began offering a free three-night cruise to the Bahamas to those who purchased certain Adventures by Disney tours. At the same time, the company announced the availability of a combination travel package, pairing one of its Adventures by Disney European itineraries with a Mediterranean cruise offered on the Disney Magic in summer 2010.[19]

The downturn in the economy proved unfortunate timing for the Disney Company as it was just beginning to get comfortable with its latest tourism venture. It is likely that the company will make additional adjustments in the promotion and marketing of the Adventures by Disney program as it waits out the recession and can then continue to try to grow its relatively young escorted tour business.

Disney Vacation Club

Long before entering the cruise and escorted tour markets, the Disney Company had already established itself as a reliable provider of quality accommodations for its theme park guests. When the Magic Kingdom at Walt Disney World opened in 1971, the company also opened the Contemporary and Polynesian Resort Hotels for visitors wanting to make the park a vacation destination.

Many other Disney-owned hotels soon followed on the Florida property. Then, in 1991, Disney devised a way to encourage repeat visitors to the Walt Disney World Resort to make a stay at a Disney-owned property a regular part of their visits to the parks. The program was called the Disney Vacation Club.

Did You Know?
When Disney Vacation Club members arrive for check-in, they are greeted by Disney cast members with the phrase, "Welcome Home."

A Different Kind of Time-Share

The Disney Vacation Club (DVC) is Disney's version of a time-share program. Participants invest in a stake in real estate at a Disney resort facility, which the company calls a "Disney vacation villa." With traditional time-share programs, customers are often required to purchase a vacation unit at a designated location and use it during a specific time period every year.

The Disney Vacation Club is based on a point system. Investors purchase a certain number of points to be allotted to them every year. Points can then be used at any time during the year and applied to a stay at any DVC resort.

The point system is what differentiates Disney from a traditional time-share program, according to one vacation club sales representative. When the company established the vacation club program, he explained, Disney wanted to move away from the stereotypical time-share concept as much as possible.[20]

The minimum number of points required to buy into the program is 160 at $112 per point—an investment of $17,920. The maximum purchase allowed is 2,000 points. Members are also required to pay monthly maintenance fees. Most families typically buy between 270-400 points.[21]

Membership in the Disney Vacation Club includes access to 10 Disney owned-properties. While the majority are in Florida, the company also owns DVC accommodations in Anaheim, Calif., and Hilton Head, S.C. Disney has agreements with a network of approximately 450 non-Disney-owned properties throughout the world as well where members can use their points to stay.

Jean and Barry Levine bought into the program in 1998. The couple from Egg Harbor Township, N.J., had been visiting the Florida parks regularly for many years and started thinking about investing in property nearby.

After coming close to buying a time-share from a competing company, said Jean Levine, they decided that the solid reputation of the Disney brand was likely to be a better investment in the long run. The Levines invested in 200 points a year, good for a period of 42 years, said Barry Levine. At the time, they paid $51 per point. Most years they use up all their points, he said. When they don't, "We've taken points and banked them to use the following year," as Disney allows owners to roll over points, provided they are used within a certain period of time.

He added that there is a site on the Internet where people will sell their unused DVC points (www.dvcbyresale.com). This gives members a way to protect their investment if they aren't able to use their banked points in the allotted time frame.[22]

Program Participants

Since 1991, Disney has sold 140,000 memberships, giving it an approximate base of 400,000+ members.[23] The company aggressively markets the program to Disney theme park and cruise ship customers. Sales representatives can be found at kiosks throughout the World Disney World Resort, giving out basic information about the DVC and offering to schedule one-on-one meetings with those interested in learning more about the program.

In addition, on each cruise ship sailing, sales representatives lead group information sessions about the program and encourage the scheduling of one-on-one meetings. Special discounts are offered to those who purchase a DVC membership while onboard a Disney cruise. Approximately 35–40% of those who attend a one-on-one DVC presentation end up investing in the program.[24]

While the majority of DVC members live outside the Orlando area, even those within driving distance of Walt Disney World find the program appealing. Kathy and Mickey O'Brien invested in DVC in 1994, while living in New Jersey. When they relocated to Leesburg, Fla., in 2002, they chose to keep their membership rather than sell it.

"We live 30 minutes from Disney, and we can't give it up," Kathy O'Brien said. Since they are so close to the parks, they have no need to stay for long stretches of time. However, they do enjoy spending an occasional night or two at one of the resorts. They have also used points toward a Disney cruise, which is one of the accommodation options allowed by the program.

One of the selling points Disney promotes at its presentations is the fact that vacation club points are transferable, which works well for the O'Briens. "We've given family and friends weekends down here, three or four days with their kids," O'Brien said. She thinks they are in the minority in doing this. "Most people don't share their points—they use them," she explained.[25]

Figure 13: Disney Vacation Club Properties

Orlando, Florida
Bay Lake Tower at Disney's Contemporary Resort
Disney's Animal Kingdom Villas
Disney's Beach Club Villas
Disney's BoardWalk Villas
Disney's Old Key West Resort
Disney's Saratoga Springs Resort & Spa
The Villas at Disney's Wilderness Lodge

Vero Beach, Florida
Disney's Vero Beach Resort

Anaheim, California
The Villas at Disney's Grand Californian Hotel & Spa

Hilton Head, South Carolina
Disney's Hilton Head Island Resort

Oahu, Hawaii
Aulani, Disney Vacation Club Villas, Ko Olina, Hawaii

Source: Disney Vacation Club, http://disneyvacationclub.disney.go.com/destinations/resorts

Expansion and Growth

At the end of 2009, Disney added 50 time-share units to its Grand Californian Hotel inside Disney's California Adventure in Anaheim, Calif. This marked the company's first West Coast DVC property. Currently, approximately 86% of DVC members live in the eastern United States. Disney's intention is to try to make the membership program more appealing to those in other parts of the country.[26]

As with Adventures by Disney, the Disney Vacation Club has felt the pinch of the recession. Nevertheless, the Disney Company continues to invest in the growth of its program in the hopes that when the economy improves, it will be ready with new properties in place.

As part of this growth, Disney will open its first facility in Hawaii in 2011. Called the Aulani, it is located in the Ko Olina Resort & Marina on the western side of Oahu. The property will include 360 hotel rooms and 481 Disney Vacation Club time-share villas.[27]

Disney also purchased 15 acres in the Washington, D.C. area in 2009, with the intention of building a similar property that could serve as a combination hotel and DVC site. At the time, there was speculation that the locale could be incorporated into the Adventures by Disney "Spirit of America" itinerary as well, which encompasses Washington, D.C., Williamsburg, and Philadelphia.[28]

Conclusion

Disney has made a strong showing in the travel and tourism industry in the last two decades, competing with much more established companies in the areas of cruising, escorted tours, and time-share vacations. The company's cruise line has expanded its fleet and itineraries since launching in the late 1990s. Likewise, the Adventures by Disney program has more than doubled its size in less than 10 years. The Disney Vacation Club has added new properties over the years to accommodate the interests of its 400,000+ members.

Disney has applied its family-friendly formula in a big way to its travel ventures. With a strong emphasis on customer service and a "something for everyone" approach, Disney has been able to meet the travel needs of people of all ages with its vacation offerings. This has contributed significantly to the popularity of these programs. ◆

Notes

1. See Jason Garcia, "Disney's Guided-Tour Business Catches Its Breath," *Orlando Sentinel*, 21 September 2009.

2. See Lucy Harding, "Disney Broadening Appeal of Cruising," *Travel Trade Gazette*, August 19,1998, 23.

3. Jeffery D. Zbar, "Disney Maps Land and Sea Strategy," *Advertising Age*, September 16, 1996, 6.

4. See Shirley Slater and Harry Basch, "Disney Sets Sail Again—and This Time It's a Wonder," *Los Angeles Times*, 17 October 1999, 9; and Jane Engle, "Disney Cruises Into San Pedro," *Los Angeles Times*, 9 May 2004, L3.

5. Christine Shenot, "Disney Cruise's Purchase of Island Sails On Through," *Orlando Sentinel*, 29 February 1996, B1.

6. "Disney Cruise Line Creating More Magic at Castaway Cay," *Leisure & Travel Week*, September 19, 2009, 40.

7. Karl Holz, public presentation at D23 Expo, Anaheim, California, September 11, 2009.

8. Elaine Dunn, in-person interview, January 20, 2010.

9. Beth Gieseking, in-person interview, January 21, 2010.

10. Holly Favazza, in-person interview, January 21, 2010.

11. Karl Holz, public presentation at D23 Expo, Anaheim, California, September 11, 2009.

12. Ibid.

13. *Disney Cruise Line Fact Sheet*, www.dclnews.com.

14. Brooks Barnes, "Disney Ventures Far From the Parks," *The New York Times*, 3 August 2008, TR3.

15. See Lori Rackl, "A Storybook Vacation; On Disney Group Tour in Germany, Fairytales Come to Life," *Chicago Sun-Times*, 9 August 2009, A16.

16. Jodi Mailander Farrell, "It's a Small World After All: New Disney Tour Company Stretches Magic Kingdom's Border to Costa Rica...and Beyond," *Miami Herald*, 29 April 2007, 1.

17. See Eileen Ogintz, "Disney Adventures Designed to De-stress, Appeal to All Ages," *The Record*, 14 September 2008, T02; and Nancy Gottfried, "Disney's Pot of Gold," *Connecticut Post Online*, 10 October 2008.

18. Matthew Link, "The World According to Mickey," *Time*, December 7, 2009, 100.

19. See "Exciting New Adventures by Disney Offer Gives Families More Vacation Time Together," *PR Newswire*, 26 October 2009; and "Adventures by Disney and Cruise Line Come Together to Create the Ultimate Mediterranean Vacation for Summer 2010," *Leisure & Travel Week*, January 2, 2010, 82.

20. Based on information from a Disney Vacation Club presentation, January 19, 2010.

21. Ibid.

22. Jean and Barry Levine, in-person interview, January 18, 2010.

23. Disney Vacation Club presentation, January 19, 2010.

24. Ibid.

25. Kathy and Mickey O'Brien, in-person interview, January 18, 2010.

26.   See "Disneyland Expands Hotel, Adds Timeshares for Increased Demand," *Orange County Register*, 19 September 2007; Sarah Tully, "Disney Debuts New Hotel Rooms; The Company Opens Its First West Coast Timeshare Units," *Orange County Register*, 24 September 2009; and Jason Garcia and Sara K. Clarke, "Disney Vacation Club Goes West," *Orlando Sentinel*, 28 September 2009.

27.   See "Aulani: A Disney Resort & Spa," Walt Disney Parks and Resorts, 2010.

28.   Thomas Heath, "Disney Buys Land for Future Resort Hotel at National Harbor," *The Washington Post*, 19 May 2009, A01.

11

Disney Sports

As Disney CEO Michael Eisner and his executive team looked for ways to stretch the entertainment holdings of the Disney Company, a move into the world of sports seemed like a natural. Sports make up one of the largest segments of the entertainment industry, encompassing both participants and spectators.[1] By adding professional and amateur sports activities into the company's growing entertainment offerings, Eisner and other Disney executives realized they had the potential to connect the dots between existing Disney properties and the vast sports industry.

Disney made its first attempt to enter the world of professional sports with the establishment of a hockey team called the Mighty Ducks in 1993. This was followed in 1995 by the purchase of the California Angels, soon renamed the Anaheim Angels. While the teams initially appeared to be a smart investment for Disney, within a few years it became evident that ownership of professional sports teams was not a good mix with the company's existing core businesses. By the mid-2000s, Disney had sold both teams and gone on to focus on other sports ventures.

One of the sports-related entities that *has* been successful for Disney is its ESPN cable television franchise. ESPN was one of the properties Disney acquired in its 1996 purchase of Capital Cities/ABC, and it has proven to be one of Disney's biggest moneymakers. While owning professional sports teams may not have lived up to the hopes and dreams of Disney executives, having the ability to broadcast the games of other teams through the ESPN network has been a tremendous boon to the Disney Company.

Disney has also has done very well in penetrating the youth and amateur sports market. Disney's Wide World of Sports complex, opened in 1997, is located on the Walt Disney World compound in Florida. It contains facilities for all kinds of sporting events and draws thousands of school and amateur groups who come to compete at the complex every year. The influx of people to the facility has also helped boost business at Disney's nearby theme parks and hotels.

One of the key events held at the complex is the annual Walt Disney World Marathon, which attracts runners from all over the world. Started in 1994, the race has been so successful for Disney that it spawned a West Coast counterpart, the Disneyland Half-Marathon, in 2006.

This chapter will look at the different dimensions of Disney's involvement in the sports market. It will assess the positives and negatives of Disney's sports-related activities over the years. It will also provide some insight into the reasons these diverse aspects of the company's sports ventures have received the reception they have from both sports and Disney fans.

Mighty Ducks

Disney's initial venture into the sports arena began with a movie. The film was called *The Mighty Ducks,* and it chronicled the trials and tribulations of a struggling hockey team that went on to win a championship. Building on the film's success, Disney proceeded to bring its fictitious team to life. The company applied for and was granted a National Hockey League (NHL) franchise to build an expansion team in 1993, in Anaheim, Calif., near Disneyland.

Marketing the Ducks

Part of the plan was to make Anaheim a "Disney destination" where visitors could come and have a full Disney entertainment experience that expanded beyond the theme park. This resulted in a highly orchestrated marketing blitz, as Disney attempted to develop the team and create a following of hockey fans and Disney fanatics who would support the company's latest enterprise.

The Mighty Ducks hockey team—named after its celluloid predecessors—played its first game on October 8, 1993. In the months leading up to the team's debut, then president of Disney Sports Enterprises, Tony Tavares, set out to build momentum with audiences and let the public know they were about to witness something they had never seen before—hockey as entertainment, not just sport.

The result was the development of Duck-related promotion and merchandising to announce the team's arrival to the public and the media. It involved a complete revamping of what hockey fans could expect to see when they attended a game. As one reporter observed at the time, "Disney looks at the Mighty Ducks as much as an entertainment spectacle as a pro sports team."[2]

Disney started by creating a "look" for the team. A logo was designed, featuring a fighting duck in bright teal, silver, and white colors. This logo was then plastered on everything from T-shirts to hockey pucks and sold well in advance of the team's opening game. That helped generate fan interest, loyalty, and pride before the players ever set their blades on the ice. The strategy resulted in the sales of millions of dollars of Mighty Ducks merchandise, and within a year, according to reporter Tom Singer, "The Mighty Ducks zoomed to the top as sports' best-selling logo."[3]

A promotion called "Operation Duck Hunt" was launched to encourage season ticket sales. As a result of this effort, the company sold out 27 of 41 home games for the team's first year.[4]

Hockey as Entertainment

Once the season began, the Mighty Ducks games became entertainment extravaganzas. According to *Orange County Register* reporter Randy Youngman, for the team's opening night at the Anaheim "Pond," the home arena for the Ducks:

> Disney spent a reported $450,000, more than the salaries of several players on the inaugural roster, for a carefully choreographed and many-times-practiced show before the franchise opener against the Detroit Red Wings on Oct. 8, 1993.[5]

Cheerleaders known as the "Decoys" cheered on the team. "Wild Wing," the team mascot, descended from the ceiling of the arena like Tinker Bell flying over Cinderella's castle. Music and laser displays filled the intervals between periods. All these activities became a regular part of each Ducks game.

To sustain ongoing interest in the team, Disney integrated the Mighty Ducks into its other Anaheim enterprise, Disneyland, wrote reporter Pablo Galarza, by having players participate in:

> ...parades, autograph sessions and the team's annual charity event at the amusement park. The concierges at the Disney-owned hotels near Disneyland push Ducks games for those guests looking for things to do. Disney also sells Duck products in 200 Disney stores throughout North America.[6]

For the first few years of the Mighty Ducks' existence, this marketing approach was extremely productive in building a following for the team, just as Disney executives had hoped. Disney then decided it was time to take its next step by making inroads into acquiring the Anaheim area's best-known sports property—the California Angels baseball team.

Anaheim Angels

The California Angels were established as an expansion team called the Los Angeles Angels in 1961, when former "singing cowboy" actor Gene Autry purchased the team for $21 million. The team was renamed California Angels in 1965, and it relocated to Anaheim, Calif., in 1966. Autry and his wife Jackie retained ownership of the team for more than 30 years, but by the 1990s, they began looking for a partner willing to invest in the team and eventually take control of its management.

Michael Eisner then approached Autry about having Disney invest in a piece of the Angels. The result was a deal that allowed Disney to acquire 25% of the team in 1995, with an option to buy the remaining 75% after Autry's death. The agreement stipulated that the Autrys would be the majority owners of the Angels, but the Disney Company would be responsible for the team's day-to-day operations.[7] After Gene Autry died in 1998, Disney did purchase the remaining interest in the team.

Awakening the Angels

From a baseball standpoint, the Angels had been considered a losing proposition for many years. Disney's CEO was hoping to change that. Eisner's vision was to create even greater synergy between the baseball and hockey teams and the Disneyland theme park.[8] Over the next few years, Disney initiated what was dubbed by reporter Peggy Hesketh as a:

...total Disney makeover: a bigger marketing budget, more community relations, new uniforms, new mascots, pregame shows, bands, videos and other entertainment designed to attract youngsters and families to the ballpark.[9]

Disney changed the name of the team from the California Angels to the Anaheim Angels in 1997, to give the team a more local focus. The biggest undertaking of the marketing effort was the renovation of Anaheim Stadium where the team played its home games. Disney invested approximately $70 million in the renovation, and the City of Anaheim contributed another $30 million.[10] The renovation included remodeled seating and the construction of a theme park-like fountain and waterfall at the far end of the stadium.

Marketing Missteps

The company then set about incorporating many of the same marketing strategies it had used in promoting the Mighty Ducks. Despite the similarity of these practices, however, the results were drastically different. What had been an effective formula for the hockey crowd didn't work quite as well for baseball fans, according to an article in the *Wall Street Journal.*

Disney added new attractions right away. A Dixieland band tooted on the dugouts. (Fans complained.) Rock music replaced the organist. (Fans complained.) Disney renamed the team the Anaheim Angels and unveiled periwinkle-pinstriped uniforms. The discontent peaked when fans learned that next year top ticket prices [would] be raised to help finance a $108 million renovation of Anaheim stadium.[11]

One explanation was that the Mighty Ducks were a novelty, a new addition to the southern California sports scene. For that reason, the hype used to stimulate curiosity and fan interest had worked. The Angels, on the other hand, were a well-known organization, as well as part of a sports institution—baseball—that was viewed with greater sanctity than hockey.

Consequently, local baseball fans were not at all amused by the "Disneyfication" of their sport. What had initially seemed to be a good business idea was quickly eroding into a question about whether or not Disney should even be in the sports business at all.

The Magic Ends

By the end of the 1990s, things were looking bleak for both the Angels *and* the Mighty Ducks. While the hockey team had started off with a bang, after several seasons, the novelty began to wear off, and fans lost interest in attending games and purchasing team-related merchandise.

Part of this was attributed to the fact that the team just wasn't that good. While Disney had invested heavily in the entertainment activities that accompanied each game, the company had been reluctant to spend money on hiring the caliber of athletes needed to produce a winning team. The more games the team lost, the more fan interest declined. By 2002, the Mighty Ducks had "the lowest attendance in the NHL," according to an article in the *Wall Street Journal.*[12]

The same was true of the Anaheim Angels. While so much effort was put into the marketing of the team, little attention was paid to the team itself, noted the same article.

> Disney spent $5 million on advertising in 1998, the first season in the new park, and attracted around 750,000 more fans than the previous year. But attendance tumbled 21% the next three seasons as the team finished last in its division in 1999 and next to last in 2000 and 2001.[13]

Some critics pointed out that Disney didn't really understand the nature of sports. While the entertainment aspects of the hockey and baseball games may have made them fun and helped boost merchandise sales, that didn't replace the fans' desires to see their teams win.

As reporter David Shoalts explained, "Sports franchises may serve to spin money for their owners, but they are also public trusts. Fans allow themselves to be exploited only because they believe the owner is doing everything possible to make the team a winner."[14] In the case of Disney, he said, winning did not appear to be a priority.

Selling Off the Teams

In fall of 2002, Disney began actively seeking buyers for both the Mighty Ducks and the Anaheim Angels. Ironically, the news was announced just as the Angels finally made it into the post-season baseball playoffs for the first time since 1986.[15] They went on to win the World Series in October 2002.

This achievement made them an attractive purchase. Soon after the World Series, Disney sold the Angels in 2003 to businessman Arturo "Arte" Moreno for $184 million. With the purchase, Moreno became the first Hispanic to own a U.S. major sports team.[16]

Then, in 2005, the company sold the Mighty Ducks for $75 million to Henry Samueli, the owner of the arena where the Ducks played.[17] Two years later, the Ducks—by then renamed the Anaheim Ducks—won the Stanley Cup for the first time.

Disney's attempt at professional sports ownership had not gone well. But the company's experiment with the Ducks and the Angels was not to be its last hurrah in an attempt to penetrate the sports industry. Other sports-related activities would follow and were to prove far more successful for the company.

ESPN

Around the same time the Disney Company was diving into the sports field with its two teams, it also received the unanticipated benefit of a sports-related windfall. As discussed in Chapter 6, when Disney purchased Capital Cities/ABC in 1996, the sale included a cable channel franchise called the Entertainment and Sports Programming Network, better known as ESPN.

Development of a Sports Powerhouse

ESPN was founded in 1979 in Bristol, Conn., by Will Rasmussen and his son Scott Rasmussen, a New England sports broadcaster, started the channel to broadcast University of Connecticut sporting events and New England Whalers hockey games.[18] Getty Oil bought the channel shortly after its founding and held on to it until 1984, when the company sold it to ABC. Eventually, ABC sold 20% of ESPN to Nabisco, which in turn sold its share to the Hearst Corporation.

In the interim, ESPN established itself as a 24/7 quality programmer of major sporting events. In the years following the sale to ABC, ESPN negotiated deals with the National Football League (NFL) to broadcast Sunday night games, as well as with Major League Baseball (MLB). This put the cable channel "in the big leagues," as the saying goes, by allowing it to compete with existing network sports programming.

By the mid-1990s, ESPN was broadcasting all over the world. The company had also launched ESPN Radio and ESPNET SportsZone, which evolved into ESPN.com.[19] When the Disney Company purchased Capital Cities/ABC in 1996, ESPN came as part of the package. This coincided with Disney's efforts in developing a presence in the world of sports.

Figure 14: The Wide World of ESPN

Television
- ESPN on ABC
- ESPN 3D
- 6 U.S. cable networks
- 46 international networks in seven continents

Radio
- ESPN Radio
- ESPN Deportes Radio
- Syndicated in 11 countries

Online
- ESPN.com
- ESPNDeportes.com

Broadband
- ESPN3.com

Publishing
- ESPN The Magazine
- ESPN Books

Wireless
- ESPN Mobile Properties

ESPN Zone
- Restaurants, games, retail

Source: ESPN Fact Sheet, http://espnmediazone3.com/wpmu

Integration and Reorganization

ABC was no stranger itself to sports programming. For many years, the network had been known for programs such as *Monday Night Football* and the *ABC Wide World of Sports*, featuring sports broadcasting legends such as Howard Cosell and Jim McKay and orchestrated by ABC Sports president Roone Arledge. When Disney bought ABC and got ESPN in the bargain, questions arose about plans for the future of both ABC Sports and ESPN.

Between 1996 and 2006, Disney slowly began integrating the two entities. ESPN announcers made regular appearances on ABC Sports. The two companies merged their sales departments and later their marketing and production units.[20]

In the fall of 2006, the blending of the two sports channels was officially completed with the announcement that ESPN would become "the overarching brand for all sports programming carried on the ABC Television Network," according to *Sports Illustrated*.[21] "ESPN said the new approach will cover all of the sports programming on ABC, encompassing all aspects of the production effort including on-air look, graphics and branding."[22] The name for the new venture was to be "ESPN on ABC."

Did You Know?

ABC Wide World of Sports was originally intended to be a summer replacement series. Instead, it became part of ABC's regular programming and stayed on the air for 40 years.

To some viewers and sports programming professionals, this change marked the end of an era. To others, such as ABC Sports veteran Frank Gifford, it appeared inevitable.[23] George Bodenheimer, co-chairman of Disney Media Networks and president of ESPN, explained that the move was ultimately an opportunity to better serve fans.[24]

Others, such as *Sports Illustrated* reporter Richard Deitsch, surmised it was a means of reaching out to a younger demographic. He said, "Do not underestimate the impact of the 18 to 34 crowd in this decision. Changing the name to ESPN on ABC appeals to younger viewers who identify sports only through ESPN."[25]

A Leader in the Field

Despite the differences of opinion about the change, members of the media and the sports community were in agreement about the fact that since its founding in 1979, ESPN had become a powerhouse that eclipsed the once reverent status of ABC Sports. As an article in the *Washington Times* noted:

> ESPN...has become a multi-billion dollar behemoth, a standard offering for nearly every cable and satellite company in America. Moreover, the network no longer is just a broadcaster of events and news but is an essential partner to nearly every sports league.[26]

Today, ESPN has expanded to include multiple channels, including one for news and one for college sports; international coverage in 200 countries; ESPN Radio; *ESPN The Magazine*; and several ESPN Zone sport-themed restaurants. The company also opened a production facility in Los Angeles in 2009.[27]

For Disney, all of this has translated into significant dollars. As an article in *Barron's* explained, "ESPN is by far the most valuable asset within Disney and perhaps in all of media."[28] This has enabled Disney to maintain a respectable presence in the world of professional sports.

Disney Wide World of Sports Complex

Perhaps the most noteworthy of Disney's sports-related activities in the last decade and a half has been the company's investment in youth and amateur sports.

Florida Sports Complex

In 1993, Disney announced plans to construct a sports complex in the vicinity of its Florida theme parks. According to information released by the company, the project was intended to "attract thousands of sports enthusiasts from around the world to Central Florida" and establish a "new center for all kinds of amateur athletes."[29]

Initial plans for the complex included a baseball stadium, playing fields, indoor basketball arena, and facilities for golf, tennis, volleyball, track and field, and other indoor and outdoor sports.[30]

When it opened in 1997, the complex was originally called Disney's Wide World of Sports in a tip of the hat to ABC *Wide World of Sports*, which was still going strong at the time. In conjunction with the creation of the facility, the Amateur Athletic Union (AAU) relocated its headquarters from Indianapolis to Orlando to work with Disney to help fill the complex with athletes. The AAU is a nonprofit sports organization that promotes sports programs by sponsoring a variety of competitive athletic events.[31]

Partnering with AAU was key to Disney's ability to develop and promote its new complex. Disney offered AAU office space on its Florida grounds, while the nonprofit organized events at the complex likely to draw crowds to the area.[32] Currently, AAU sponsors more than 40 events a year on the Disney property.[33]

Did You Know?

The Atlanta Braves inaugurated what is now Champion Stadium at Disney's Florida sports complex with an exhibition game against the Cincinnati Reds on March 28, 1997.

Corporate Sponsorships

Over the years, Disney has also partnered with major sponsors who have purchased naming rights to the different pieces of the sports complex. The 5,500 seat arena, for example, was called the Milk House, a result of a deal struck with the Milk Processor Education Program, creators of the "Got Milk?" campaign.[34]

In 2002, the facility's 9,500-seat baseball stadium was dubbed Cracker Jack stadium as part of an arrangement with PepsiCo's Frito Lay, maker of the popular snack food. The stadium was renamed the Champion Stadium a few years later when a deal with Hanesbrands Inc. superceded the arrangement with PepsiCo.[35]

Youth Sports Programs

According to the Disney Company, the sports complex plays host to more than 200 sporting events a year. "Nearly two million athletes from more than

70 different countries have competed at the sports complex in front of millions of spectators since the venue opened in March 1997."[36] In addition to accommodating competitions organized by AAU, the complex serves as a training facility for high school and college students each year during their spring breaks.[37]

Craig Stein is the assistant coach of the varsity baseball team at Cheltenham High School in Cheltenham, Penn. Each spring, he and his coaching colleagues bring a group of 20 students to the Walt Disney World Resort to play at the sports complex.

"They have a program for high school sports teams to come down and use the facilities to practice and get practice games and scrimmage games while you're down there," he explained. [38]

The cost of the program includes accommodations, transportation to the field, and a three-day Park Hopper pass for each student. They've also been able to arrange for meal plans at Disney's eateries. Generally, Stein said, they will play three or four games and do another three or four practices. He and his colleagues let the students practice and play during the day so they can go to the parks in the evening.

> The nice thing about Disney is that everything is so self-contained. We don't have to worry about renting a bus. They can eat when they want. We don't have to worry about them getting into trouble or getting alcohol. That's really for us the biggest advantage to Disney. They really try to maintain a nice, family atmosphere and just shoot for having fun. For us, it's been a great experience.[39]

Drawing a Crowd

Although primarily equipped for amateur and youth sporting groups, two professional sports teams have also made use of the facility. The Atlanta Braves hold spring training in the Champion Stadium ballpark each spring. The Tampa Bay Buccaneers also hold their summer training camp at the complex. Both teams attract spectators to their games and practice sessions.

Drawing crowds to the area was a big incentive behind Disney's development of the Wide World of Sports complex, and that has proven its worth in gold, according to an article in the *Orlando Sentinel*.

Every event brings business to Disney World's four theme parks and 22 hotels, creating an economic boon for Central Florida.... Many guests stay at the Disney resort, spend money at Disney's eateries and visit Disney theme parks, a price tag that easily could top more than $1,000 for a family of four over a week's stay. The result? A strategic corporate integration of sports and leisure.[40]

Disney has four hotels near the sports complex that are priced below a number of the other resorts on the Walt Disney World property, and many of the school groups that come to compete stay in these facilities. One is appropriately named the "All Star Sports Resort."

Merchandising Programs

There is also the inevitable merchandising benefit that accompanies the crowds, noted an article in the *Orlando Business Journal*. "For every one of the events at Disney's Wide World of Sports, there's a separate line of merchandise. And that merchandise is purchased by about 90 percent of the people attending sporting events at the complex."[41]

For the high school teams that use the facilities, for example, "They print up T-shirts for each of the sports that are going on that lists all the schools that are coming down that year," Craig Stein said. These are then offered for sale to the student athletes.[42]

Rebranding and Expansion

As a means of strengthening the synergy between the company's Wide World of Sports complex and its well-known ESPN franchise, in 2010, Disney re-branded the sports facility as the ESPN Wide World of Sports complex.[43] *Orlando Sentinel* reporter Jason Garcia assessed the strategic thinking behind the move.

Disney hopes the association with ESPN—one of the best-known brands on the planet—will help it lure larger and more varied athletic events to Wide World of Sports...as a way to drive new traffic to its theme parks and hotels.... Disney will add in each of its nearly 30,000 hotel rooms a cable-TV channel devoted to events at Wide World of Sports.... For ESPN, developing a bigger presence at Disney World is part of an effort to reach out to younger athletes and sports fans—all potential future viewers.[44]

The change prompted further expansion of the sports complex facilities, including the addition of a 100-lane bowling alley. This paved the way for a partnership between Disney and the U.S. Bowling Congress, which sponsors annual events that draw 80,000 people a year—more potential customers for the Disney parks.[45]

ESPN planned to retain its headquarters in Bristol, Conn. However, in late 2009, the sports broadcasting company opened an ESPN Innovation Lab at the Wide World of Sports complex, designed to add a touch of sports-related Imagineering to the existing facility.[46] The lab was to be used to help develop 3-D technology, as well as "test a variety of cutting-edge on-air telecast applications by using the sporting events held at the complex year-round," explained an article in the *Osceola News Gazette*.[47]

One new feature has been the addition of cameras all over the complex to film the different games going on. These are then edited for participants to see. "You can sit and watch the clips and see your team playing its game," said Stein. This has proven to be a big hit with his ballplayers.[48]

Disney Marathons

Disney's sports complex has been the site of hundreds of events, and one of these is an annual marathon. Soon after the wheels were set in motion to build the Florida complex in the early 1990s, Disney announced plans for its first public sporting event—a Walt Disney World Marathon.

Walt Disney World Marathon

The initial 26.2 mile race was to take place on the Walt Disney World grounds, with runners passing through the company's theme parks and hotel properties. At the time, company executives were hoping the mild Florida weather and Disney sponsorship of the race would combine to make the event attractive for both professional and amateur runners from all over the world.

Approximately 8,000 people participated on January 16, 1994, in the first of what was to be many Disney marathons. Since 1994, the race has been held annually, and the crowds have grown significantly.

Today the Walt Disney World Marathon is ranked by the Association of International Marathons and Distance Races (AIMDR) as one of the 10 largest marathons in the country and the top 15 in the world.[49] In January 2010, approximately 24,000 runners competed in the race.[50]

Over the years, Disney added other activities and turned the annual gathering into a two-day weekend event. In addition to the full marathon held on a Sunday, the program now features a half-marathon on the previous Saturday, a 5K Family Fun Run, a Kids' Fest race, and a Health and Fitness Expo. There is also a "Goofy Race and a Half Challenge," for die-hard runners who want to run the half-marathon one day and the full marathon the next.[51]

As initially hoped, runners come from all over the world to participate in the weekend festivities. Runners have come from all 50 states and 34 different countries. The marathon is also used as a fundraiser for the Leukemia and Lymphoma Society and raises approximately $7 million in donations.[52]

Disneyland Marathon

Building on the success of the Florida race, Disney introduced an annual half-marathon at its Disneyland Resort in Anaheim, Calif., in 2006. The 13.1 mile course goes through Disneyland and California Adventure as well as through parts of the City of Anaheim.

In the race's inaugural year, 12,000 runners participated, while another 3,000 took part in a Family Fun Run and Kids' race. By 2010, half marathon numbers had increased to 14,000 runners from 50 states and 16 countries.[53]

Dara Vazin was one of the participants in the first Disneyland half-marathon in 2006. She became aware of the race through a running club she belonged to and decided to give it a try.

> I wanted to challenge myself. It was something fun and interactive. Knowing it was Disney made it even more appealing. There were other races I could have done, and Disney was a little more expensive. But, I knew it would be organized well, and it would be fun with all the characters.[54]

Vazin was impressed by how well-orchestrated all the details of the race were. "You felt safe, you felt like you were in good hands, and even though it was early and you weren't quite awake, it was fun," she explained.[55]

Both the Walt Disney World and Disneyland Marathons work well to bring crowds to the parks during the off-season—January in the case of Disney World, and September in the case of Disneyland. Those cheering on the runners add to the crowd. They also fill Disney hotels and increase attendance at the theme parks before and after each race. In many regards, the marathons at both Disney properties have been winning propositions for the company.

Runner Dara Vazin shows off the medal and T-shirt she received for participating in the first annual half-marathon held at the Disneyland Resort in 2006.

Conclusion

Since the 1990s, Disney has dabbled in several different areas of the sports industry in an attempt to find its niche in the marketplace. While ownership of professional sports teams was not good for business, covering sports through the company's well-known ESPN cable television brand has proven to be extremely profitable.

Likewise, a venture into the youth and amateur sports market has been a better fit for the company in integrating sports into its existing core entertainment businesses. As a result of these two ventures, Disney has been able to have a respectable impact on the wide world of sports. ♦

Notes

1.   See Andi Stein and Beth Evans, *An Introduction to the Entertainment Industry* (New York: Peter Lang Publishing, 2009): 153.

2.   John Horn, "Disney Has Mighty Marketing Effort for Mighty Ducks," *Seattle Times*, 26 September 1993, C1.

3.   Tom Singer, "Ducks for Bucks," *Orange County Metropolitan*, 15 October 1994, 22.

4.   Ibid. Also see Horn, "Disney Has Mighty Marketing Effort for Mighty Ducks," C1.

5.   Randy Youngman, "Saluting The Pond in Its Waning Days," *Orange County Register*, 2 October 2006, 1.

6.   Pablo Galarza, "The Mighty Bucks," *Financial World* 164:25 (December 5, 1995): 28.

7.   See Dave Cunningham, "Disney Buys into Angels," *Press-Telegram*, 19 May 1995, S1.

8.   See Thomas R. Ring, "Disney to Acquire 25% of Baseball's California Angels," *Wall Street Journal*, 19 May 1995, B12.

9.   Peggy Hesketh, "Disney to Triple Angels' Marketing, Target New Fans," *Orange County Business Journal* 19:23 (June 3, 1996): 1.

10.   See Howard Fine, "Disney and Sports," *Orange County Business Journal*, August 12, 1996, 1.

11.   Stefan Fatsis, "Money-Losing Angels Seem Immune to Disney Magic," *Wall Street Journal*, 19 September 1997, B1.

12.   Stefan Fatsis and Bruce Orwall, "Throwing in the Towel: For Disney, Owning Teams Conflicts With Bottom Line Media," *Wall Street Journal*, 29 August 2002, A1.

13.   Ibid.

14.   David Shoalts, "Sport Doesn't Belong in Disney World," *The Globe and Mail*, 21 November 2001, S3.

15.   See Christopher Grimes, "Disney in Talks to Sell Sports Franchises," *Financial Times*, 27 September 2002, 1.

16.   See "Historical Moments, Los Angeles Angels of Anaheim," *Sports E-Cyclopedia*, http://www.sportsecyclopedia.com/al/anaca/angels.html.

17.   See "League Approves Sale of Mighty Ducks," *Daily Breeze*, 17 June 2005, D2.

18.   See "ESPN, Inc.," *Encyclopedia Britannica 2010*, http://www.britannica.com/EBchecked/topic/ 192762/ESPN-Inc>.

19.   "ESPN's 30th Anniversary: Fact Sheet," http://www.espnmediazone.

20.   See Richard Sandomir, "ABC Sports Is Dead at 45; Stand By for ESPN," *The New York Times*, 11 August 2006, D2.

21.   Richard Deitsch, "Worldwide Leader Expands," *SI.com*, August 11, 2006.

22.   Ibid.

23.   See Sandomir, "ABC Sports Is Dead at 45; Stand By for ESPN," D2.

24.   See Paul J. Gough, "Goodbye ABC Sports, Hello ESPN on ABC," *MSNBC.com*, August 12, 2006.

25.   Deitsch, "Worldwide Leader Expands," August 11, 2006.

26.   Tim Lemke, "ESPN Evolves With New Media," *Washington Times*, 24 September 2006, A01.

27.   See "ESPN's 30th Anniversary: 30 Facts About ESPN," http://www.espnmediazone.

28.   Michael Santoli, "The Magic's Back," *Barron's* 88:8 (February 25, 2008): 27.

29.   "Walt Disney World Announces International Sports Center," PR *Newswire*, 19 November 1993, 1.

30.   Ibid.
31.   See Amateur Athletic Union website, www.aausports.org.
32.   See Alan Byrd, "Disney Has Designs on More Than AAU," *Orlando Business Journal* 11:16 (September 23-29, 1994): 5.
33.   Amateur Athletic Union website, www.aausports.org.
34.   Alan Byrd, "Waterhouse, Move Over: The Milk House Is Here," *Orlando Business Journal* 17:49 (May 18, 2001): 14.
35.   See Barry Janoff, "Disney's Quest to Brand and Market Its Sports Division Is a Complex Matter," *Brandweek* 44:3 (January 20, 2003): 10; and "Hanesbrands Inc. and the Walt Disney Parks and Resorts Announce Multiyear Strategic Marketing Alliance," *Business Wire*, 31 October 2007.
36.   "Disney's Wide World of Sports Complex Fact Sheet," Walt Disney World Public Affairs, 2010, http://www.wdwpublicaffairs.com. See also ESPN Wide World of Sports website, http://espnwwos.disney.go.com.
37.   See Doug Smith, "And They Will Come," *USA Today*, 10 September 2008, 01C.
38.   Craig Stein, in-person interview, July 11, 2010.
39.   Ibid.
40.   Andrew Astleford, "Spanning the Globe: Disney's Wide World Complex Has Seen It All During Its 10-Year Run," *Orlando Sentinel*, 1 April 2007, 1.
41.   Alan Byrd, "Disney Sports Rolls Out New Logo, Merchandise," *Orlando Business Journal* 16:4 (June 25-July 1, 1999): 3.
42.   Craig Stein, in-person interview, July 11, 2010.
43.   See "America's Youth Athletes to Enter All New 'World' at ESPN Wide World of Sports Complex at Disney," *Business Wire*, 25 February 2010.
44.   Jason Garcia, "ESPN to Rule at Disney Venue," *Orlando Sentinel*, 6 November 2009, A1.
45.   See Mark Albright, "Disney Adds ESPN Cachet," *St. Petersburg Times*, 25 September, B4.
46.   See "ESPN Innovation Lab Opens Today at ESPN Wide World of Sports," *Business Wire*, 16 October 2009.
47.   Peter Covino, "Sports-plex at Disney Now Has ESPN Tag," *Osceola News Gazette*, 3 March 2010. See also Andrea Adelson, "ESPN Puts Name on Complex," *Orlando Sentinel*, 26 February 2010, C7.
48.   Craig Stein, in-person interview, July 11, 2010.
49.   Association of International Marathons and Distance Races website, http://www.aimsworldrunning.org/statistics/World's_Largest_Marathons.html.
50.   Kyle Hightower, "Bastos Snares 6th Race in Row at Chilly Disney," *Orlando Sentinel*, 11 January 2010, C3.
51.   See "Walt Disney Marathon Weekend," ESPN Wide World of Sports website, http://espnwwos.disney.go.com/events/wdw-marathon.
52.   Ibid.
53.   See "Inaugural Disneyland Half Marathon to Take Thousands of Runners on Magical 13.1-Mile Experience Through Disneyland Resort and Streets of Anaheim," *PR Newswire*, 14 September 2006; and "Paul Ngeny, 31, of Auburn, Calif., Wins Fifth Annual Disneyland Half Marathon," *PR Newswire*, 5 September 2010.
54.   Dara Vazin, in-person interview, April 10, 2010.
55.   Ibid.

12

Disney Home Entertainment and Interactive Media

The popularity of Disney stories and characters has enabled them to go beyond the films and television programs for which they were originally developed. Over time, Disney properties have been repackaged for a variety of home entertainment and interactive media. The evolution of technology has contributed toward making Disney media accessible through a wide range of formats. These include DVDs, home computers, mobile phones, and digital books.

The home video market blossomed in the 1980s with the advent of videocassette recorders (VCRs). Disney took advantage of this trend by repackaging some of its classic films and making them available for home viewing. The emergence of DVD and Blu-ray technology has allowed the company to refine and enhance these films to make them even more appealing to audiences.

Since the mid-1990s, Disney has maintained an online presence with its Disney.com website. Today the site is an electronic gateway to the wonderful world of Disney, offering users the opportunity to watch videos, learn about their favorite characters, play games, and interact with other Disney fans online.

A growing interest in online interaction has led the company to develop social networking sites and virtual world programs that feature some of the organization's biggest franchises. Disney has also developed a line of video games based on its films, TV shows, and characters, which can be played on home computers as well as mobile devices.

While not as technologically sophisticated as other media, print products such as books, magazines, and comics also offer Disney audiences a form of home entertainment. Disney's publishing division is rooted in the company's past but also has made inroads into the future with the introduction of a new digital book program.

This chapter will explore the different versions of home entertainment and interactive media the Disney Company has created for its audiences and fans. It will discuss the various types of home entertainment media produced by Disney and explain how they have evolved over time to keep people engaged and entertained in their own living rooms.

Home Video and DVDs

While the theatrical releases of Disney films have traditionally comprised a large portion of the company's bottom line, since the early 1980s, the sale of home videocassettes and DVDs has added significantly to this bottom line. Technological innovations and changing audience tastes have led to a shift in people's viewing habits. This has turned the home entertainment video and DVD market into a billion dollar business.[1]

Initial Market Entry

Compared to other Hollywood studios, Disney was initially a late bloomer when it came to the home video market. The company began packaging pieces of its vast film library for sale and rental in the early 1980s under the watch of former Disney CEO Ron Miller.

Miller and others in the company at the time were reluctant to release the company's more popular feature films, however. They were afraid the products would dilute the economic impact of the company's practice of re-releasing its classic animated features to theaters every seven years. Consequently, some of the early video releases included lesser-known live action films and animated features such as *Dumbo* and *Alice in Wonderland*, which had not exhibited as much box office muscle as some of the company's other films.

When Michael Eisner and Frank Wells took over the reins of the company in 1984, they recognized the potential capital that was to be realized by releasing to video more of Disney's film library, which was estimated to be worth approximately $400 million. The home video market was growing by leaps and bounds, and Disney had the chance to jump on the bandwagon.[2]

By 1985, the company had begun remastering many of its films to prepare them for release on video and developing large-scale advertising campaigns to promote these releases with great fanfare. The move, as predicted, proved extremely profitable for the company.[3]

Disney employed the same strategy it had used with the theater releases of its films. The movies were released on video for a certain window of time, heavily promoted during this time period, and then relegated to the Disney "vault" for a number of years before they were to be released again for the next generation of children.

Direct-to-Video Releases

By the mid 1990s, the company had also begun a practice of releasing direct-to-video sequels of some of its newer animated films such as *Aladdin, Beauty and the Beast, Pocahontas,* and *Mulan.* To the surprise of many in the industry, this approach was well received by Disney audiences, explained an article in *Discount Store News,* written during the program's initial phase.

> Once scoffed at, direct-to-video children's titles have been elevated to a high art form at Disney's home video division.... At Disney, direct-to-video titles help feed the demand for new adventures of already popular franchises and have all but replaced theatrical sequels, thus freeing up the company's theatrical movie division to develop new blockbusters.[4]

The resulting success of this approach led Disney executives to begin creating sequels of older classics, resulting in direct-to-video films such as *Lady and the Tramp II: Scamp's Adventure* (2001); *Cinderella II: Dreams Come True* (2002); and *Bambi II* (2006).

The Impact of DVDs

As the home video market began to shift from VHS cassettes to DVDs in the late 1990s, Disney was forced to readjust its approach to distributing films for this market. In 1999, Disney announced plans to release many of its titles on DVD and make them available to the public on a permanent basis rather than continue with the limited release timetable used for its VHS cassettes. This resulted in a vast number of Disney animated and live action titles suddenly becoming available to consumers.

At the same time, the company announced that 10 of its more popular animated films would continue to be held back and released on a 10-year cycle. These were dubbed the Platinum Collection and included classics such as *Snow White and the Seven Dwarfs, Cinderella, The Little Mermaid,* and *Beauty and the Beast.*[5] One film from the collection was to be released each year.

The strategy behind this approach was to generate significant buzz and excitement around each film's release and to use the opportunity to develop tailor-made marketing and merchandising campaigns to accompany the debut of each Platinum Collection video.

Disney's first release was *Snow White and the Seven Dwarfs* in October 2001. It was supplemented by a marketing campaign that included tie-ins to the Disney Channel, ABC, Radio Disney, and Disney's various theme parks.[6] The strategy worked—on the first day of its availability, *Snow White* sold one million copies, more than any other home video release.[7]

When *Cinderella* was released a few years later, it, too, was accompanied by a promotional blitz that included "a TV campaign and a national sweepstakes [with] a $75,000 prize and the opportunity to build a Disney Princess bedroom, courtesy of Home Depot," noted *Brandweek* reporter Todd Wasserman.[8] The release also included "a flood of new *Cinderella* merch[andise], including bedding, stationery, books, footwear and toys."[9]

Disney ultimately modified its approach to the Platinum Collection. Beginning in 2003, the company began releasing two films from the collection each year rather than just one. It also adjusted the films' release schedule, so movies would become available every seven years rather than every 10 years.[10]

Value-Added Material

Part of Disney's initial success with its DVD line was the ability to include bonus features to supplement the main film. This was crucial in marketing the films to parents who may have already owned VHS copies of the movies.

When Disney released the 60th anniversary edition of *Dumbo* on DVD, for example, one of the bonus features was a segment about the original Dumbo ride at Disneyland and how it had been refurbished and redesigned. A crew was sent to film the ride and interview park visitors about what the ride meant to them, explained composer Joe Alfuso, who worked on the musical portion of the segment.

"It was a very touching moment," Alfuso said. People talked about how they rode the Dumbo ride as children and now brought their own children and grandchildren to Disneyland to ride it. "They also had cool footage of the ride before it was redesigned and then morphed that into the present-day Dumbo ride," he explained.

Alfuso scored the segment to *Baby Mine*, the well-known lullaby from the *Dumbo* film. "It was very tender, very nice," he said.[11]

As one Disney executive noted:

> Value-added material is critically important. A lot of our customers already have a large Disney video library. Additional features are very instrumental in helping parents feel good about upgrading, building a DVD library. It's a whole new experience.[12]

Twenty-First-Century Technology

With the advent of high definition television and Blu-ray discs, Disney modified its approach to home video sales once again. The company released its first Blu-ray disc with the 50th anniversary edition of *Sleeping Beauty* in 2008.

Then in 2009, Disney announced a new series called the Diamond Collection. It was to include 14 titles to be released over a period of time in Blu-ray format, including several that were already part of the Platinum Collection.

Once again, *Snow White and the Seven Dwarfs* launched the series. It debuted at the top of the national video sales charts when it was released in October 2009.[13]

The impact of the recession in the late 2000s began to have a negative effect on Disney DVD sales, causing the company to explore other options for bolstering its home entertainment sector. One idea currently in development is called "Keychest." It involves allowing consumers to purchase a Disney movie that can then be viewed on multiple platforms including computers, DVD players, and mobile phones, explained reporter Ethan Smith.

"Keychest would essentially reinvent the notion of what it means for a consumer to buy a movie by redefining ownership as access rights, not possession of a physical product like a DVD."[14] At the time of this writing, Disney was still in the discussion stages with its cable distributors and online retailers about the economic feasibility of Keychest.[15]

Figure 15: Disney Platinum and Diamond Collections

Disney Platinum Collection DVDs

Film	Release Date
Snow White and the Seven Dwarfs	2001
Beauty and the Beast	2002
The Lion King	2003
Aladdin	2004
Bambi	2005
Cinderella	2005
Lady and the Tramp	2006
The Little Mermaid	2006
Peter Pan	2007
The Jungle Book	2007
101 Dalmatians	2008
Sleeping Beauty	2008
Pinocchio	2009

Source: UltimateDisney, http://www.dvdizzy.com/disneyreleasetypes.html

Disney Diamond Collection Blu-ray

Film	Release Date
Snow White and the Seven Dwarfs	2009
Beauty and the Beast	2010
Bambi	2011
The Lion King	2011

Source: Blu-ray.com, http://www.blu-ray.com/news/?id=4757

Disney Online

Disney's Interactive Media Group includes two divisions that loom large in the company's home entertainment activities. Disney Interactive Studios produces video games for personal computers and mobile devices, while Disney Online manages the company's websites.

The Disney.com website is a key part of the company's interactive media presence in addition to being a crucial marketing tool for the organization. Disney first launched a website in 1996, but it has only been in recent years that the site has been highly developed.

One of CEO Bob Iger's goals upon assuming his position was to upgrade the company's use of interactive technologies to reach today's tech-savvy youth. This resulted in a major overhaul of the website in 2007, and an additional tweaking in 2008.

The revamped version of the website has played an important role in helping Iger accomplish his goal. In July 2009, the site was ranked as the number one community-family and parenting site on the web with close to 34 million viewers.[16]

Part of the site's appeal is that it allows users to multitask. As *Wall Street Journal* reporter Merissa Marr explained, "Disney.com…is Disney's take on social networking for mainstream America. In it, kids can chat while watching video clips, listening to music and playing a game, all at the same time."[17]

Online Gaming

Disney.com features a variety of options to keep its audiences entertained, including numerous interactive games, which hold great appeal for tween users, according to one Disney executive.

> This group is all about gaming. It's by far the most popular activity across Disney online, whether it's games linked to films or characters, or games in virtual worlds. That's what they come to the sites for and what they're expecting to see.[18]

Running a close second are the video clips featured on the site that include "extras" from Disney's films and TV shows, he noted.

Creative Activities

The company regularly updates the website and adds new features to compensate for the short attention span of its youthful audience. Some features are designed to promote innovation and creativity. A mini-site within the site called Create, for example, offers users a chance to paint onscreen using an assortment of electronic artists' tools.[19]

Another feature called The Possibility Shop contains a video series from the Jim Henson Company that offers ideas on artistic projects children and families can work on at home.[20] This is the kind of programming that might have been delivered in the form of an educational television series in the past and underscores the movement of today's youngsters away from traditional media and toward their computer screens.

Disney Online Mom and Family

In addition to reaching out to children through Disney.com, Disney uses other websites to connect with parents, particularly mothers of small children. In 2009, the company purchased a series of parenting websites from Kaboose, Inc., and bundled them as the Disney Online Mom and Family Portfolio. They include DisneyFamily.com, a general interest parenting site; Babyzone.com, for expectant and new mothers; Kaboose.com, offering information on crafts and other activities for children; and DisneyFamilyFun.com, an offshoot of the company's magazine of the same name.[21]

Social Networking and Virtual Worlds

In the last few years, Disney has had to work to keep up with some of its competitors to develop a social networking presence to compete with sites such as Webkinz and Neopets. The company has tried to accomplish this by purchasing existing social networking sites and developing some of its own.

Club Penguin

Disney made significant inroads into the market when it purchased Club Penguin in 2007. Founded by three fathers from British Columbia, Club Penguin is one of the most popular social networking sites for the preteen set.

Disney inked a deal with the site's creators that offered them $350 million upfront and another $350 million if the site met certain growth targets by 2010.[22] At the time of the purchase, the site had 700,000 users. According to the *Wall Street Journal*, Club Penguin offers users:

> ...the ability to customize their own penguin in an online community. Armed with their penguin avatars, children can chat with their friends, play games and earn coins to buy items such as furnishings for their igloo homes.[23]

While the site is free, advanced features can only be accessed for a subscription fee of $5.95 a month.

Club Penguin has been expanded to reach 190 countries in four languages—English, French, Spanish, and Portuguese. While the site has added to Disney's social networking capabilities as expected, the economic recession of the late 2000s led to a decline in site traffic.

As a result, by 2010, Club Penguin did not meet the target set by Disney as an incentive for the second half of payment to the site's founders—ultimately saving Disney $350 million in payouts.[24]

Pirates of the Caribbean Online

As a tie-in to the company's successful *Pirates of the Caribbean* film franchise, Disney launched a *Pirates of the Caribbean* virtual world site in 2007. The site, primarily aimed at boys, offered users a chance to customize their own swashbuckler avatars and take part in virtual pirate battles on the high seas.

To help promote the site at the end of its first year, Disney launched a first-anniversary celebration that included a video contest. Players were asked to "submit a short video documenting how much they love Pirates Online and demonstrating how they 'Live the Pirates Life.'"[25]

Since its launch, the Pirates site has been plagued by technical issues, which have affected the site's traffic, according to the *Los Angeles Times*. Between 2008 and 2009, the number of users fell from 500,000 to 192,000, resulting in a need to retool the program.[26]

Pixie Hollow

Disney has had better success with a virtual world program based on its Disney Fairies franchise. Pixie Hollow debuted in 2008 in conjunction with the release of the direct-to-video film, *Tinker Bell*. The program allows users to take on a fairy identity and maneuver around Tinker Bell's online fairy world. Like Club Penguin, basic access to Pixie Hollow is free with a chance to upgrade for a $5.95 monthly fee.[27] Since its debut, the site has attracted approximately 1.6 million monthly users.

World of Cars

Disney's latest entry into the social networking arena is the World of Cars, which debuted in summer 2010. Similar to the Club Penguin and Pixie Hollow concepts, World of Cars gives users the chance to create and customize their own online car personas.

Like Pixie Hollow, one aim of World of Cars is to tie several Disney properties together, explained reporter Dawn Chmielewski.

> The launch marks the latest exercise in corporate cross-branding for Disney, which hopes it can leverage the movie's popularity into monthly subscription payments from boys and their NASCAR dads in advance of the release of *Cars 2* in summer 2011 and the Cars Land attraction that opens in 2012 at Disney's California Adventure theme park.[28]

Interactive Games and Media

In addition to developing games for its online sites, Disney produces a wide range of video games for home computer platforms such as PlayStation, Xbox 360, Nintendo DS, and Nintendo Wii. Many of these are based on the company's films and television shows. Some are issued in conjunction with the release of new films. Disney works with several software developers to produce its games. These include Avalanche Software, Wideload Games, Junction Point Studios, and Propaganda Games.

A number of Disney's key franchises have accompanying video games. The PlayStation and Nintendo Wii versions of "Disney Princess: Enchanted Journey" complement the Princess line, while a PlayStation offering called "Hannah Montana: Rock Out the Show" is designed to appeal to fans of the popular Disney Channel television series.[29]

Did You Know?

The first Disney home video game based on a theme park ride was "Toy Story Mania," modeled after the attraction of the same name. It was released for the Wii in 2009.

Some games come with additional features and "extras" that tie them to other Disney properties. When "Pirates of the Caribbean: At World's End" was released for the Nintendo DS, for example, the company tied the release to a theme park promotion. Game owners were encouraged to bring their games with them to Disneyland or the Walt Disney World Resort so they could "download new video game content at specific 'X-marks-the-spot' hotspots hidden near the Pirates of the Caribbean attraction."[30]

Disney has also worked to connect its video games to those franchises with virtual world sites. For the Nintendo DS version of "Disney Fairies: Tinker Bell and the Lost Treasure," for example, players can upload fairy avatars from the video game into the Pixie Hollow virtual world.[31]

Disney recently released a game that is designed to bring renewed attention to Mickey Mouse. Called "Epic Mickey," the game is distributed for the Nintendo Wii and places Mickey inside a "cartoon wasteland" where he encounters other classic Disney characters such as Donald Duck and Oswald the Rabbit.[32] Part of the rationale behind the game is to make Mickey Mouse more recognizable to youngsters as more than just a Disney corporate symbol.

Mobile Apps

Ever since Disney CEO Bob Iger struck a deal with Apple Computer in 2006 to make Disney/ABC shows available through iTunes as discussed in Chapter 3, the company has worked to increase the accessibility of its content through mobile devices. Many of Disney's computer games can now be integrated into cell phones and other mobile platforms.

Disney has also released several apps for the iPhone, iPod Touch, and iPad. A free general interest Disney app, released in 2009, offers users access to information about videos, games, music, and Disney characters.[33]

When the Apple iPad made its debut in early 2010, Disney launched an app allowing users to download and watch ABC shows on the new device with a wi-fi connection. With the release of the movie *Toy Story 3* in June 2010, Disney introduced an accompanying "read-along" app that allowed children to listen to the story being read while they watched 3-D animated effects on the iPad screen.[34]

A mobile phone app called "Disney Digicomics" was launched in 2010. The application offers users the ability to download comics with ongoing storylines featuring classic Disney characters. The app is based on comics originally developed for magazines and newspapers in Italy.[35]

As mobile devices become increasingly more integral to people's everyday lives, Disney appears committed to broadening its reach to audiences through as many different mobile applications as possible.

Publishing

While they may seem "old fashioned" compared to the other forms of home entertainment discussed in this chapter, books and magazines are still quite popular with Disney audiences. The Disney Company has been in the publishing business since its early beginnings. Back in 1930, Walt Disney elected to build on the success of his Mickey Mouse cartoon shorts by sanctioning the creation of comic strips featuring the popular mouse. These were soon followed by others starring Donald Duck and assorted Disney characters.

The company's print efforts eventually grew beyond the early comic strips into a full-blown publishing enterprise. Today, Disney Worldwide Publishing (DPW) falls under the company's Consumer Products division and includes a variety of books, magazines, and comics. According to the company's press materials, DPW products are published in approximately 75 countries and 85 languages.[36]

Books

Within DPW, Disney publishes books for both children and adults under several different brands—Disney-Hyperion, Disney Editions, Disney Press, Disney Jump at the Sun, and Disney Libri. Many of the company's publications are based on Disney characters or films and often support the release of the organization's feature films and DVDs.

Disney has contractual agreements with a stable of authors who have produced successful book series. These authors include Rick Riordan (Percy Jackson series); Sara Pennypacker (Clementine series); and Eoin Colfer (Artemis Fowl series).

Some authors are brought in specifically to develop products that will ultimately become Disney film properties. Gail Carson Levine, for example, author of *Ella Enchanted*, was commissioned by Disney to write a novel based on the character Tinker Bell. The resulting book, *Fairy Dust and the Quest for the Egg*, became the basis for what is now the Disney Fairies franchise.

In 2010, former Baltimore Oriole and National Baseball Hall of Famer Cal Ripken, Jr., signed an agreement with DPW to develop a series of baseball-related books aimed at grade school students.[37] Disney also publishes books written by some of its Disney Channel stars such as Miley Cyrus and the Jonas Brothers. These publications are intended to complement other merchandise used to promote the TV channel stars.[38]

Did You Know?

Disney En Familia was Disney's first Spanish-language magazine developed for the U.S. market.

Magazines

The bulk of Disney's magazines are sold internationally under DPW's global magazine division. According to the company's press materials, "Disney represents approximately 45 percent of all children's magazines sold in the world."[39]

Key characters such as Mickey Mouse and Donald Duck have their own publications. *Mickey Mouse Magazine*, for example, is published in 22 different countries.[40] Other popular titles featuring Disney characters include *Disney Princess Magazine*, *Winnie the Pooh Magazine*, *Hannah Montana Magazine*, and *Disney Fairies*.[41]

Disney has had less success with its magazines aimed at U.S. audiences. In recent years, the company shuttered several of its periodicals, including *Disney Magazine*, *Disney Adventure*, and *Wondertime*.[42] Presently, the company produces two magazines with U.S.-based circulations: *Family Fun Magazine* and *Disney En Familia.*

Comics

As noted earlier, Disney comics date back to Walt Disney's creation of a Mickey Mouse comic strip in 1930. Since then, comic books have been a steady part of the Disney Company's publication offerings and have been drawn by artists such as Floyd Gottfredson and Carl Barks.

Over the years, Disney has used several outside companies to produce and distribute its comic books, including Western Publishing, Gladstone Publishing, Gemstone Publishing, and BOOM! Studios.[43]

Disney's 2009 acquisition of Marvel Entertainment adds a new dimension to the company's production of comics. Marvel is the "#1 comics publisher in the U.S., claiming a little over 45% of [the] comics market in units," noted an article in *Publishers Weekly.*[44] As Disney determines how to best integrate Marvel into its existing properties, the role of the comic book may well become more prominent within Disney's publishing sector.

Disney Digital Books

The newest publishing venture launched by Disney is an electronic book service called Disney Digital Books (DDB). Inspired by the success of other electronic book endeavors such as the Amazon Kindle, DDB operates on a subscription basis rather than relying on individual downloaded product sales. For an annual fee, subscribers have access to more than 600 titles online through a web-based platform.

According to the *New York Times,* Disney launched the service with a marketing campaign that included postcards distributed at Disney film screenings, demonstrations at Apple stores, and a "social media and advertising component…intended to reach 14 million mothers."[45] The site is expected to be launched internationally in 2011.

Conclusion

Disney has become a key player in the home video and DVD markets by making its classic films available for affordable home viewing by children and adults. The company has also established a strong online presence through its

Disney.com website and has created a line of video games that complement some of its most popular film and character franchises. Additionally, Disney has maintained a steady footing in the publishing industry, producing books, magazines, and comics that have global appeal.

Disney CEO Bob Iger has expressed a commitment to keeping the company at the forefront of technology in the creation of new products and services that address the diverse interests of today's tech-savvy children and tweens. This may well set the bar for future home entertainment and interactive media endeavors undertaken by the company. ◆

Notes

1. See *DEG Year-End 2009 Home Entertainment Report*, Digital Entertainment Group, http://www.dvdinformation.com.

2. See Ron Grover, *Disney Touch: How a Daring Management Team Revived . an Entertainment Empire* (Homewood, IL: Business One Irwin, 1991): 138.

3. Ibid.

4. "Kids Still the Kings of Home Video," *Discount Store News* 36:3 (February 3, 1997): 48.

5. See Bruce Orwall, "Disney Plans Strategic Shift in Home Videos," *Wall Street Journal*, 17 August 1999, B1; and Diane Garrett, "Disney Reworks Catalog Strategy," *Video Business* 19:46 (November 15, 1999): 1.

6. See Robert Scally, "Buena Vista Fine-Toons DVD Line Up," *Discount Store News* 39:1 (January 3, 2000): 39.

7. See "*Snow White and the Seven Dwarfs* Sells One Million Units on First Day," *DVD News* (October 11, 2001); and Stephanie Loughran, "HD Technology, Classic Stories Drive Sales of Animated Video," *Supermarket News* (October 22, 2001): 56.

8. Todd Wasserman, "Disney's *Cinderella* Belle of $150M Ball," *Brandweek* 46:5 (January 31, 2005): 4.

9. Ibid.

10. See Laura Dunphy, "Disney on Platinum Push for Earnings," *Video Business* 23:18 (May 5, 2003): 6.

11. Joe Alfuso, telephone interview, June 21, 2010.

12. Gordon Hoe quoted in Catherine Applefeld Olson, "The Young Generation Wants its DVD," *Billboard* 114:33 (August 17, 2002): 58.

13. See "Walt Disney Studios Home Entertainment Unveils the 'Diamond Collection,'" *Entertainment Business Newsweekly* (September 27, 2009): 219; and Thomas K. Arnold, "'Snow White' Still the Fairest of Them," *Home Media Magazine* 31:42 (October 19-25, 2009): 16.

14. Ethan Smith, "Disney Revamps Its Movie Marketing—Single Team Will Handle Distribution From Theaters to Pay-TV, DVDs and Online," *Wall Street Journal*, 12 November 2009, B3.

15. See Matthew Garrahan, "Disney and Rivals Square Up in New Movie Distribution Battle," *Financial Times*, 6 January 2010, 20.

16. See "Disney Online Breaks All-Time Traffic Records in July With 34 Million Unique Visitors," *Business Wire*, 13 August 2009.

17. Merissa Marr, "Updated Disney.com Offers Networking for Kids," *Wall Street Journal*, 2 January 2007, B1.

18. Alan Welsman quoted in Luan Goldie, "Tweens Online: Kids Rule," *New Media Age* (February 11, 2010): 19.

19. See Warren Buckleitner, "A Full Palette of Tools for Little Artists at Disney.com," *The New York Times*, 3 September 2009, B8.

20. "Disney Online Launches 'The Possibility Shop,' Web Site Featuring Original Web Series From the Jim Henson Company and Sponsored Exclusively by The Clorox Company," *Entertainment & Travel* (December 12, 2009): 15.

21. See Mike Shields, "Disney Eyes Mommies," *Mediaweek* 19:22 (June 1, 2009): 8; and "Disney Online Completes Acquisition of Kaboose, Inc. Internet Assets," *Business Wire*, 1 June 2009.

22. See Brooks Barnes, "Wary of Losing Out Online, Disney Buys Site for Children," *The New York Times*, 2 August 2007, C3.

23. Merissa Marr and Peter Sanders, "Disney Buys Kids' Social-Network Site," *Wall Street Journal*, 2 August 2007, A6.

24. See Brooks Barnes, "Club Penguin Misses Goals, Giving Disney a Half-Price Deal," *The New York Times*, 13 May 2010, B3.

25. "Pirates of the Caribbean Online Celebrates One Year of Pirating and Adventures on the High Seas," *Business Wire*, 30 October 2008.

26. See Dawn C. Chmielewski, "Disney Hoping Kids Will Test-Drive World of Cars," *Los Angeles Times*, 24 February 2010, B1.

27. See "Disney Online Launches Pixie Hollow Virtual World," *Business Wire*, 23 October 2008.

28. Chmielewski, "Disney Hoping Kids Will Test-Drive World of Cars," B1.

29. See "Disney Unveils 'Princess' Video Games," *Wireless News* (November 1, 2007): 1; and "Drawing Anticipation From Fans and Girls Globally Disney Interactive Studios Ships Hannah Montana PSP PlayStation Portable Game Hannah Montana: Rock Out the Show," *Leisure & Travel Week* (August 22, 2009): 25.

30. "Pirates of the Caribbean Fans With a Nintendo DS™ Can Search for Hidden Treasure at Disney Parks," *Business Wire*, 21 May 2007.

31. See "Disney Interactive Studios Announces Disney Fairies: Tinker Bell and the Lost Treasure for Nintendo," *Business Wire*, 2 June 2009.

32. See Paul Thompson, "Why After 80 Years Mickey Has Stopped Being Mousy," *Daily Mail*, 6 November 2009, 27; and "Warren Spector Revisits a Cartoon Icon's Legacy in Disney Epic Mickey," *Business Wire*, 28 October 2009.

33. See "Free Disney App Now Available on App Store," *Business Wire*, 28 October 2009.

34. See The Walt Disney Company, "Disney, ABC and ESPN to Offer New Applications and Content for Apple's iPad," press release, April 1, 2010; and "Disney Publishing Worldwide Launches Original 'Toy Story 3' Read-Along Application for the iPad," *Business Wire*, 17 June 2010.

35. See "Disney DigiComics' Global Launch," ICv2.com, December 17, 2009, http://www.icv2.com/articles/news/16506.html.

36. "About Disney Publishing Worldwide" Fact Sheet, Disney Consumer Products, 2010.

37.   "Cal Ripken Jr. Signs Middle Grade Book Deal With Disney Book Group," *Business Wire*, 30 June 2010.

38.   See "Burning Up: On Tour With the Jonas Brothers Hits Bookstores Today," *Business Wire*, 18 November 2008; and "Miles to Go—First Ever Book From Superstar Miley Cyrus—Is a #1 Best Seller," *Business Wire*, 23 March 2009.

39.   "About Disney Publishing Worldwide" Fact Sheet, Disney Consumer Products, 2010.

40.   Ibid.

41.   See "Disney Launches Fairies Magazine," *Marketing* (June 1, 2006): 6.

42.   See Owen Boss, "*Wondertime* Magazine, Web Site Shutting Down," *Daily Hampshire Gazette* (January 23, 2009): A1.

43.   See David Gerstein, "Disney Comics History, 1930-1984, http://stp.lingfil.uu.se/~starback/dcml/history.html; and "New Adventures for 'Walt Disney's Comics and Stories'!" *Disney Fans Insider*, January 26, 2010, http://home.disney.go.com/foryou/disneyfans/insider/article/?date=20100126.

44.   Heidi MacDonald, "Disney Buys Marvel," *Publishers Weekly* 256:36 (September 7, 2009): 5.

45.   Brooks Barnes, "Disney Tries to Pull the Storybook Ritual Onto the Web," *The New York Times*, 29 September 2009, B3.

13

Disney Marketing and Promotion

Throughout the various chapters of this book, the recurring themes of marketing and promotion have been shown to be significant contributors to the popularity of the Disney brand. When overlaid on the wide range of products and services produced by Disney, these elements become a force to be reckoned with known as Disney corporate synergy. As author Janet Wasko explained, "'Disney synergy' is the phrase typically used to describe the ultimate in cross-promotional activities."[1]

A variety of marketing strategies have been used to promote Disney films since the early days of Mickey Mouse and Snow White. As the company has grown and expanded to include theme parks, television programs, theater, travel, musical performances, and sports activities, among other corporate ventures, marketing and promotion have been woven into the fabric of nearly every aspect of the Disney Company.

Marketing is evident in corporate partnerships, advertising campaigns, and theme park promotions. It encompasses the use of traditional media such as print and broadcast, as well as digital media such as blogs and YouTube videos.

This chapter will examine the marketing and promotional strategies implemented by Disney to spread the magic word about the company's multitude of products and services. It will begin with a discussion of the concept of corporate synergy and look at the many ways Disney has used synergized marketing practices to keep the Disney name and brand alive and well in the minds of consumers of all ages.

Disney Synergy

Synergy is a buzzword that became popular during the merger and acquisition craze of the 1980s. It has been described as the synchronized interaction of a company's assets to form something greater than the total of the individual parts.[2]

Since the mid-1980s, the word synergy has been closely associated with the Walt Disney Company. The organization has become a master at spinning off multiple products from a single Disney movie or character, often turning an animated film into a theme park attraction, Broadway show, television special, or even a parade subject, to offer just a few examples.

Writer Frank Roost observed, "For decades the concept of synergy has been a key to Disney's economic success.... It is used more thoroughly and comprehensively than in any other media company."[3]

In reality, however, synergy is not a new concept for Disney. As a *New York Times* editorial explained, "The very idea of corporate synergy, the mantra of modern media corporations, begins with Walt."[4]

Creating Synergy Magic

As discussed in earlier chapters, Walt Disney applied synergy to his company long before anyone knew what the word meant. Back in the 1950s, he used his *Disneyland* television program to help promote the Anaheim theme park he was building—a park based on animated films and characters his company had created.

Under the leadership of Michael Eisner, the Disney Company seemingly perfected the art of corporate synergy, making it a routine part of operations and hiring employees with the word "synergy" specifically embedded in their job titles.[5] During this period, consumers began to see more and more examples of integrated campaigns used to promote Disney films through a multitude of complementary media.

When the company celebrated the 50th anniversary of *Snow White and the Seven Dwarfs* in 1987, for example, the re-release of the film at theaters across the United States was accompanied by Snow White parades at Disneyland and Disney World; a television special featuring Linda Ronstadt singing, "Someday

My Prince Will Come"; appearances by Snow White herself at the Easter Egg Roll at the White House and as the grand marshal at the annual cherry blossom parade in Washington, D.C.; and a host of Snow White merchandise ranging from clothes to commemorative coins.[6]

New Opportunities for Cross-Promotion

When Disney purchased ABC in 1995, evidence of cross-promotion became even more apparent as characters from ABC television sitcoms such as *Roseanne* and *Sabrina the Teenage Witch* began making trips to Walt Disney World as part of the storylines of their shows. This cross-promotion has intensified even further in the last two decades as the synergy concept has been applied to Disney Channel shows and their spin-off musical acts.

Today, corporate synergy is a given in the marketing activities the Disney Company uses to promote its brand, build a relationship with its audiences, and encourage consumers to become and remain loyal customers of Disney products. As a result, noted an article in *Advertising Age* about the company, "The emotional connection [Disney] enjoys with its audience is its greatest asset."[7]

Disney cross-promotional practices have become synonymous with success when it comes to building a brand. As author Janet Wasko explained, "The Disney Company has developed the strategy so well that it represents the quintessential example of synergy in the media/entertainment industry."[8]

Corporate Partnerships

Since the days of Walt Disney, one of the Disney Company's tried and true marketing techniques has been the establishment of partnerships with other corporations. These relationships have proven to be mutually beneficial to both Disney and the corporate giants with which the company has joined forces, such as Coca-Cola, General Motors, Wal-Mart, and Kodak among others.

By partnering with other companies, Disney has been able to use the financial resources of these organizations to help promote its own business enterprises. The corporations, in turn, have gained added recognition as a result of regular exposure to Disney audiences.

As discussed in previous chapters, one of the company's earliest partnerships resulted from Walt Disney's relationship with ABC in the 1950s during the construction of Disneyland. Coca-Cola was another company that got in on the ground floor of Disney's theme park project. The beverage company agreed to invest in Disneyland in exchange for the right to become the park's sole soft drink supplier. That relationship has continued to this day, allowing Coca-Cola to market its products to Disney customers at all 11 theme parks.[9]

Figure 16: Disney Corporate Partners and Sponsors

The following companies have had corporate partnership or sponsorship relationships with the Walt Disney Company.

Disneyland

ABC Television	Dole
Bank of America	Energizer
Carnation	Hunt-Wesson
Chevron	Kodak
Coca-Cola	Monsanto

1964 World's Fair

Ford Motor Company	Pepsico
General Electric	State of Illinois

Walt Disney World Resort

Alamo/National Car Rental	Josten's
American Express	Kraft
AT&T	McDonald's
General Motors	Nestlé
Hanes/Champion	Siemen's AG
Hess Corporation	Stanley Works

World's Fair Partnerships

The 1964 World's Fair offered Walt Disney the opportunity to develop additional corporate partnerships. As discussed in Chapter 2, Disney was hired to design several exhibits for the fair that would be sponsored by four different outside organizations. These included General Electric's Carousel of Progress; Ford Motor Company's Magic Skyway; the State of Illinois' Great Moments with Mr. Lincoln; and Pepsico's It's a Small World. Several of these exhibits were later moved to Disneyland to become permanent attractions.

Disney's exhibits helped draw fair attendees to the World's Fair pavilions sponsored by these organizations. At the same time, they exposed fair visitors to the entertainment company in a new way, making Disney magic accessible to thousands of people who had never set foot in Disneyland.

"The 1964–65 World's Fair proved to be a critical step for Walt Disney and his creative empire.... The fair tightened connections between Disney and corporate America," noted Disney biographer Steven Watts.[10]

After Walt Disney's death in 1966, the Disney Company continued to cultivate relationships with a wide range of corporations. The opening of the Epcot theme park in 1982, for example, led to the sponsorship of park attractions by companies such as General Motors, Monsanto, and American Express.

Other Corporate Partners

Perhaps the most highly publicized of Disney's corporate partnerships was its 10-year arrangement with McDonald's between 1996–2006. After a string of animated hits in the early to mid-1990s (*Beauty and the Beast, Aladdin, The Lion King*), Disney struck a deal with the fast-food giant, explained *Los Angeles Times* reporter Rachel Abramowitz.

> Under the terms of the agreement, said to be worth $1 billion to Disney, McDonald's paid $100 million in royalties and conducted 11 promotions a year for Disney films, videos and TV shows, with seven aimed specifically toward the young Happy Meal consumers. Disney also agreed to let McDonald's set up shop inside its theme parks.[11]

Initially, the arrangement seemed ideal for both companies. Ultimately, however, the partnership was not quite as lucrative for McDonald's as it had promised to be. A number of the animated Disney films produced after the agreement was signed turned out to be duds—films such as *Treasure Planet* and *Atlantis: The Lost Empire.*

The Disney/McDonald's partnership came to an end when the 10-year contract expired on January 1, 2007. With a national spotlight shining brightly on the hazards of childhood obesity, Disney ultimately wanted to distance itself from a corporate partner whose claim to fame was its high fat, cholesterol-laden fast foods and vowed to focus on selling more healthy alternatives at its theme parks. The move also freed up McDonald's to begin negotiations with other film companies. By 2008, the chain's fast-food outlets had disappeared from Disney's parks.[12]

In recent years, Disney has developed a successful relationship with Wal-Mart stores to aid the company in its promotion of its Disney Channel blockbusters such as *Hannah Montana* and *High School Musical.* A partnership with Kodak has led to additional promotion of Disney Channel programs as well as of the Disney Cruise Line.[13]

According to an article in *Marketing Week,* "Disney now has about 20 global partners with about the same number of companies sponsoring attractions locally at its park complexes in the U.S., France, Hong Kong and Japan."[14] Overall, from a marketing standpoint, the practice of partnering with large corporations has proven to be a profitable one for Disney.

Advertising Campaigns

Advertising plays a significant role in the overall marketing efforts of the Disney Company and encompasses print, broadcast, and electronic media. According to *Advertising Age* magazine, Disney spent approximately $2.22 billion on advertising in 2008, and was ranked seventh in the publication's annual survey of the 100 Leading National Advertisers in 2009.[15]

Over the years, Disney has developed some innovative advertising campaigns, particularly for its theme parks. One that has been seen by millions of sports fans in the last two decades is the company's "I'm Going to Disneyland" campaign.

The first of these television spots aired in 1987 and featured New York Giants quarterback Phil Simms soon after his team clinched Super Bowl XXI. Since 1987, more than two dozen sports stars including Kareem Abdul-Jabbar, Joe Montana, Jerry Rice, and John Elway, have been asked the question

"What's Next?" on camera soon after their teams' victories and have responded with the now legendary phrase, 'I'm Going to Disneyland.'[16]

In keeping with its focus on corporate synergy, Disney often combines advertising with other media. When preparing for the 1998 launch of the Disney Cruise Line, for example, the company ran promotions on the Disney Channel and trailers on Disney videos in addition to developing traditional print and TV ads. Disney also tied the advertising of the cruise line to the promotion of the 25th anniversary of Walt Disney World in 1996, as a means of encouraging visitors to combine a visit to the park with a voyage on the fledgling cruise line.[17]

One of Disney's biggest theme park advertising and marketing campaigns in recent years was its promotion of the 50th anniversary of Disneyland on July 17, 2005. A centerpiece of the 18-month marketing blitz, "The Happiest Celebration on Earth," was a television commercial titled, "Coming Home." The ad showed classic Disney characters such as Dumbo, Goofy, Donald Duck, and Cinderella heading toward Disneyland from all over the globe for the celebration. It ended with the tagline, "The only one missing is you."[18]

In addition to relying on traditional media for advertising purposes, Disney also uses electronic options such as mobile phones to reach younger audiences. According to an article in *Mobile Marketer*, "The company is using mobile to connect and enhance larger campaigns for films and TV shows.... Disney has found that ads promoting a specific TV show or movie are more successful than general Disney-branded ads."[19]

Did You Know?

The television ad campaign for the Disneyland 50th anniversary celebration launched during the Tournament of Roses Parade on January 1, 2005.

Film Marketing

Disney relies on a variety of techniques when promoting the release of a new film. Over the years, the company has gotten more and more innovative with some of its marketing practices.

The Princess and the Frog

The 2009 animated film, *The Princess and the Frog*, marked the Disney Studio's return to hand-drawn animation after nearly a decade of only releasing computer graphic animated films. Because of apprehension as to whether or not audiences would respond positively to the film, Disney ramped up its marketing and promotional efforts for the film.

At the keynote session of the D23 Expo in Anaheim, Calif., in September 2009, Disney CEO Bob Iger talked about the forthcoming film and then, to the surprise of attendees, showed the first 30-minutes of the movie. As *Los Angeles Times* reporter Dawn Chmielewski noted, "First rule of movie marketing: With a hard sell, sell the faithful first."[20] Since the Expo attracted Disney fans from all over the world, the screening served to pique their interest in hopes that when the film was officially released several months later, they would lead the charge to theaters.

Toy Story 3

Similar strategic marketing efforts were used to promote the Disney/Pixar film *Toy Story 3*. The third of the successful *Toy Story* franchise films opened in June 2010, and was released in 3-D in keeping with a growing industry trend. To get *Toy Story* enthusiasts excited about the 3-D project, Disney re-released 3-D versions of the original *Toy Story* and its sequel, *Toy Story 2* as a double-feature in theaters eight months before the opening of *Toy Story 3*.

Disney/Pixar also took an unusual approach to the third film by targeting college students who were children when the original films were released in 1995 and 1999. In the months leading up to the film's release, Disney sponsored "cliffhanger" showings of *Toy Story 3* on 84 college campuses around the United States. Viewers got to see about 65 minutes of the film before the lights came on before the ending.

Students were told ahead of time that they would not get to see the entire film. What they saw instead was an advertisement at the end of the movie that said, "Make sure to check out the full 3-D experience of *Toy Story 3* when it hits theaters nationwide. The toys are depending on you."[21]

New York Times reporter Brooks Barnes commented on the method behind the marketing strategy.

By reigniting these core fans—and withholding the ending—Disney hopes that they will not only buy tickets to opening weekend, but also bring their friends and chatter on Facebook and Twitter in the meantime about how much they liked the opening two-thirds of the film…. The ploy demonstrates how a recently overhauled Walt Disney Studios is thinking about marketing.[22]

Theme Park Promotions

A great deal of marketing muscle is put into promoting Disney's theme parks. As discussed earlier in this chapter, extensive advertising campaigns have been used to promote the parks, as was the case during the Disneyland 50th anniversary celebration in 2005. Since then, Disney has tried to keep the momentum going with several innovative park promotions.

Year of a Million Dreams

In the last few years, theme park marketing efforts have used a more personalized approach with the focus on the experiences of park guests rather than the parks themselves. One example is the "Year of a Million Dreams" promotion, which ran from 2006–2008, where park guests saw their Disney dreams come true in a variety of ways.

Each day at both Disneyland and Walt Disney World, Disney cast members randomly tapped visitors on the shoulder and awarded them prizes. According to reporter Bob Retzlaff, the dream winnings included:

…Disney Vacation Club memberships, travel around the world as parade grand marshals in each Disney resort destination, exclusive pins and Mouse ears, Disney Cruise Line sailings and private shopping sprees at popular Disney shops.[23]

What Will You Celebrate?

Disney followed up its "Year of a Million Dreams" promotion with one that had even more of a personal touch. In 2009, the company invited theme park guests to celebrate their birthdays at Disneyland or Walt Disney World for free as part of the parks' "What Will You Celebrate?" campaign.

More than 4 million people initially registered for the promotion online, according to the *Orlando Sentinel,* and approximately 30%—or 1.2 million— followed through and took advantage of the free birthday present from

Disney.[24] Since most of these individuals brought other paying customers with them to share in the celebration, the promotion helped generate revenue for the parks during a year where a tough economy had forced people to cut down on their leisure spending.

Give a Day, Get a Disney Day

Another park promotion called "Give a Day, Get a Disney Day" added an element of social responsibility to Disney's marketing endeavors. Launched in 2010, the promotion encouraged people to sign up to volunteer for a day at a local nonprofit organization. In exchange, Disney offered them a free day at a California or Florida Disney theme park once they had completed their service.

Disney worked with HandsOn Network, a nationwide volunteer networking service, to get people to register for the promotion. Individuals or groups could use the network's database to sign up and donate a day of volunteer service with the nonprofit of their choice. They were then issued a voucher good for a free day at a Disney theme park.[25]

Disney began the promotion on January 1, 2010, and planned to run it until the end of the year or until one million people had volunteered. The promotion was so popular that by the end of March, it had ended. Suzi Brown, director of media relations for Disneyland, said the promotion inspired a million people to volunteer in just three months.[26]

For local organizations, the Give a Day, Get a Disney Day promotion proved to be a tremendous boon. Giving Children Hope (GCH), a nonprofit organization in Buena Park, Calif., is one of the organizations that was willing to host volunteers as part of the promotion. To publicize the nonprofit's involvement, "We put it on our website, we promoted it through our e-newsletter, we sent out a press release," said Harmony Trevino, GCH director of communications.

Within a few days, GCH was flooded with offers from potential volunteers. "The majority were new people who didn't know who we were," she said. "With the Disney promotion, we were able to really get our name out in the community."

Although the Disney promotion ended sooner than anticipated because so many people did volunteer, Trevino said that some of those who came as a result of the promotion have continued to donate their time. In addition, GCH has received internship inquiries and financial donations.

"The people that have stayed, they've gotten involved in a great way, be it financial or by giving their time," she said. I would definitely do this promotion again. Being associated with Disney has brought us a lot of attention."[27]

Did You Know?

The Muppets were used to promote Disney's "Give a Day, Get a Disney Day" promotion. It was the first time the company used them in its theme park marketing campaign efforts.

Marketing Through Digital and Social Media

As Disney's audience has become more technologically savvy, the Disney Company has escalated its reliance on digital and social media to market itself to this audience. While Disney has had an Internet presence since the late 1990s, as discussed in Chapter 12, in the last few years the company has made a concerted effort to connect with its existing fans and potential customers through a variety of digital media. These have included theme park blogs and forums and a YouTube channel.

Park Blogs

A multitude of independent blogs about Disney exist on the Web, and in 2009, the company opted to join in the online chatter. The Disney Parks Blog was created as a means of encouraging those seeking information about the company's theme parks to get it directly from the official source rather than from outside entities.

The primary focus of the blog is to keep visitors updated about vacation-related topics pertaining to Disneyland, Walt Disney World, and the Disney Cruise Line.[28] Readers are encouraged to submit comments; however, a disclaimer on the site explains that comments are moderated and selectively posted. The majority of information posted on the blog comes from Disney personnel, so those looking for more unbiased opinions about the parks may still find non-Disney blogs to be more objective.

Moms Panel

In a similar vein, Disney launched an online forum in 2008 called the "Walt Disney World Moms Panel" as another way to provide park guests with information to help them plan their theme park vacations. The company invited those with in-depth knowledge of the Florida parks to apply for the panel by responding to essay questions followed by a telephone interview.

Those selected for the panel are responsible for answering questions posted on Disneyworldmoms.com. The company promotes the panelists as "everyday parents who have mastered the art of planning a vacation for their own families and are excited to share their pearls of wisdom with others."[29] In exchange for their services, Disney gives participants free passes to Walt Disney World. Although called the "Moms Panel," dads are included on the panel as well.[30]

Disney Living YouTube Channel

Given the popularity of YouTube with children and teens, Disney created its own YouTube channel to market its products and services through promotional videos. Called "Disney Living," the channel is billed as "a place for families and fans to get the latest information on Disney products and swap stories and experiences."[31]

The YouTube videos feature new products such as fashion, accessories, and toys, as well as information related to upcoming films. Prior to the opening of *The Princess and the Frog*, for example, Disney launched a video series on the channel that promoted some of the merchandise created in tandem with the film and featured interviews with Anika Noni Rose, who supplied the voice for the film's Princess Tiana.[32]

So far, the channel has been quite popular, according to an article in *MediaWeek*. A tween fashion show posted on the site, for example, resulted in 330,000 views, among the most any video has received when launched on YouTube.[33]

Conclusion

Marketing and promotion have played major roles in the success of Disney's many enterprises since the early days of Mickey Mouse and Snow White. Over the years, the company has built its brand by carefully coordinating its marketing efforts, resulting in a perfect blend of cross-promotion that permeates all aspects of the organization.

The company's keen focus on its marketing and promotional practices has earned Disney a reputation as a master of corporate synergy, respected and envied by companies worldwide. It is one of the key factors that have helped position the Disney Company as a leader in today's entertainment industry. ◆

Notes

1. Janet Wasko, *Understanding Disney* (Cambridge, England: Polity Press, 2001): 71.
2. See Dictionary.com, http://dictionary.reference.com/browse/synergy; Cambridge Dictionaries Online, http://dictionary.cambridge.org/dictionary/british/synergy; and Merriam-Webster Online, http://www.merriam-webster.com/dictionary/synergy.
3. Frank Roost, "Synergy City: How Times Square and Celebration Are Integrated Into Disney's Marketing Cycle," in Mike Budd and Max H. Kirsch, eds., *Rethinking Disney* (Middletown, CT: Wesleyan University Press, 2005): 263.
4. Verlyn Kinkenborg, "Marking Walt Disney's Centennial," *The New York Times*, 6 December 2001, A34.
5. See Christine Shenot, "When It Comes to Cross-Promotion, Disney Dominates," *Orlando Sentinel*, 1 December 1996, H1.
6. See Aljean Harmetz, "A Promotional Blitz for Snow White," *The New York Times*, 29 April 1987, C19.
7. Michael Mendenhall, "Emotional Equity Is Still Disney's Key Asset," *Advertising Age* 76:7 (February 12, 2005): 24.
8. Wasko, *Understanding Disney*, 71.
9. See Matthew Garrahan, "Sponsors With a Taste for Mickey Mouse Marketing," *Financial Times*, 5 March 2008, 14.
10. Steven Watts, *The Magic Kingdom: Walt Disney and the American Way of Life* (Columbia, MO: University of Missouri Press, 1997): 418.
11. Rachel Abramowitz, "Disney Loses Its Appetite for Happy Meal Tie-Ins," *Los Angeles Times*, 8 May 2006, A1.
12. See Dawn C. Chmielewski, "McNuggets' Ride Is Over at Disneyland," *Los Angeles Times*, 8 August 2008, C2.
13. See "Disney Channel Stars Ahoy! Kodak and Disney Cruise Line Bring Exclusive Fan Experience to the High Seas," *Leisure & Travel Week* (May 30, 2009), 54.
14. Christian Sylt, "Can Disney Really Become Bigger Sponsorship Vehicle Than the Olympics?" *Marketing Week* (April 16, 2009): 16.
15. See "About Ad Age's Marketer Profiles," *Advertising Age* 80:43 (December 28, 2009): 18.
16. See Felix Sanchez, "The Super Bowl Spawns Buying, Eating and a Few Urban Legends," *Knight-Ridder Business News*, 31 January 2006, 1; and "History of the 'I'm Going to Disney World' Ad Campaign," LaughingPlace.com, www.laughingplace.com/news-id10001330.asp.

17. Jeffrey D. Zbar, "Disney Maps Land and Sea Strategy," *Advertising Age* 67:38 (September 16, 1996): 6.

18. See Becky Ebenkamp, "Disneyland at 50: Ear to Ear," *Brandweek* 46:17 (April 25, 2005): 32.

19. Giselle Tsirulnik, "Disney Takes Fourth Place: 2009 Mobile Marketer of the Year," *Mobile Marketer* (January 12, 2010), www.mobilemarketer.com.

20. Dawn C. Chmielewski, "Disney Hopes Its 2-D Movie Doesn't Fall Flat," *Los Angeles Times*, 11 September 2009, B1.

21. See Brooks Barnes, "Disney Uses Cliffhanger to Market *Toy Story 3*," *The New York Times*, 1 May 2010, C1.

22. Ibid.

23. Bob Retzlaff, "Disney's Positively Dreamy," *Post-Bulletin*, 21 September 2007.

24. See Jason Garcia, "More Than a Million People Visited Disney Free on Their Birthdays," *Orlando Sentinel*, 4 January 2010.

25. See "Give a Day of Volunteer Service in 2010, Get a Day of Disney Theme Park Fun," *PR Newswire*, 29 September 2009; and Cigi Ross, "Disney Promotion Floods Nonprofits With Volunteers," *North County Times*, 7 March 2010.

26. Suzi Brown, public presentation at Cal State Fullerton, April 28, 2010.

27. Harmony Trevino, telephone interview, July 27, 2010.

28. See "About the Disney Parks Blog," http://disneyparks.com.disney.go.com/blog/about.

29. "The Walt Disney World Moms Panel Boasts 43 Panelists in 2010, Featuring 21 New Members," *PR Newswire*, 4 January 2010.

30. See Medina Roshan, "Columbia Resident Rewarded for Love of Disney: Frequent Visitor Earns Spot on Disney Moms Panel," *Columbia Flier*, 21 January 2010; and "Celebrating the Start of the Third Year: Disney Expands Walt Disney World Moms Panel and Seeks New 'Mouse' Experts for 2010," *PR Newswire*, 10 September 2009.

31. Disney Living, http://www.youtube.com/DisneyLiving.

32. See "Disney's *The Princess and the Frog* Merchandise in High Demand Weeks Before the Film's Debut," *Marketing Weekly News*, December 5, 2009.

33. Dawn Wilensky, "Licensing Landscape 2010," *MediaWeek* 20:8 (February 22, 2010): IPI 1.

14

Disney Merchandising

For every Disney film, for every Disney TV show, for nearly every Disney *anything*, there is a corresponding piece of merchandise. Be it a T-shirt, plush toy, or character watch, Disney merchandise encompasses thousands of products representing a wide range of the company's characters, films, television shows, and theme park attractions, among others.

Some of this merchandise is sold directly by Disney, while much is licensed to outside vendors who are granted the rights to sell Disney products in exchange for licensing fees. Since the late 1980s, the company has sold a good deal of its merchandise through its chain of retail outlets known as Disney Stores. Although the chain has undergone a financial roller coaster ride in the last two decades, it has recently been retooled and is currently positioned to become a growth area for the company.

Disney merchandise is often sought after by collectors who are eager to recapture memories of their childhood through Disney products. They purchase these products through Internet sites like EBay or at Disneyana conventions.

Part of Disney's merchandising success has come from its careful targeting of specific demographic groups. The Princess line of products, aimed at young girls, for example, has grown to be a $4 billion business. Products based on the company's Disney Channel programs such as *Hannah Montana* and *High School Musical* have proven to be top sellers with the tween market.

Disney has also created a line of products for adults, which includes clothing, jewelry, and even home furnishings. As part of its sales efforts toward the adult market, the company has been successful in selling not only products but also a unique experience known as the Disney Fairy Tale Wedding.

This chapter will examine the many different ways Disney has been able to reach its audiences through its merchandising efforts. An overview of these practices will be provided, along with an explanation of how Disney has been able to showcase its brand through a steady supply of merchandise.

Merchandising Overview

As noted in previous chapters, Disney's merchandising efforts can be traced to the early days of Mickey Mouse. In 1929, as the mouse's popularity began to grow, a businessman offered Walt Disney $300 for the rights to produce school tablets adorned with Mickey Mouse's image on the cover. This launched the beginning of the company's merchandising activities, which today fall under the corporate umbrella of Disney Consumer Products (DCP).[1]

DCP's merchandise ranges from "apparel, toys, home décor and books and magazines to interactive games, goods and beverages, stationery, electronics and fine art," according to the company's website.[2] Several of the product areas within DCP do extremely well against their competitors.

If the company's Disney Toys division operated as an independent toy company, for example, it would be the third largest in the world. Likewise, Disney's clothing brand is ranked 15th worldwide.[3]

Merchandise related to well-known Disney characters makes up a large percentage of annual revenues. Products are also routinely developed in conjunction with the release of Disney films as part of the company's overall synergy efforts.

Disney sells much of its merchandise through licensing agreements with outside vendors. According to *License! Global* magazine, Disney Consumer Products (DCP) earned $27.2 billion from licensed product sales in 2009, making it the largest licensor in the world.[4]

Examples of early Mickey Mouse merchandise including toys, books, clocks, and watches can be seen on display at The Walt Disney Family Museum in San Francisco.

Photo by Cesar Rubio, Courtesy The Walt Disney Family Museum.

Merchandising Through The Disney Store

While Disney has been peddling its merchandise for decades through its licensees and theme park shops, in the late 1980s, the company took the next step by opening its own chain of retail outlets. The first official Disney Store opened in Glendale, Calif., on March 28, 1987, and started a new trend in themed retailing.[5]

The first Disney Store carried, "2,800 different items, ranging from 50-cent Mickey Mouse erasers to a $3,200 diamond-studded Dumbo brooch," according to the *Wall Street Journal*.[6] Subsequent stores were modeled after the Glendale prototype and featured a wide array of Disney products. Customers heard Disney music played over loudspeakers while they shopped, and strategically placed video monitors played an endless stream of Disney films that they could stop and watch periodically while browsing through the store.

The success of the initial store led to a burst of expansion for the company. By 1991, Disney had opened 100 stores in North America and its first international store on Regent Street in London. Other companies such as Warner Brothers soon imitated the Disney Store model, and for the next decade, it seemed as though the company knew no bounds.

During the 1990s, Disney opened stores all over North America as well as in Japan and France where the company had its two international theme parks. By 1999, Disney had 749 stores, including a 40,000-sq.-ft. flagship store in Manhattan.[7]

Consequence of Overexpansion

By the early 2000s, however, the chain was suffering from signs of overly rapid growth, and Disney began making drastic changes to its retail enterprise. In 2002, the company leased its Japanese stores to the Oriental Land Company, operator of Tokyo Disneyland, to reduce management costs.

Then, in 2004, Disney extricated itself even further from the retail management business when it licensed the rights to its North American Disney stores to New Jersey-based retailer The Children's Place. The shift was attributed to "overexpansion, a failure to respond quickly to changing times and a falloff in demand for merchandise featuring its animated characters," explained reporter Richard Verrier.[8]

The arrangement involved a 15-year licensing agreement, where Disney granted The Children's Place a two-year royalty-free period so it could restructure and remodel the existing Disney Stores. Disney then began collecting royalties in 2006.

Initially, the deal seemed to work for both organizations. Just two years later, however, the arrangement had soured. Disney was unhappy with the slow pace of the store remodeling and resulting lackluster sales figures.

Regrouping and Reorganization

In 2008, Disney dissolved its agreement with The Children's Place and took back control of its chain of Disney Stores, naming Jim Fielding as president to resurrect the ailing retail business.[9] The result has been a complete retooling of Disney Store operations to make the stores more interactive and oriented specifically toward children ages 12 and under. The mantra behind the restructuring was to make a visit to a Disney Store "the best 30 minutes of a child's day," a magical experience rather than just a routine shopping trip. [10]

The first retooled store opened in Montebello, Calif., in June 2010. A New York store opened in Times Square less than six months later in the heart of Broadway's theater district, as a retail companion to Disney's New Amsterdam Theatre.

As the time of this writing, there were 229 Disney Stores in North America and 105 in Europe. In March 2010, Disney also announced it had taken back control of the Disney Stores managed by the Oriental Land Company in Japan, adding more than 40 stores to the chain's international holdings. [11]

Disney Collectibles Merchandise

Not only is Disney merchandise sold by the Disney Company and its licensees, it is often resold by independent vendors who sell to Disney collectors. Collectibles are sold at conventions, such as the Disneyana Fan Club annual meeting, held each summer in Anaheim, Calif.

Jim Jensen and his wife Leila operate SACC collectibles in Garden Grove, Calif. They sell Disney merchandise through their store, on the Internet through EBay, and at Disneyana conventions.

Jensen has been selling Disney collectibles for 23 years. The bulk of his customers are over 30, and many live overseas, especially in Japan. Over the years, Jensen has sold all kinds of Disney products—figurines, watches, coins, beanbag toys, and pins, among others. In the last few years, he said, Disney Vinylmation figures have become extremely popular. "We can't get enough of them," he said.

The most expensive item Jensen ever sold was a hand-painted mural by Charles Boyer, "a well-known Disney artist," which sold for $9,000. "It had different scenes from Disney movies. It was very detailed," he said.

Some customers will buy anything and everything, while others will specialize in one subject—Mickey Mouse or Tinker Bell, for example. Others collect memorabilia from older Disney movies.

Jensen believes people collect Disney merchandise because it "brings back the memories of their childhood. They buy a few things and then seem to get hooked on it, and they keep buying. It sort of makes you feel young to collect," he said.[12]

Did You Know?

The first official Disneyana collectibles convention was held at the Contemporary Resort Hotel at Walt Disney World in 1992.

Targeted Youth Merchandising

One of Disney's merchandising strengths has been its ability to identify key market segments and create lines of merchandise aimed at specific groups. Some of these products, such as those aimed at girls and tweens, have been wildly successful, while others, such as products aimed at boys, are still struggling to hit their mark.

Merchandising for Girls: The Disney Princesses

In recent years, Disney's greatest success in its merchandising efforts toward young girls has been its Princess line of products, as discussed in Chapter 4. The Disney Princess line was originally created to highlight eight female royal figures from Disney's animated films—Snow White, Cinderella, Sleeping Beauty, Ariel, Belle, Jasmine, Mulan, and Pocahontas.

In March 2010, following the release of *The Princess and the Frog*, Disney officially added the film's star, Princess Tiana, as the ninth member of the royal court and Disney's first African-American princess.[13] Another princess, Rapunzel, star of the 2010 film *Tangled*, was added to the court shortly after that film's release.

When packaged together by Disney Consumer Products' Andy Mooney in the early 2000s, the Disney Princesses quickly became a marketing wonder that has become a $4 billion a year business for the company.

In addition to vending Princess-related products, Disney has capitalized on its Princess power by selling youngsters a magical experience—the chance to dine with their royal heroines. At the Grand Floridian Resort & Spa in

Orlando, Princess fans are given the opportunity to have afternoon tea with their favorite Disney Princesses.[14]

Young princess wannabes can also experience the process of seeing themselves transformed into royalty at the Bibbidi Bobbidi Boutique in Walt Disney World's Downtown Disney. The styling salon opened in 2006 and sells three different Princess packages that include hairstyling, makeup, and costumes, depending on the cost of each package.[15]

Merchandising for Girls: Tinker Bell and Company

Building on the success of the Disney Princess line, Disney has worked hard to hold onto its youthful female customers by offering them a slightly more sophisticated follow-up franchise—Tinker Bell and the Disney Fairies.

The debut of the Disney Fairies marked the first time Disney tried to build a brand through its publishing division rather than through feature films.[16] Gail Carson Levine's *Fairy Dust and the Quest for the Egg* was released in 2005 by Disney Publishing and stayed on the *New York Times* bestseller list for 20 weeks.[17] It was followed by nearly 600 Disney Fairies-related additional titles, including a second book by Levine called *Fairy Haven and the Quest for the Wand.* By 2010, more than 18 million Disney Fairies books had been sold. A companion magazine, *Disney Fairies,* sold 7.5 million copies.[18]

The publication of the first book was accompanied by a line of Tinker Bell products—clothes, accessories, toys, and electronic gadgets. Then, in 2008, Disney released *Tinker Bell,* the first of a series of computer graphic animated, straight-to-DVD films that complement the fairy books.

By 2010, Disney Fairies were bringing in about $850 million in annual revenues,[19] which did not come close to the sales generated by the Disney Princesses. However, much may depend on the success of the subsequent DVDs and the marketing strategies Disney uses to promote them and their spritely star in the future.

Merchandising for Boys

While Disney has done well in creating merchandise aimed at young girls, it has been less successful in reaching out to boys. This is partly because so many of Disney's films and characters tend to have more appeal for females than males. It has presented a challenge for the company as it works to develop corresponding merchandising possibilities that are likely to attract a wider male audience.

Disney made some progress in recent years with merchandise from its *Pirates of the Caribbean* films. The company has also had success in reaching out to boys through merchandising efforts related to its Pixar films. A number of these films such as *Toy Story, Monsters, Inc., Finding Nemo,* and *Cars* have males as main characters. This has provided Disney with potential merchandising opportunities.

The 2009 acquisition of Marvel holds great promise for Disney in its attempt to expand its reach to boys through product merchandising. With an array of superhero characters in the Marvel storehouse, the product possibilities are seemingly endless. Much will depend on the characters Disney chooses to cultivate and how well they resonate with a young male audience.

Did You Know?

Disney Channel merchandise sales peak at back-to-school time, as school-related items featuring stars from the channel's shows are snatched up by the tween crowd.

Merchandising for Tweens

Disney has been able to reach out to the tween market through its merchandising of products related to its hit Disney Channel shows and stars. *Hannah Montana* and *High School Musical,* in particular, have become their own franchises.

Part of Disney's success in this area has been the company's strategy of developing merchandise at the same time it develops its shows, just as it does with its films, explained *Women's Wear Daily* (WWD) reporter Sharon Edelson. "Rather than wait years to see if a show will succeed, Disney is developing products at the first whiff of a hit. It is also trying to create franchises with lasting appeal."[20]

The *High School Musical* franchise is a good example of this. With three hit movies in a five-year time frame, Disney has been able to extend its merchandising opportunities over a period of several years without having to pull merchandise from shelves because of loss of interest.

Fashion and accessories have made up a large segment of the *Hannah Montana* franchise. As noted in the previous chapter, in 2008, Disney developed a corporate partnership with Wal-Mart to promote the brand. "Wal-Mart set up mini 'Hannah Montana Shops' in 750 stores to display the clothes and accessories" related to the hit TV show, noted an article in *USA Today*.[21]

Even within the tween market segment, however, Disney has not had as much success selling its products to boys as to girls. With the recent launch of the Disney XD Channel and the programs and characters it has created for that channel, the company is hoping to change this.

Targeted Adult Merchandising

While Disney has devoted a great deal of energy to developing merchandising strategies for children and tweens, it has also put a considerable amount of thought into how to reach adults. Disney has created products specifically geared toward grown-ups who still have a penchant for all things Disney. Some of these products are quite high-end, as they encompass designer clothes, jewelry, furniture, and even wedding gowns.[22]

Fashion and Jewelry

Disney enlisted the help of designer names such as Kidada Jones, Paul Smith, Vivienne Tam, and Dolce & Gabbana in its attempt to give its clothing and accessories an added upscale touch. The products are sold in upper echelon department stores, such as Neiman Marcus, as well as in high-end boutiques rather than in the company's theme parks and Disney stores.

Part of Disney's strategy has been to flag the attention of Hollywood stars with these products in hopes that their fans will follow suit in purchasing them. When the company launched its "Disney Vintage" line of sweaters, sweatshirts, and tank tops, for example, "Disney started stuffing the newly fashionable retro-wear into Hollywood gift bags. Celebrities such as Jennifer Aniston, Leonardo DiCaprio, and Jennifer Garner wore them," noted reporter Dawn Chmielewski.[23]

Furniture

Disney also partnered with several furniture manufacturers to produce a line of home furnishings called the "Disney Signature Collection." While the collection draws on the tradition of the Disney name and features products such as the "storyteller sofa" and "studio club chair," no trace of Disney characters can be found in the merchandise design.[24]

Wedding Gowns

Building on the popularity of the Disney Princess craze, Disney has even released a line of princess-themed wedding gowns. The Kirstie Kelly for Disney's Fairy Tale Weddings collection, which made its debut in 2007, features wedding gowns that are promoted as capturing the essence and personality of the individual princesses.

The creation of the wedding collection was Disney's way of appealing to women who were far past the princess phase of their childhoods but who still harbored the desire to feel like a princess on their wedding day.

All of these high-end adult products in many ways showcase the versatility of the Disney brand when it comes to merchandising. DCP's Andy Mooney has been quoted as saying,

> Disney is the only brand that can sell a shirt in the same city on the same day for $1,400 and $14.00.... There are only a handful of brands in the world that have the emotional depth that Disney has. If you produce the appropriate product for the demographic, it'll reach the consumer.[25]

Disney Fairytale Weddings

One of the merchandising inspirations for the Kirstie Kelly wedding gown line is not actually a product but a unique Disney experience the company has been successfully selling for many years called Disney Fairy Tale Weddings. Since 1991, Disney has offered couples the opportunity to tie the knot at the company's Walt Disney World or Disneyland Resorts.

What started as a small sideline program has grown to a full-time business with a full-time staff at the parks. Walt Disney World alone plays host to more than 1,600 weddings every year. Disney offers a variety of wedding packages ranging in price from approximately $4,800 to $65,000 and upwards, depending on the level of sophistication and added amenities of each wedding package.[26]

The wedding program was so popular from the start that in 1995, the company built a special wedding pavilion near the Grand Floridian Hotel in

Walt Disney World, which can host up to six weddings a day. The pavilion features a small chapel with a view of Cinderella's castle that is visible to the bride and groom as they take their vows. For an additional fee, Disney will even throw in a guest appearance by Mickey and Minnie Mouse at the wedding reception.

Disney will also arrange for a Fairy Tale Honeymoon at one of its theme parks or on one of its Disney Cruise Line ships. The company has a service called the Honeymoon Registry, which allows wedding guests to contribute to a Disney honeymoon fund by paying for something like cocktails on the beach or couples massages at a spa in lieu of a more traditional gift like a toaster or set of flatware.[27]

While some choose a Disney wedding for the novelty of it all, others use the Disney setting as a chance to live out their fairytale fantasies. For Disney, the payoff comes not only in the fees generated from the weddings themselves but from the money spent on accommodations and theme park tickets by wedding guests. For the bride and groom, it is billed as an experience to remember for a lifetime.

Conclusion

Merchandising contributes to the overall success of the Disney brand by offering consumers a tangible and lasting reminder of the company's products and services. Disney's merchandising activities are designed to complement the company's many properties and capture the interests of audiences of all ages and income brackets.

Disney's Consumer Products division has been able to rely on steady sales of merchandise based on its franchises. At the same time, Disney constantly strives to develop products that keep pace with the company's release of new entertainment media. Disney has also succeeded in targeting its merchandising efforts toward specific markets and in selling products and experiences that embody the omnipresence of Disney magic. ◆

Figure 17: Global Licensees of Disney Products

These are just some of the companies licensed to sell the Disney Company's products around the world.

Fashion and Home

BBC Apparel Group
Carrefour
Hallmark
Kardstadt
Kids Headquarters
Oviesse

Playtex
Rooms to Go Furniture
Target
Tesco
Wal-Mart
Zak Industries

Toys

Bandai America Inc.
Fisher-Price
Jakks Pacific
Mattel
Playmates Toys

Techno Source
Thinkway Toys
Tomy
WowWee
Zizzle

Stationery

Crayola
Hallmark
Innovative Designs

Mead
National Design
Trends International

Health and Beauty

Bic
The Gillette Co./Oral-B

Kimberly-Clark
Procter & Gamble

Food

Breyers
Imagination Farms
Kellogg Company

Morinaga & Co., Ltd.
Nestlé
Pez Candy

Source: Disney Consumer Product Fact Sheets, www.disneyconsumerproducts.com

Notes

1. See The Walt Disney Company "Company Overview," http://corporate.disney.go.com/corporate/overview.html.
2. Ibid.
3. See Disney Consumer Products, http://www.disneyconsumerproducts.com.
4. See Tony Lisanti, "Disney's New Decade," *License! Global* 13:2 (March/April 2010): 34.
5. See "Disney Store Unveils a Bouquet of Earth Day Activities," *Business Wire*, 2 April 2009.
6. Daniel Akst, "Disney Plans Large-Scale Expansion Into Retailing Starting Next Spring," *Wall Street Journal*, 23 December 1987, 1.
7. Based on information from Disney Store president Jim Fielding, public presentation at D23 Expo, September 12, 2009. See also, "Disney's Fifth Avenue Showplace," *Chain Store Age* 73:3 (March 1997): 110.
8. Richard Verrier, "Disney Puts Its Stores Up for Sale," *Los Angeles Times*, 23 May 2003, C1.
9. See Dawn C. Chmielewski, "Disney to Take Back Namesake Retail Outlets," *Los Angeles Times*, 21 March 2008, C3; Peter Sanders, "Disney to Buy Back Most Namesake Stores," *Wall Street Journal*, 21 March 2008, B4; and "The Walt Disney Company Takes Control of Disney Stores in North America," *Business Wire*, 1 May 2008.
10. See Brooks Barnes, "Disney's Retail Plan Is a Theme Park in Its Stores," *The New York Times*, 13 October 2009, A1.
11. See Disney Consumer Products, "Disney Retail," www.disneyconsumerproducts.com; "Disney Store Launches Magical New Store Design in Major Markets Across the U.S. and Europe in Summer 2010," *Business Wire*, 12 May 2010; and The Walt Disney Company, "Disney Acquires Stores in Japan," *News From Investor Relations* (March 2010): 6.
12. Jim Jensen, telephone interview, July 28, 2010.
13. See "Princess Tiana Officially Joins the Disney Princess Royal Court at Star-Studded Crowning Event in New York City," *Entertainment Newsweekly* (April 2, 2010): 127.
14. See Phil Kloer, "Tween Dreams: Young Girls Who Would Be Princess Reign Supreme," *The Atlanta Journal-Constitution*, 13 June 2004, LS1; and Eileen Ogintz, "Little Girls Are Disney Princesses for a Day," *The Ledger*, 11 April 2010.
15. See Bibbidi Bobbidi Boutique, http://disneyworld.disney.go.com/tours-and-experiences/bibbidi-bobbidi-boutique.
16. See David Litterick, "Disney Says It Does Believe in Fairies," *The Daily Telegraph*, 5 September 2005, 28.
17. Dawn C. Chmielewski, "Pixie Gets Star Role as Vault Dust Flies," *Los Angeles Times*, 4 August 2008, C1.
18. "The World's Most Beloved Fairy Returns in an All-New Magical Adventure," *PR Newswire*, 8 June 2009.
19. Disney Consumer Products, "Disney Fairies," www.disneyconsumerprodutcs.com.
20. Sharon Edelson, "Disney Taps Into Tween TV Hits," *WWD* 193:132 (June 21, 2007): 11.

21. Laura Petrecca, "Wal-Mart, Hannah Montana Join Forces," USA *Today*, 30 January 2008, B1.
22. See Dawn C. Chmielewski, "Disney Seeks High-End Cachet," *Los Angeles Times*, 19 June 2007, C1.
23. Ibid.
24. See Brooks Barnes, "Disney, by Design," *The New York Times*, 6 November 2008, E1.
25. Andy Mooney quoted in Dawn C. Chmielewski, "Disney Seeks High-End Cachet," *Los Angeles Times*, 19 June 2007, C1.
26. Walt Disney World Resort, "Disney's Fairy Tale Weddings Fast Facts," http://wdwnews.com/viewpressrelease.aspx?pressreleaseid=99882&siteid=1. See also Disney Fairy Tale Weddings, http://disneyweddings.disney.go.com/weddings.
27. See Carley Petesch and Nicole Lyn Pesce, "Nothing Makes Travel-Loving Couples Happier Than a Honeymoon Registry," *Daily News*, 11 February 2007, Travel 4.

15

Disney and the Global Marketplace

When Richard M. and Robert B. Sherman wrote their now-famous song, *It's a Small World*, they could just as well have been writing about the Disney Company itself. Almost since the company's inception, Disney characters and products have been embraced and consumed by people all over the globe.

In the beginning, it was the characters featured in Disney's cartoon shorts that drew worldwide attention. As Disney began producing feature-length animated films, these developed an international following, particularly in European countries.

On the television front, the growth and popularity of the Disney Channel in the United States prompted the company to expand the channel overseas to increase its exposure to international markets. As a result, Disney Channel sitcoms such as *Hannah Montana* and *Sonny With a Chance* are now watched by tweens in South Africa and Australia as well as in New York and Los Angeles.

In recent years, Disney has begun targeting what had once been untapped regions with its products in an attempt to make inroads into these locations. China and India are especially appealing to Disney because of their large populations. Other areas such as Russia and parts of Latin America have proven to be receptive to the Disney brand as well.

Through a combination of appealing products and targeted marketing, the Disney Company has succeeded in making the Disney name one that is recognized worldwide. This chapter will examine some of the efforts that have gone into building the Disney brand on an international scale. It will discuss the types of Disney products that have done well abroad and look at what Disney has done to make this happen.

Disney as a Global Phenomenon

The Global Disney Audiences Project was a major study undertaken by a group of Disney researchers in the 1990s and published in 2001 by Janet Wasko, Mark Phillips, and Eileen Meehan. The project looked at the impact Disney has had on consumers in 18 different countries across six continents and concluded that Disney appears to be a "global phenomenon."[1]

Based on a survey of participants, the authors noted, "nearly 98 percent of the respondents had seen a Disney film, nearly 82 percent were familiar with Disney books, and around 79 percent had experienced Disney television programs and merchandise."[2]

Mickey Mouse and the World

The recognition of Disney products on an international level actually began in the 1920s with the creation of Mickey Mouse, long before the term "globalization" had been coined. The success of Mickey Mouse cartoon shorts in the United States led to their distribution abroad, and within a few short years, Mickey and his friends—Minnie Mouse, Donald Duck, Pluto, Goofy, etc.—had gained an international following.

According to authors Bevis Hillier and Bernard Shine, Mickey was known by a variety of names around the world—Topolino in Italy; El Raton Miki in Spain; Michel Souris in France; and Miki Kuchi in Japan, among others.

> In his infancy he was more popular in England and France than in America. As early as 1930, his effigy in wax, playing the piano in *The Opry House* (1929) went on show at Madame Tussaud's in London.[3]

As the Disney Studio began releasing full-length animated feature films, these, too, received international as well as domestic attention. *Snow White and the Seven Dwarfs*, for example, was shown in cities all over Europe and Asia, including Shanghai in the late 1930s.[4] Disney films became so popular in Europe that the company felt a significant financial pinch when it was unable to distribute its films in that region during World War II.[5]

Even today, Disney films do a brisk business overseas because of their popularity with international audiences. The live action film *Alice in Wonderland*, directed by Tim Burton, for example, hit the $1 billion mark in global box office sales within three months of its release in March 2010.[6]

Sequels of Disney movies often generate positive response from international audiences. "Sequels in this country don't necessarily do as well, but sequels abroad do very well," said Philippe Perebinossoff, associate professor of Radio-TV-Film at Cal State Fullerton.[7]

Did You Know?

Toy Story 3 took in more than $980 million in global box office ticket sales within three months of its opening and broke a record as the highest grossing animated film of all time.

Disney Channel Programming

Television has helped popularize Disney characters and films by exposing them to viewers via TV channels in other countries. Disney has also done extremely well in recent years in using its Disney Channel programming to reach audiences abroad.

At the end of 2009, the company claimed more than 100 million subscribers in countries in Europe, Asia, Africa, Australia, and Central and South America.[8] In some cases the programming is shown in English with subtitles, while in others such as Israel and Taiwan, it is dubbed in the language of the country where it is being shown.[9]

As with the company's programming in the United States, regular showings of some of the Disney Channel's tween-oriented sitcoms have helped build the company's key franchises across borders. Miley Cyrus, aka Hannah Montana, for example, is "the most recognized Disney Channel star in South Africa," according to the *Himalayan Times*.[10]

In 2010, Disney Channel South Africa held a contest where viewers could design their own Hannah Montana T-shirts and compete for a chance to "be whisked off to Hollywood to meet a stylist from the smash hit show and have their T-shirt design produced in a limited edition run to share with friends," noted an article in the Durban *Sunday Tribune.*[11]

Maeve Sheen, age 10, lives in Cape Town, South Africa, and is a regular viewer of *Hannah Montana.* She watches the show every day, including reruns. "One of them she's seen a million times, but she'll always watch it again," said Maeve's 11-year-old sister Katie.[12]

Like many other fans of the tween superstar, Maeve also has a collection of Hannah Montana merchandise. "I have purses, tops, and jammies. I used to have a Hannah Montana guitar. Once I had a Hannah Montana birthday party," she said.[13]

Figure 18: Global Reach of the Disney Channel

Region	Subscribers
United States	98.2 million
Europe	39.5 million
Asia	25.8 million
Latin America	24.0 million
Middle East	2.6 million
Australia/New Zealand	2.4 million
Africa	1.9 million

Source: *Disney Factbook 2009*; based on data from 10/09

Targeted Global Marketing

While Disney has succeeded in maintaining a longstanding global presence through its films, television programs, and merchandise, in recent years the company has made more of a concerted effort to solidify its global reputation. Under the watch of Bob Iger—first as Disney president and now as CEO—the company has begun to target specific regions where it can beef up consumer awareness of its products and services. Part of this strategy has involved a shift in the company's approach to how it markets itself abroad.

In the past, the company's practice had been to export films, television programs, and merchandise that was already popular in the United States in hopes they would be welcomed in other countries simply because they were

Disney products. More recent efforts, however, have been made to assess the needs and interests of consumers in different countries and tailor the products sold in these countries accordingly, as noted in Disney's 2009 annual report.

> To achieve this, more accountability and decision-making authority are being shifted to local managers so they can determine which Disney brand, franchise and characters are most relevant and emotionally resonant to consumers in their markets.[14]

From a television standpoint, this new strategy has resulted in the creation of local programming that complements the Disney Channel's existing shows. On the film front, it has involved partnering with local filmmakers to develop movies likely to appeal to audiences in specific countries while still maintaining the family-friendly focus that has come to be associated with the Disney brand.

The Disney Company has focused on four regions that have been identified as potential growth areas for the organization: China, India, Russia, and Latin America. These areas have traditionally not had much of a Disney presence, but they hold great potential for future corporate growth because of the size of their populations.[15]

Marketing Disney in China

With a population of 1.3 billion, China has been on the Disney Company's radar screen for many years as a key growth area for its brand. In the last decade in particular, Disney has been able to enter the Chinese market on several fronts, including retail, theme parks, film, and television.

Strict government regulations have made access to some of these areas somewhat challenging. However, Disney has gradually been able to introduce its products to Chinese audiences in hopes of eventually becoming an instantly recognized brand in that country, as it is in other parts of the world.

Disney has had a small presence in China for a number of years, according to *Time* magazine.

> In 1995 *The Lion King* became one of the first Western films to premiere in theaters since the Communists took over China in 1949. More than 15 other movies have followed—including *The Incredibles* and *National Treasure*—an impressive record, given that Beijing allows only 20 foreign films to be shown in the country each year. Disney on Ice has been performed in Beijing, Guangzhou and other cities since 1996.[16]

Part of the challenge for the company has been a lack of awareness of Disney products on the part of the Chinese. During the reign of Mao Tse-Tung, Disney characters were banned from the region. Consequently, several generations of children—now parents themselves—had no familiarity with or emotional connection to the heart of Disney's enterprise.

When the decision was made to build theme parks in China, first in Hong Kong and ultimately in Shanghai, Disney executives knew they had to lay a lot of groundwork in order to ensure these parks would actually mean something to those who visited them. This prompted some strategic planning on behalf of the company to try and build a following for its products and services.

Disney Corners Retail Outlets

Part of the strategy to prepare Chinese audiences for the Disney experience was to introduce them to the company's characters through merchandising. This was accomplished by setting up "Disney Corners" in existing Chinese stores. These mini retail outlets sold branded merchandise from among Disney's biggest franchises such as Mickey Mouse, Winnie the Pooh, and the Disney Princesses. One example of this approach was a trendy Hong Kong clothing store that sold apparel and shoes adorned with images of Mickey Mouse.[17]

While products such as clothing, books, and toys have been hot ticket items for the Disney Corner outlets, the company has been less successful with home entertainment media. Piracy is a longstanding problem in China and, as a result, "legitimate Disney DVDs cost up to 10 times as much as knock-offs, restricting sales to a trickle," noted author Jeffrey Ressner.[18]

The Disney Corner concept was developed in the early 2000s. By 2007, there were approximately 4,200 Disney Corner outlets established in more than 25 Chinese cities, according to the *China Business Review*.[19]

With the success of these outlets, Disney went on to open a network of Disneykids and Toonsland stores throughout China as well. In 2010, Disney also opened a high-end retail outlet in Shanghai called "Man Is in the Forest," in anticipation of the eventual opening of Disneyland Shanghai.[20]

Did You Know?

Disney merchandise is sold in more than 5,000 retail locations throughout China, including department stores, shopping centers, and airports.

Theme Park Preparations

As noted in Chapter 7, Hong Kong Disneyland opened in 2005, and, in many respects, is still finding its footing in the Chinese market more than five years later. As a result of the lessons learned from the opening of Euro Disney in 1992, a number of concessions were made from the beginning at the Hong Kong park to accommodate the cultural differences between Chinese park patrons and the American audiences for whom the original Disney parks were constructed.

Even with these accommodations, however, the challenge of getting Chinese visitors to relate to existing Disney stories and characters was still a hurdle to overcome. One step taken by Disney was the formation of a partnership with local youth groups run by China's Communist Youth League prior to the opening of the park.

Through this partnership, "Mickey Mouse and other Disney representatives visited 500 children at two youth centers in Guangzhou, in southern China," explained an article in the *Los Angeles Times*.[21] Guangzhou is approximately 100 miles from Hong Kong and was expected at the time to be a prime feeder of visitors to the park. The company also sent Mickey Mouse and other Disney figures to shopping malls, libraries, and assorted public places to try and build awareness of the characters children were likely to encounter at Hong Kong Disneyland.

As time draws closer to the eventual opening of Disneyland Shanghai, it is anticipated the Disney Company will use similar efforts to boost awareness of its characters and products in northern China, where many of that park's visitors are expected to hail from.

Forging Film Partnerships

Partnering with local filmmakers has proven to be a profitable way for Disney to make its mark with the Chinese movie-going public. While the Chinese government limits the number of foreign films that can be released in China each year, it does not place the same restrictions on local filmmakers who work with foreign companies to produce films. Consequently, to date, Disney has produced three films through partnership arrangements with various local Chinese directors and producers.

The Secret of the Magic Gourd or *Baohulu de Mimi*, based on a story by children's author Zhang Tianyi, was the first of these projects. Combining live action with computer animation, the film was directed by John Chu of China's Centro Digital Pictures and released in 2007. It grossed approximately $2.7 million at the box office.[22]

According to *China Daily*, "While the film was made by Centro rather than Disney's famous animators, the production process was collaborative, with Disney contributing perspectives and suggestions."[23]

The success of *The Secret of the Magic Gourd* led to a second co-produced film. *Trail of the Panda* was released in 2009, in conjunction with Castle Hero Pictures and Ying Dong Media. This was followed by *Disney's High School Musical: China*, released in 2010 and based on the 2006 Disney Channel hit.

Co-produced with the Shanghai Media Group and Huayi Brothers Media Corporation, the movie was directed by Chen Shizheng, a leading Chinese director, and filmed in Shanghai using local actors.[24] It featured mostly new music by local artists but included one hit from the original film—*We're All in This Together*—which was retooled with Mandarin lyrics.[25]

Developing a Television Presence

In the television arena, Disney has encountered a number of roadblocks in reaching Chinese audiences. Strict regulations in China prohibit foreign companies from producing and distributing their own media over Chinese airwaves. This has prevented Disney from launching its own Disney Channel, as it has been able to do in other countries.[26]

As a result, Disney's efforts to establish a television presence in China have been steady but slow. Ten years after the death of Mao Tse-Tung, Disney was first able to air some of its Mickey Mouse cartoon shorts on Chinese

Central Television in 1986. Since then, the company has been able to broadcast only a limited amount of Disney content over Chinese television.

In 1994, Disney developed a partnership with Beijing TV to produce a children's program similar in nature to *The Mickey Mouse Club*. The show combined Disney content with local programming. Disney was not able to use the name Mickey Mouse in the title, however, so the show was ultimately called the *Dragon Club*.[27]

Creating Instructional Programs

One of Disney's newest efforts to connect with the Chinese public is not part of the company's entertainment offerings but is actually a form of educational media with an entertainment twist. Disney English is an instructional program launched in Shanghai in 2008. It is designed to teach English to Chinese children, using Disney characters, stories, and songs as teaching tools.

The program provides 96 hours of instruction and includes lessons for children ages 1 to 12. The curriculum is infused with activities that not-so-subtly introduce students to different aspects of the Disney brand while helping them learn to read, write, and speak English, noted an article in the *Wall Street Journal*.

> Classroom and homework exercises introduce the kind of Disney books, TV shows and movies that China's government otherwise tightly restricts.... In class, a strong singing voice earns students 'magic tokens' that are exchangeable into 'reward gifts' like Disney pens and hats on display in the lobby. Students can also get Mickey Mouse book bags as well as bilingual books, flashcards and CDs that feature Disney characters, much of them otherwise unavailable in China.[28]

Although only a few years old, Disney English has taken off in China. By 2010, Disney had 12 locations in Shanghai and Beijing and planned to expand to more than 100 by 2015.[29]

Marketing Disney in India

Like China, India has been an untapped market for Disney for many years. It is only recently that the company has begun to make headway in connecting with the country's residents, largely through television programming and consumer products. While Disney has made some progress in breaking into the local film market, that has been more difficult—as it has for many outside entertainment companies—because of India's own strong Bollywood film industry.

Establishing a Television Foothold

Disney has been able to establish itself as a player in the Indian television market, primarily because the company's family-friendly approach to entertainment meshes nicely with Indian cultural values. "India's burgeoning middle class places near-obsessive focus on family and is increasingly paying for cable television," explained *Wall Street Journal* reporter Merissa Marr.[30]

Consequently, in 2004, Disney was able to establish both the Disney Channel and Toon Disney in India. (Toon Disney has since become Disney XD.) The company bought a local children's channel, Hungama, two years later for $30.5 million. Disney also invested $30 million in UTV Global Broadcasting, which encompasses several movie channels.[31]

Not only has Disney shown its existing programming on these channels, the company has worked at the local level to develop original programs that Indian audiences can relate to, focusing on three core themes: "believe in yourself, express yourself, and celebrate your family."[32]

According to the *Wall Street Journal*, these shows have "created a new genre of children's programming in India they call 'aspirational storytelling,' aimed at a generation of children with broader ambitions than their parents."[33]

Marketing Consumer Products

The sale of Disney products in India runs a close second behind television in generating revenue for the company. As with TV, it is only in the last decade that Disney has been able to move into the market. It has done so by developing some product lines that feature Disney characters as well as non-character merchandise that simply carries the Disney name.

The company has developed licensing relationships with a number of local businesses to market its products. A line of apparel called Disney Jeans, for example, was launched in 2006 by Indus Clothing and features non-character jeans, T-shirts, and accessories aimed at children and teens.[34]

A similar arrangement was made the following year to sell craft and stationery products through a network of stores called Disney Artist, operated by the Delhi-based Ravi Jaipuria Corporation. The local licensee markets

"Disney branded greeting cards, stationery, arts, crafts, and party products through specialty stores," according to the *Times of India.*[35]

Disney books and magazines have also become popular sellers in India and have been released in several Indian languages, including Hindi, Marathi, and Malayalam.[36]

Making Strides With Film

As noted earlier, breaking into the film business in India has been more difficult for Disney than reaching the public through television and consumer products. As with China, forming partnerships with local filmmakers and using local talent has been one solution to this problem.

Roadside Romeo, released in 2008, was the result of a joint venture between Disney and Yash Raj Films. The animated film surpassed box office sales for other Disney films previously released in India including *Toy Story* and *The Incredibles*. However, overall, it was dubbed a "critical and commercial failure" by the media for failing to generate sufficient profits.[37]

Roadside Romeo was followed by *Zokkomon*, a live action movie filmed in Hindi, which opened in 2010. A third project, a yet-to-be-titled Telegu-language film aimed at southern Indian audiences, was in the works at the time of this writing and slated for release in 2011.[38]

Disney executives are still trying to determine whether or not this localization approach will work in India as well as it has in China. Ultimately, the company aims to make its movie sector in India one that will complement its other divisions. "The hope is that the new generation of locally produced Disney movies can propel the group's other businesses, as Disney movies do in the US," noted the *Financial Times.*[39]

Marketing Disney in Russia

Disney's efforts to penetrate the Russian market have also been primarily focused on developing partnerships on a local level. Unlike India, however, Russia has proven to be more receptive to Disney's film endeavors, while television has been stalled in bureaucratic red tape.

254 | *Why We Love Disney*

Localized Films With a Disney Touch

The Book of Masters, or *Kniga Masterov,* was a joint project between Disney and a Russian film production team. Released in 2009, it was Disney's first attempt to produce a feature film specifically aimed at a Russian audience.

The movie featured Russian cast members who portrayed characters from well-known local folk tales but with a Disney twist. Reporter Michael Schwirtz explained:

> The film, a live-action adventure story aesthetically similar to recent productions like *The Chronicles of Narnia* series, is quintessentially Disney down to the inevitable happy ending—not always a given in Russian fairy tales.[40]

The Disney touch combined with local flavor resonated with Russian moviegoers. *The Book of Masters* earned $10 million in box office sales by the end of its second week and $11.5 million overall. As a result, by 2010, plans were already under way for a follow-up effort.[41]

Television and the Internet

While Disney's efforts on the Russian film front have been positive, the company's attempts to break into television have not worked out quite as well. An announcement was made in 2008 that Disney had formed a partnership with a local Russian broadcaster, MediaOne. The company planned to launch a family-oriented channel similar to the Disney Channel, which would air on 30 Russian television stations. Just a year later, however, the deal was stalled by the Russian government and currently remains in limbo.[42]

Disney did sign an agreement in 2010 with Mobile TeleSystems, a local telecommunications company, to make Disney films and TV shows available through the Internet. At the time of this writing, implementation of that agreement was still pending.[43]

Other Media in Russia

The Disney Company has been able to generate Russian audience interest in some of its other properties. Disney movies including *Pirates of the Caribbean* and *Alice in Wonderland* have done well at the Russian box office. The stage version of *Beauty and the Beast* opened in Moscow in 2008, and was positively received by audiences. In addition, Disney's publishing division produces 13 different magazines sold in the country.[44]

Marketing Disney in Latin America

Disney has had a small presence in several Latin American countries for a number of years but has recently ramped up its marketing efforts to expand this presence. The company first began to see a surge of interest in its merchandise in Latin America in the 1990s, long before any serious efforts were made to boost consumer awareness of Disney in this region.

Between 1989 and 1993, for example, sales of Disney merchandise swelled from $150 million to over $600 million, according to the *South Florida Business Journal*.[45] This was an early indication of the growth possibilities for this market.

High School Musical Goes to the Movies

With the entree of the Disney Channel into several Latin American countries a decade later, awareness of the Disney brand intensified. The company debuted *High School Musical* in the region with much success in 2006. Two years later, Disney produced several localized versions of the hit film called *High School Musical: El Desafio* and released them in theaters. According to *Billboard* magazine, this was:

> ...the first Disney-branded feature film made in Latin America. It was produced entirely in triplicate for Mexico, Argentina and Brazil...with three local casts, three distinct scripts and three versions of the soundtrack.[46]

In addition, cast members for each production were drawn from *American Idol*-type reality shows produced by Disney in each market, which generated their own set of fans. *Billboard* reported that the local versions of *High School Musical* "opened a slew of new revenue streams in the region, including longterm mobile sponsorship, a traveling ice dancing show, CDs spawned from the local reality programs and concert tours."[47]

Localized Television Programming

In the late 2000s, Disney also adapted its popular ABC television series *Desperate Housewives* for Latin American viewers. Three different versions of the show were produced for markets in Argentina, Colombia, and Ecuador. According to writer Ed Waller:

> The show was one of the first US dramas to be adopted for Latin American audiences, and the move was a neat reversal of how so many Latino telenovela formats, such as *Ugly Betty*, were then being re-developed for the more lucrative US network primetime market.[48]

Conclusion

Disney's global presence dates back to the early days of Mickey Mouse and the company's beginnings as a creator of cartoon shorts. As the company began developing its repertoire of feature films and television programs, Disney was able to firmly establish itself as a producer of high quality family entertainment that appealed to audiences abroad as well as in the United States.

Disney continues working to extend its reach into previously untapped international markets. Using a variety of strategic approaches, Disney has endeavored to introduce its characters and stories to children and adults of all ages who may not have had previous exposure to the company's creations. As a result of these efforts, Disney has become one of the most easily recognized brands around the world. ♦

Notes

1. Janet Wasko, Mark Phillips, and Eileen R. Meehan, eds., *Dazzled by Disney? The Global Disney Audiences Project* (London: Leicester University Press, 2001): 330.
2. Ibid.
3. Bevis Hillier and Bernard C. Shine, *Walt Disney's Mickey Mouse Memorabilia* (New York: Harry N. Abrams, 1986): 25.
4. See Jeffrey Ressner, "Disney's Great Leap Into China," *Time* 166:3 (July 11, 2005), 52.
5. See Bob Thomas, *Walt Disney: An American Original* (New York: Disney Editions, 1994): 161.
6. The Walt Disney Company, "Disney's *Alice in Wonderland* Reaches Exclusive $1 Billion Global Box Office Club," press release, May 27, 2010.
7. Philippe Perebinossoff, in-person interview, July 29, 2010.

8. The Walt Disney Company, "Update on Cable Subscribers," *News From Investor Relations*, June 2010, 14.

9. See David Brinn, "Israel Joins the Mickey Mouse Club," *Jerusalem Post*, 31 August 2009, 24; and Sally D. Goll, "Asian Marketing," *Wall Street Journal*, 21 April 1995, 4.

10. "The Rising Star," *Himalayan Times*, 7 November 2009.

11. "Have You Got Hannah Montana Style?" *Sunday Tribune*, 14 March 2010, 7.

12. Katie Sheen, in-person interview, July 3, 2010.

13. Maeve Sheen, in-person interview, July 3, 2010.

14. The Walt Disney Company, *2009 Year in Review*, 53.

15. Ibid.

16. Ressner, "Disney's Great Leap Into China," 52.

17. See Simon Parry, "Mickey Mao," *Travel Retailer International*, October/November 2004, 16.

18. Ressner, "Disney's Great Leap Into China," 52.

19. Paula M. Miller, "Disneyland in Hong Kong," *The China Business Review* 34:1 (January/February 2007): 31.

20. See "Disney to Launch First High-End Store in Shanghai," *China Knowledge Press*, July 5, 2010.

21. "Disney Markets Mickey Mouse in China," *Los Angeles Times*, 24 September 2004, C2.

22. See "Disney Taps Sophomores for *High School Musical*," *China Daily*, 24 November 2009.

23. Liu Wei, "Sowing Seeds of Magic," *China Daily*, 30 June 2007, 8.

24. See "Disney Taps Sophomores for *High School Musical*," *China Daily*, 24 November 2009; and "Disney to Add Chinese Flavor in Shanghai," *China Daily*, 23 April 2010.

25. See "Making a Song and Dance for China," *China Daily*, 10 August 2010.

26. See Jane Leung and Kate Nicholson, "Disney Seeks to Consolidate Reputation in China," *Media*, November 19, 2009, 16.

27. See Clay Chandler, "Mickey Mao," *Fortune* 151:8 (April 18, 2005): 170.

28. James T. Areddy and Peter Sanders, "Chinese Learn English the Disney Way," *Wall Street Journal*, 20 April 2009, B1.

29. See "Mickey Mouse and Donald Duck Impart English Education Amongst Chinese Toddlers," *Meri News*, 12 July 2010.

30. Merissa Marr, "Small World: Disney Rewrites Script to Win Fans in India," *Wall Street Journal*, 11 June 2007, A1.

31. See "Disney to Set Up 150 Stores in India," *Times of India*, 12 October 2006; and Anusha Subramanian, "Disney's India Waltz," *Business Today*, May 31, 2009.

32. See Marr, "Small World: Disney Rewrites Script to Win Fans in India," 11.

33. Ibid.

34. "Walt Disney to Roll Out Disney Jeans for Kids," *The Economic Times*, 28 September 2006.

35. "Disney to Set Up 150 Stores in India," *Times of India*, 12 October 2006. See also "First Disney Franchise Store Opened in India," *FinancialWire*, 19 March 2007.

36. See "Disney Publishing to Woo More Readers With Local Editions," *Businessline*, February 26, 2008, 1.

37. Naman Ramachandran, "A Passage Into India," *Variety*, 12 March 2010, 8. See also Anupama Chopra, "Stumbling Toward Bollywood," *The New York Times*, 22 March 2009, 18.

38.   Ramachandran, "A Passage Into India," 8.

39.   Matthew Garrahan, "Disney Indian Adventure Rewarded," *Financial Times*, 12 November 2008, 18.

40.   Michael Schwirtz, "Home of the Mouse Finds Box Office Success in the Land of the Bear," *The New York Times*, 14 November 2009, C1.

41.   Ibid. See also Marc Graser and Dave McNary, "Mouse Taps Topper for O'Seas Pics," *Variety*, 11 February 2010, 5.

42.   See Schwirtz, "Home of the Mouse Finds Box Office Success in the Land of the Bear," C1. See also Peter Sanders, "Disney Will Launch TV Channel in Russia," *Wall Street Journal*, 17 December 2008, B1; and "The Walt Disney Company and Media-One Form JV to Launch Disney-Branded TV Channel in Russia," *Wireless News*, December 21, 2008.

43.   See "MTS/Disney to Deliver Content to Russia," *Telephone IP News* 21:5 (May 1, 2010).

44.   Matthew Garrahan, "Disney Is Aiming for a Fairytale Start in Russia," *Financial Times*, 26 October 2009, 21.

45.   Christopher Hosford, "Garsh! Latin America Digs Disney," *South Florida Business Journal*, December 17-23, 1993, 3.

46.   Ayala Ben-Yehuda, "Big Hit, Local Tastes," *Billboard* 120:29 (July 19, 2008): 14.

47.   Ibid.

48.   Ed Waller, "Latin Moves for Mouse," *C21 Media.net*, May 21, 2010, www.c21media.net.

Postscript

This book has attempted to shed some light on the inner workings of the Walt Disney Company in an effort to understand why so many people love Disney. By providing an overview of the organization's history, products, management, and marketing practices, it has offered a glimpse into a company whose brand is recognized and embraced by millions of people worldwide. An examination of the many facets of Disney clearly shows the strategic steps the company has taken over the years to build this brand.

While Disney may not appeal to everyone, there is no denying that the company has had an unrivaled impact on the entertainment industry. Beginning as a small studio in the 1920s, the Disney Company has grown to be one of the most influential organizations in the business.

Walt Disney once said, "All our dreams can come true—if we have the courage to pursue them."* Disney's continuous stream of family-friendly products and services, coupled with innovative management and marketing practices, have firmly established the Disney brand in the consciousness of consumers all over the globe. This is truly the stuff that corporate dreams are made of.

*Walt Disney quoted in Pat Williams and Jim Denney, *How to Be Like Walt: Capturing the Disney Magic Every Day of Your Life* (Deerfield Beach, FL: Health Communications, 2004): 69.

Suggested Readings

Art and Animation

Andrae, Thomas. *Carl Barks and the Disney Comic Book: Unmasking the Myth of Modernity*. Oxford, MS: University Press of Mississippi, 2006.

Bailey, Adrian. *Walt Disney's World of Fantasy*. New York: Gallery Books, 1982.

Bain, David, and Bruce Harris, eds. *Mickey Mouse: Fifty Happy Years*. New York: Harmony Books, 1977.

Blitz, Marcia. *Donald Duck*. New York: Harmony Books, 1979.

Canemaker, John. *Walt Disney's Nine Old Men and the Art of Animation*. New York: Disney Editions, 2001.

Finch, Christopher. *The Art of Walt Disney: From Mickey Mouse to the Magic Kingdoms*. New York: Harry N. Abrams, 2004.

Koenig, David. *Mouse Under Glass: Secrets of Disney Animation & Theme Parks*. Irvine, CA: Bonaventure Press, 1997.

Kurtz, Bruce D. *Keith Haring, Andy Warhol, and Walt Disney*. Munich, Germany: Prestel-Verlag, 1992.

Peri, Don. *Working With Walt: Interviews With Disney Artists*. Jackson, MS: University Press of Mississippi, 2008.

Thomas, Frank, and Ollie Johnston. *The Illusion of Life: Disney Animation*. New York: Disney Editions, 1981.

Walt Disney's Donald Duck: 50 Years of Happy Frustration. London: HP Books, 1984.

Biography

Barrier, Michael. *The Animated Man: A Life of Walt Disney*. Berkeley, CA: University of California Press, 2007.

Eisner, Michael. *Work in Progress*. New York: Random House, 1998.

Flower, Joe. *Prince of the Magic Kingdom: Michael Eisner and the Re-making of Disney.* New York: John Wiley & Sons, 1991.

Funicello, Annette. *A Dream Is a Wish Your Heart Makes.* New York: Hyperion, 1994.

Gabler, Neal. *Walt Disney: The Triumph of the American Imagination.* New York: Alfred A. Knopf, 2006.

Green, Amy Boothe, and Howard E. Green. *Remembering Walt: Favorite Memories of Walt Disney.* New York: Hyperion, 1999.

Greene, Katherine, and Richard Greene. *Inside the Dream: The Personal Story of Walt Disney.* New York: Disney Editions, 2001.

Greene, Katherine, and Richard Greene. *The Man Behind the Magic: The Story of Walt Disney.* New York: Viking, 1998.

Miller, Diane Disney, and Pete Martin. *The Story of Walt Disney.* New York: Henry Holt, 1957.

Thomas, Bob. *Building a Company: Roy O. Disney and the Creation of an Entertainment Empire.* New York: Hyperion, 1998.

Thomas, Bob. *Walt Disney: An American Original.* New York: Disney Editions, 1994.

Tumbusch, Tom. *Walt Disney the American Dreamer.* Dayton, OH: Tomart Publications, 2008.

Watts, Steven. *The Magic Kingdom: Walt Disney and the American Way of Life.* Columbia, MO: University of Missouri Press, 1997.

Company History/Corporate Information

Bazaldua, Barbara, Steve Bynghall, Jo Casey, et al. *Pixarpedia: A Complete Guide to the World of Pixar...and Beyond!* New York: DK Publishing, 2009.

Grover, Ron. *The Disney Touch: Disney, ABC and the Quest for the World's Greatest Media Empire.* New York: McGraw-Hill, 1996.

Grover, Ron. *The Disney Touch: How a Daring Management Team Revived an Entertainment Empire.* Homewood, IL: Business One Irwin, 1991.

Holliss, Richard, and Brian Sibbey. *The Disney Studio Story.* London: Octopus Books, 1988.

Jackson, Kathy Merlock. *Walt Disney Conversations.* Jackson, MS: University Press of Mississippi, 2006.

Kaufman, J.B. *South of the Border With Disney: Walt Disney and the Good Neighbor Program, 1941-1948.* New York: Disney Editions, 2009.

Masters, Kim. *The Keys to the Kingdom: How Michael Eisner Lost His Grip.* New York: William Morrow, 2000.

Palk, Karen. *To Infinity and Beyond!: The Story of Pixar Animation Studios.* San Francisco: Chronicle Books, 2007.

Price, David A. *The Pixar Touch: The Making of a Company.* New York: Alfred A. Knopf, 2008.

Shale, Richard. *Donald Duck Joins Up: The Walt Disney Studio During World War II.* Ann Arbor, MI: UMI Research Press, 1982.

Smith, Dave, and Steven Clark. *Disney: The First 100 Years.* New York: Disney Editions, 2002.

Stewart, James B. *Disney War.* New York: Simon & Schuster, 2005.

Taylor, John. *Storming the Magic Kingdom: Wall Street, the Raiders, and the Battle for Disney.* New York: Alfred A. Knopf, 1987.

Telotte, J.P. *The Mouse Machine: Disney and Technology.* Urbana, IL: University of Illinois Press, 2008.

Critical Analysis

Booker, M. Keith. *Disney, Pixar and the Hidden Messages of Children's Films.* Santa Barbara, CA: Praeger, 2009.

Bryman, Alan. *Disney and His Worlds.* London: Routledge, 1995.

Bryman, Alan. *The Disneyization of Society.* Thousand Oaks, CA: Sage Publications, 2004.

Budd, Mike, and Max H. Kirsch, eds. *Rethinking Disney: Private Control, Public Dimensions.* Middletown, CT: Wesleyan University Press, 2005.

Dorfman, Ariel, and Armand Mattelart. *How to Read Donald Duck: Imperialist Ideology in the Disney Comic.* International General, 1984.

Eliot, Marc. *Walt Disney: Hollywood's Dark Prince.* Secaucus, NJ: Carol Publishing Group, 1993.

Frantz, Douglas. *Celebration, U.S.A.: Living in Disney's Brave New Town.* New York: Henry Holt, 1999.

Giroux, Henry A. *The Mouse That Roared: Disney and the End of Innocence.* Lanham, MD: Rowman & Littlefield, 1999.

Hiaasen, Carl. *Team Rodent: How Disney Devours the World.* New York: Ballantine, 1998.

Pinsky, Mark I. *The Gospel According to Disney: Faith, Trust, and Pixie Dust.* Louisville, KY: Westminster John Knox, 2004.

Ross, Andrew. *The Celebration Chronicles: Life, Liberty, and the Pursuit of Property Values in Disney's New Town.* New York: Ballantine Books, 1999.

Sammond, Nicholas. *Babes in Tomorrowland: Walt Disney and the Making of the American Child, 1930-1960.* Durham, NC: Duke University Press, 2005.

Schickel, Richard. *The Disney Version: The Life, Times, Art and Commerce of Walt Disney.* Chicago: Irwin R. Dee, 1997.

Schweizer, Peter, and Rochelle Schweizer. *Disney: The Mouse Betrayed.* Washington, D.C.: Regnery Publishing, 1998.

Smoodin, Eric, ed. *Disney Discourse: Producing the Magic Kingdom.* New York: Routledge, 1994.

Wasko, Janet. *Understanding Disney: The Manufacture of Fantasy.* Cambridge, England: Polity Press, 2001.

Wasko, Janet, Mark Phillips, and Eileen R. Meehan, eds. *Dazzled by Disney? The Global Disney Audiences Project.* London: Leicester University Press, 2001.

Film

Allan, Robin. *Walt Disney and Europe: European Influences on the Animated Feature Films of Walt Disney*. Bloomington, IN: Indiana University Press, 1999.

Maltin, Leonard. *The Disney Films*, 4th ed. New York: Disney Editions, 2000.

Merritt, Russell, and J.B. Kaufman. *Walt Disney's Silly Symphonies*. Gemona, Italy: La Cineteca del Friuli, 2006.

Merritt, Russell, and J.B. Kaufman. *Walt in Wonderland: The Silent Films of Walt Disney*. Baltimore, MD: Johns Hopkins University Press, 1993.

General Interest

Grant, John. *Encyclopedia of Walt Disney's Animated Characters*. New York: Hyperion Books, 1998.

Peterson, Monique. *The Little Big Book of Disney*. New York: Disney Editions, 2001.

Smith, Dave. *Disney A to Z: The Official Encyclopedia*, 3rd ed. New York: Disney Editions, 2006.

Smith, Dave. *The Quotable Walt Disney*. New York: Disney Editions 2001.

Williams, Pat. *How to Be Like Walt: Capturing the Disney Magic Every Day of Your Life*. Deerfield Beach, FL: Health Communications, 2004.

Merchandising

Heide, Robert, and John Gilman. *Disneyana: Classic Collectibles 1928-1956*. New York: Hyperion, 1994.

Hillier, Bevis, and Bernard Shine. *Walt Disney's Mickey Mouse Memorabilia*. New York: Harry N. Abrams, 1986.

Music

Hischak, Thomas, and Mark A. Robinson. *The Disney Song Encyclopedia*. Lanham, MD: Scarecrow Press, 2009.

Hollis, Tim, and Greg Ehrbar. *Mouse Tracks: The Story of Walt Disney Records*. Jackson, MS: University Press of Mississippi, 2006.

Tietyen, David. *The Musical World of Walt Disney*. Milwaukee, WI: Hal Leonard Publishing, 1990.

Television

Bowles, Jerry. *Forever Hold Your Banner High!* New York: Doubleday, 1976.

Cotter, Bill. *The Wonderful World of Disney Television*. New York: Hyperion, 1997.

Santoli, Lorraine. *The Official Mickey Mouse Club Book*. New York: Hyperion, 1995.

Telotte, J.P. *Disney TV*. Detroit, MI: Wayne State University Press, 2004.

Theater

Bianco, Anthony. *Ghosts of 42nd Street*. New York: Harper Perennial, 2004.

Lassell, Michael. *Disney on Broadway*. New York: Disney Press, 2002.

Schumacher, Thomas, and Jeff Kurtti. *How Does the Show Go On? An Introduction to the Theater*. New York: Disney Editions, 2007.

Theme Parks

Fjellman, Stephen M. *Vinyl Leaves: Walt Disney World and America*. Boulder, CO: Westview, 1992.

Koenig, David. *Mouse Tales: A Behind-the-Ears Look at Disneyland*. Irvine, CA: Bonaventure Press, 1994.

Koenig, David. *Realityland: True-Life Adventures at Walt Disney World*. Irvine, CA: Bonaventure Press, 2007.

Kurtii, Jeff. *Since the World Began*. New York: Hyperion, 1996.

Kurtti, Jeff. *Walt Disney's Imagineering Legends and the Genesis of the Disney Theme Park*. New York: Disney Editions, 2008.

Lainsbury, Andrew. *Once Upon an American Dream: The Story of Euro Disneyland*. Lawrence, KS: University Press of Kansas, 2000.

Littaye, Alain, and Didier Ghez. *Disneyland Paris: From Sketch to Reality*. Paris: Nouveau Millenaire Editions, 2002.

Marling, Karal Ann. *Behind the Magic: 50 Years of Disneyland*. Dearborn, MI: The Henry Ford, 2005.

Walt Disney Imagineering: A Behind the Dreams Look at Making Magic More Real. New York: Disney Editions, 2010.

Index